SUSPICION NATION

# SUSPICION
# *NATION*

*The* INSIDE STORY *of the*

TRAYVON MARTIN INJUSTICE

*and* WHY WE CONTINUE

*to* REPEAT *it*

## LISA BLOOM

COUNTERPOINT
BERKELEY

Photo credits: Pages 26, 59 APVideo. Page 58 © Istock / RonBailey. Page 61 CrimeTimeVids. Page 114 © POOL/Reuters/Corbis. Page 116 © JACOB LANGSTON / POOL/epa/Corbis. Every effort has been made to trace or contact all copyright holders. The publishers will be pleased to make good any omissions or rectify any mistakes brought to their attention at the earliest opportunity.

Library of Congress Cataloging-in-Publication Data is available.
ISBN 978-1-61902-327-7

Cover design by Faceout Studio
Interior design by Megan Jones Design

COUNTERPOINT
1919 Fifth Street
Berkeley, CA 94710
www.counterpointpress.com

Printed in the United States of America
Distributed by Publishers Group West

10 9 8 7 6 5 4 3 2 1

*To my mother, Gloria Allred,*
*In honor of her fervent, relentless, lifelong fight against injustice.*

# CONTENTS

*"We are always paid for our suspicion by finding what we suspect."*

—HENRY DAVID THOREAU

# FOREWORD

# by Jeffrey Toobin

B Y THE STANDARDS of most criminal trials, there were few issues
in dispute in the matter of *State of Florida v. George Zimmerman*.
This was no whodunit. The identity of the killer, the murder weapon, the
time and cause of death—all were agreed upon by both the prosecution
and defense. In that regard, it was a simple case.

At the same time, the Zimmerman trial touched upon some of the
most haunting and complex issues in American life. Race, violence, guns,
the fairness of the criminal justice system—these are the subjects at the
heart of Lisa Bloom's *Suspicion Nation*. With the mind of a lawyer and
the eye of a journalist, Bloom achieves a remarkable double success:
meticulously examining the evidence in this case while also placing the
whole Zimmerman saga in a broad historical and cultural context.

The heart of Bloom's book is her critique of the presentation of the
case against Zimmerman by Florida's State Attorneys. There was really
only one issue in the trial. What was Zimmerman's intent when he fired
the fatal shot into Trayvon Martin's heart? Did his actions reflect the
recklessness necessary to find him guilty of second-degree murder, as
the prosecution contended? Or was Zimmerman merely acting in self-
defense, as his lawyers maintained? It was not an easy case for either

side, and we all now know that Zimmerman was swiftly acquitted. But Bloom argues that the prosecutors could have won this case—but, in simple terms, they blew it. As Bloom writes, "The overlooked evidence, lack of witness preparation, and poor strategic choices made by the state's attorneys were nothing short of astonishing."

Bloom expertly picks apart the evidence in the case to show the missed chances by the prosecution. Consider one example. In his statements to the police and the news media, Zimmerman asserted that he shot Martin because he believed the young man was reaching for Zimmerman's gun. But as Bloom carefully examines the evidence, we see that Zimmerman's gun was actually hidden inside his waistband—and behind his back. How could Martin have seen the gun, much less reached for it in a way that prompted Zimmerman to shoot first? Bloom writes, "And yet Trayvon, somehow, on that wet, black, low-visibility night, saw through the bulk of Zimmerman's body, through Zimmerman's shirt, through his jacket to a matte black gun concealed in a matte black holster clipped inside his waistband. Can anyone possibly believe this story?" Bloom, for one, clearly does not.

In the end, Bloom places the death of Trayvon Martin in the larger context of the history of race and violence in the United States. She unpacks the story of the Stand Your Ground defense (which Zimmerman's lawyers ended up not using) and explores Trayvon's own history in the Florida school system as a way of looking at its systemic flaws—flaws that are unfortunately shared in many school systems across the country. She looks, too, at another part of the story that is essential but often ignored: the question of gun laws and gun rights. It is a simple truth that Trayvon Martin would be alive today if George Zimmerman did not buy his gun.

Bloom's story is about Zimmerman, Martin, and the subsidiary cast of lawyers, cops, and witnesses, as well as her exclusive interview with the one non-white juror sitting on the case, who all became national figures for a brief moment in 2013. But the greatest significance of *Suspicion Nation* is that it is also about us. As she writes, "At the root of all of it is fear—overblown fear of crime, inordinate fear of strangers, deep-seated fear of difference, and in particular, lingering, unspoken fear that African Americans are criminals. So many of us are suspicious. We eye each other warily. And in twenty-first-century America, that fear is often armed, locked and loaded. And so the body count continues to rise, in an atmosphere of lawlessness."

Bloom maintains that our nation's biases and cultural blind spots created the conditions that led to the death of Trayvon Martin and made George Zimmerman's acquittal the most likely outcome. There is no better way than reading *Suspicion Nation* to learn how and why this sad story unfolded the way it did.

# INTRODUCTION

## *The Sixth Juror*

**M**ADDY[1] HAD HAD it. The trial wasn't over, but she was out of there. Rules or no rules, she was leaving. "If they had to put me in jail for going home, then put me in jail." Three weeks of sequestration with five white women who didn't understand the first thing about her, who demeaned and mocked and trivialized her, was more than enough. As the only minority juror in the nation's most watched and most racially charged case in decades, she was *done*.

As a thirty-six-year-old olive-skinned Puerto Rican woman, Maddy had been doubly lonely since the first week of trial. (Most juries in America have twelve members; Florida has six-person juries in all but death penalty cases, and in this case all six were female.) Judge Debra Nelson had ordered the six women sequestered, requiring them to leave their families for the duration of the trial, booking them in a local hotel under the careful watch of the sheriff's deputies, with occasional phone calls and weekly visits with family members. But Maddy had isolated herself even further, mostly staying in her room, away from the other jurors, securing herself from their words and cruel laughter and judgments about her.

She had no idea how bewildering and hurtful it would all be, nor how huge this trial was for Sanford, Florida, and the nation, which became captivated by the explosive case. On February 26, 2012, the night that Trayvon Martin was shot, Maddy wasn't even living in Florida, but in faraway Chicago, with her husband and seven children. Who had time to watch the news about a crime in a distant state? Between work and raising her family, Maddy was busy. Besides, the news was depressing. She got the weather on her phone, and that was all she felt she needed to know.

Just four months after Maddy and her family moved to central Florida in early 2013, Maddy's jury summons appeared. She couldn't believe it. And she'd just had a new baby girl. She could have easily evaded jury duty by saying she was breastfeeding, she learned, but she refused to lie, because lying is wrong.

As a nursing home caregiver, Maddy had no experience with the American court system, which seemed alien to her, conducted in a harsh foreign tongue. While being questioned at length by meticulous defense attorney Don West during jury selection, she felt confused and intimidated—Was she on trial? What had she done wrong? Why did he keep asking her what TV shows she watched, what newspapers she read? Was he accusing her of lying? Of being stupid? "They made me feel so guilty of something I didn't even do," she said. Only bad people had to go to court, she believed—just being in the courtroom made her feel like she must have done something wrong. "I don't know who George Zimmerman is, I really don't!" She kept telling them, but they kept asking anyway, the same question from different angles, because they wanted to be sure to seat jurors like Maddy who had not been tainted by pretrial publicity. It was exhausting her. The unnerving way Don West looked directly at her, as if he could read her mind—she'd never experienced anything like it and hoped never to feel so cross-examined again. "He scared the hell out of me. I cried when I came out [of jury selection]," she said.

"There he is!" other jurors whispered to her when they first saw stone-faced George Zimmerman, the accused murderer, across the small courtroom. They already knew more than she did. *Who?* Maddy thought, knowing that she was already falling behind. Business suits were so alien to her that she called them *tuxedos.* "I believed anybody who's got a tuxedo on is a lawyer," she said. So she concluded that Zimmerman, in his suit, was a lawyer too.

Assistant state attorney John Guy began the proceedings with, "Fucking punks! These assholes, they always get away." Rattled by the obscene language, Maddy did not hear the explanation, that these were Zimmerman's words on his recorded police call, which he made upon seeing Trayvon Martin for the first time, words that would become important later, so the prosecutor was using them now for dramatic effect.

All she knew was that the solemnity of the courtroom was shattered as the first attorney to speak at the trial was unnervingly profane.

During his defense opening statement, Don West awkwardly tried to break the tension in the courtroom with a knock-knock joke:

Knock knock!
Who's there?
George Zimmerman.
George Zimmerman who?
All right, good, you're on the jury.[2]

Maddy didn't understand the joke: "I just didn't get it." Who was George Zimmerman? Why did everyone in the courtroom except her seem to know all about him? Was he one of the lawyers, or the one accused of the shooting? But he'd admitted to the shooting, right? So why was a trial happening?

"I felt naive and dumb from the beginning," Maddy said. And her gnawing unease mounted each day the trial went on.

No OTHER CASE in recent memory grabbed and held the American public's attention like the Zimmerman murder trial. CNN, Fox News, and MSNBC covered the proceedings extensively, throughout the court day, with soaring ratings,[3] blowing out all other news coverage in order to broadcast opening statements, the testimony of key witnesses, and then, as viewers couldn't get enough, *all* witnesses. CNN's sister network, HLN, broadcast every moment of the trial, gavel-to-gavel, beginning to end. Many cable evening news shows covered the trial and only the trial, night after night, poring over every lame joke, analyzing juror body language, or replaying each smackdown of counsel by the judge. Prime-time specials were devoted to analyzing the trial. Network television—NBC, CBS, ABC—covered the story daily on morning shows and nightly on national news programs. Print media, highbrow and low, from the *New York Times* to TMZ.com, published thousands of stories about the proceedings, from pretrial wrangling over screams on a 911 call through the final Saturday late-night not-guilty verdict. The public's demand for stories about the trial was insatiable and continued well after its unsatisfying conclusion. Outside the United States, the world watched any of the three million YouTube videos that were posted about Zimmerman, mainly chunks of the trial.

For once, this intensive coverage was worthy. The public, especially African-American journalists and activists, had clamored for the media to pay attention to the story since shortly after February 26, 2012, when it became known that Trayvon Martin, a seventeen-year-old boy walking to a friend's home carrying only his cell phone, Skittles, and an Arizona watermelon drink, had been gunned down by a neighborhood-watch coordinator named George Zimmerman. Then Zimmerman's recorded call to the police was released, and we learned that he had looked out the window of his SUV and described Trayvon, a stranger to him, as "a real suspicious guy" who was "up to no good," adding, "these assholes, they always get away" and "fucking punks." (I refer to adults by their last names and minors by their first names throughout this book.) To many, Zimmerman appeared to have racially profiled Trayvon and shot and killed him based on the deepest, ugliest stereotypes still embedded in the American psyche: that blacks are criminals, dangerous—"they" get away with their crimes— "they" must be watched, followed—*those assholes*. Most of black America grasped immediately that a boy was dead from those prejudices.

Despite the strides America has made in the civil rights movement, eradicating Jim Crow laws, teaching tolerance, and electing an African-American president, racial inequality endures, as the shooting vividly illustrated. Any false belief that we lived in a post-racial America was shattered, as mothers of black boys spoke out about the excruciating warnings they privately gave their sons: *don't run, especially from police; don't carry anything in your hands; don't talk back to authority figures*. Yet Zimmerman was not police, and Trayvon was not running or speaking to him (at least not initially), nor was he holding anything in his hands. Many African-American commentators spoke about the personal pain they felt in hearing Trayvon lumped in with "these assholes" and "fucking punks"—that recorded language confirming their fears that they were constantly misjudged, stereotyped, suspicious merely for *walking while black.*

Some of white America was hostile to the idea that this case was significant. In a nation, sadly, with so many shootings, why did this one catch fire? Because a "bottom-up" grassroots movement insisted on it. The black community had heard it all before, too many agonizing times, the one about the unarmed dark-skinned man gunned down because he touched his waistband, or reached for a doorbell, or the cell phone in his hand had magically transformed into a gun in the eyes of his shooter. The community remembered Kimani Gray, Kendrec McDade, Timothy Russell, Sean Bell, Oscar Grant, and dozens of other names of young black men, weaponless, feared, gunned down, their shooters usually freed or facing only minimal sentences. Bruce Springsteen said, "Trayvon Martin is Amadou Diallo,"[4] invoking the unarmed African immigrant gunned down by New York City police in 1999, holding only his wallet, and sang, "you can get killed just for living in your American skin." Oprah Winfrey and others compared Trayvon to civil rights icon Emmett Till,[5] the fourteen-year-old black boy, also returning from a store with candy, who was shot in the head in 1955 in another small Southern town by a stranger with easy access to a gun, who, like Zimmerman, raised substantial funds for his legal defense fund and was quickly acquitted.

State and local officials spoke out, even at the highest levels. In no other state criminal case has President Barack Obama weighed in— twice—as he did here. First, in March 2012, carefully handling his comments about the matter, as it was then an open criminal case, he said only: "If I had a son, he'd look like Trayvon Martin."[6] No sympathetic words were offered to Zimmerman. Identifying with Trayvon, our first

African-American president, who generally avoided talk of race, under-stood that racial profiling was at the heart of the case.

After the acquittal in July 2013, as demonstrations erupted in dozens of cities nationwide, President Obama shocked the Washington press corps by making unannounced, seemingly off-the-cuff comments on the case. Speaking in the most personal terms we'd heard from him on any subject since he took office, President Obama upgraded his connection to the story, mirroring the popular "I Am Trayvon" placards at demon-strations: "When Trayvon Martin was first shot, I said this could've been my son. Another way of saying that is, Trayvon Martin could have been me, thirty-five years ago."

He continued: "There are very few African-American men in this country who haven't had the experience of being followed when they were shopping at a department store, and that includes me."[7] President Obama spoke about hearing locks click on car doors while crossing the street, something he said he personally experienced before he was sena-tor, and of women nervously clutching their purses while in elevators with African-American men like him.

Seeming to attempt to explain the black outrage about the acquittal, President Obama said: "I don't want to exaggerate this, but those sets of experiences inform how the African-American community interprets what happened one night in Florida. It's inescapable for people to bring those experiences to bear."[8]

*Understand our history*, President Obama seemed to say. *Understand that we are still living it. Grasp our pain that racial profiling happens, and it can end in death—death of our children.*

For many, the Florida verdict was a beginning, not an end. A civil rights movement was reignited, and a bright media spotlight shined on racial profiling not only in Florida, but also in New York City and nationwide. Stand Your Ground laws, which expanded traditional self-defense doctrine to allow those who felt threatened in virtually any location to use deadly force even if they could have escaped without violence, were decried, even though the law should have been inapplicable in the Zimmerman trial. Calls came for stricter gun laws, including prohibiting neighborhood-watch volunteers from carrying firearms. Yet deep divisions about race, guns, and Stand Your Ground still fester since they were put into motion when Zimmerman, on a rainy Florida night, decided to ignore the police recommendation to stay in his car, and instead ran after, as he put it, "this kid."

A verdict that could have provided accountability, vindication, and healing did not happen. But we are a nation of laws. The outcome would have to be accepted if the trial was fair. The community would have to just move on if Zimmerman's acquittal was based on the evidence at trial.

But that was not the case. Because the same suspicions and unexamined biases that Zimmerman harbored in one way or another coursed through the significant players in that courtroom: the defense attorneys, prosecutors, judge, and jury.

Before and after each day in court, tensions mounted between the jurors. "I had never looked at myself by color before," Maddy said. "The more we think about differences and negativity the more situations we have like this." She didn't think of herself as a minority. Months after the trial, she struggled with the question of whether she identified as Hispanic, black, or both. ("Hispanic," she settled on, but she also considered African Americans as members of "my culture.") But whatever category she belonged to, the trial and the behind-the-scenes group dynamics reminded her constantly that she was different, "other." The five white women seemed to inhabit another world.

A class divide, too, loomed large. Maddy bristled when other jurors complained about hotel housekeeping, for example. She identified more with the maids, a job she'd once had, than with the women she was sequestered with who griped about their service. One of the other jurors grumbled that she had no towels. "I gave her my towels," Maddy said, exasperated. "I only need one towel. I don't deal with face towel, hand towel. I have one towel. A towel's a towel, no big deal."

Other jurors told her to stop making her own hotel bed each morning. "Let the maid do it!" Maddy shook her head at the memory. "Do you really think a woman who has eight kids, who's worked her whole life, doesn't want to make her own bed? I used to work at Red Roof Inn, I had twenty rooms a day," Maddy said with pride. "I can make my own bed, clean my own room. If I can make that woman's life easier, I'm going to do it."

To some of the others, that was so funny!

After a group restaurant meal, Maddy wanted her uneaten food wrapped up for later. The other jurors teased her and told her not to— all their meals were being paid for by the state, so why save leftovers? Wasting food was anathema to Maddy. She couldn't do it. "I couldn't tell them I'd lived in a shelter with my kids, that I got some government assistance, that I've had a hard life. What would they think of me?"

Maddy didn't want to believe it, but the racial and class differences seemed to pop up everywhere in their daily interactions. "It's not about color, it's about how people are raised," she often says. Yet even in the TV room, the one safe space for the jurors to relax after stressful days in court, the gulf between Maddy and her fellow jurors widened. There the jurors watch monitored television shows and movies in the evenings and weekends, yet the group elected to watch shows with predominately white casts that Maddy disliked and even found offensive. HBO's blood-soaked, sexually explicit *Game of Thrones* was the group's favorite, and they watched it constantly. The violence and nudity disgusted Maddy: "I couldn't see it," she said. She'd asked to watch some of her beloved reality shows, like *Bridezillas*. "It's mostly white people on that show so I figured they would like it," she said, but the group vetoed it, on the grounds that it was "so dramatic." *Bad Girls Club* was one of Maddy's favorites, a popular reality show featuring a multiethnic group of aggressive, quarrelsome women living together in a luxury mansion, "but I knew they wouldn't go for it," she said. "I didn't want them to think I was ghetto and covering it up. I was trying to fit in."

One of the other jurors assumed control of the remote from the beginning and took it upon herself to decide what the group would watch. Maddy was granted one request for one thirty-minute show in three weeks, *Bridezillas*. No one could understand why she enjoyed it. As a result, Maddy removed herself from the social setting of the TV room, preferring the isolation of her room.

They weren't all bad. Just different from her. There were moments of kindness, certainly. A well-meaning fellow juror gave Maddy a music CD to listen to, telling her she'd probably like it since it was in Spanish. "It wasn't Spanish. It was French!" Maddy told her, returning the CD.

"I felt very alone," Maddy said. She felt small compared to the other women. "I'm in this bubble, I'm inside with these women. Everyone was talking about what they've done with their lives, how important they've been, and all I had to talk about was me and my kids because that's my life. I didn't sound too important. There wasn't too much interest in me from the other women. So I stayed in my room." There she would read her Christian books, like one by African-American megachurch bishop T.D. Jakes. She'd also do puzzles, and color in coloring books. The only bright spot in the calendar for Maddy was on Sundays, when her kids and husband would visit for one hour, with a sheriff's deputy sitting near her door.

Was it just a coincidence that Maddy's room was the only one with an officer stationed just outside? She couldn't tell. Did they see her as suspicious? She wondered. "I go to a lot of places and they get people to follow me sometimes,"[9] she said, recounting the common experience of Americans of color.

The juror designated as B37 treated Maddy the worst. (Maddy's the only one who's used even her first name in post-trial interviews. Her last name is withheld here to protect her privacy.) Early on in the trial, Maddy had called ramen noodles "Roman noodles," and B37 ridiculed her mercilessly. "You talk so funny!" All the other jurors laughed, and at first Maddy laughed uneasily along with them. Then she realized, *They're not laughing* with *me, they're laughing* at *me.* B37 referred to "they" or "them" a lot, Maddy said, and she knew who she was referring to. People like her.

"I didn't know I didn't speak proper English," Maddy said, until B37 kept making fun of Maddy's word choices.

Several of the white jurors were animal lovers. "We can't afford a dog," Maddy said, but she "respect[s] that love." As the trial wore on, one juror made a special request, which was granted, to spend an entire weekend day with her dog. The dog was brought to the hotel and she enjoyed nine hours with him.

Maddy, aching for her children, thought that if the dog visit was granted, she should have a full day with her baby, rather than one hour per week, which felt so brief. "I would have loved nine hours with my baby," she said. She summoned her courage, spurred on by another juror, and made her request, which was denied on the ground that children can talk. Her infant daughter was three months old. (She was granted just one extra hour with her baby on Sunday.) Maddy's belief that she was singled out for different treatment continued.

By the final week of trial, "I felt I had no voice," Maddy said. "My voice had been taken away. No matter what I would say it wouldn't make a difference. I was not important." On Monday, Maddy had uncharacteristically failed to come out for her telephone call with her family. Later, she emerged from her room, crying. A kind deputy asked her gently why she had not come out earlier. "I am going through a lot," Maddy said, and he seemed to implicitly understand. "Only those who come from my culture understood my pain," Maddy said.

The deputy made it clear that Maddy needed to stay on the jury. He sat with her and talked about his kids. He told her he had just become a law enforcement officer, and that his wife was a lawyer. "I'm African American," he told her. "For other people this comes easy." But he'd had to work hard, stay strong. That resonated deeply with Maddy. Here was someone who got it, that feeling of difference. He talked about his pride in his job, and what he had overcome to get there.

"That man inspired me so much," Maddy said. "I prayed for him, asking God to bless him financially, physically, mentally. He made me feel he's here to protect *all* of us, no matter what color. I kept strong and stayed with it to show people what I could do."

But three days later, on Thursday of the final week, Maddy was losing it again. She didn't realize the trial was almost over. For her, it felt like an endless pressure cooker, and she wanted to get out. B37 was back at it, insulting Maddy for the way she spoke, and now, mocking another juror for drinking more than her allotted two glasses of wine or beer per day ("you shouldn't be drinking because you don't know how to act when you drink") or making rude comments about another juror's disabled child. "I swear to you, you seriously have to stop talking," Maddy told her. "If you have nothing positive to say, don't talk to me. You need to stop talking about people."

The stress was too much. Maddy broke down crying and again decided she had to go home. Another deputy, a Hispanic woman, came and spoke to her. "Why am I being abused?" Maddy asked. "Why do I feel so bad?" She felt again that she had no voice, that she was always drowned out by the others, that "whatever [she] said wasn't going to matter." This deputy too insisted that she stay. She soothed her, telling Maddy she was almost done, pleading with her not to go. She could do it. She *needed* to do it. Ultimately, the officer convinced her to stay, hugging Maddy, listening to her, and "making me feel important."

The isolation, the shunning, was almost more than Maddy could bear, but the efforts of these two sensitive deputies, whom Maddy felt comfortable with, kept her there.

Closing arguments and then deliberations on Zimmerman's fate began the next day. In her heart, Maddy believed that he should be convicted of second-degree murder, the top charge.

But two other jurors, who strongly favored acquittal from the beginning, seemed to know so much more about the facts and the law than she did. That feeling of naiveté and ignorance overwhelmed her. One juror would mention that she knew things about the case that hadn't come up at trial, and that she had a lawyer for a husband; another juror's son was a lawyer too. These two seemed to understand the law far better than Maddy did. They possessed an authority that Maddy couldn't begin to counter.

For a layperson like Maddy, the inconsistent, long-winded legalese found in the booklet of jury instructions was impossible to fathom, much less follow. "For them to tell me to make a decision on someone's life, and then to give me a whole booklet that I couldn't understand . . . I don't understand," Maddy said, still puzzled and disturbed months after the conclusion of the trial.

How could Maddy persuade the others to convict? What resources could she draw upon? Just her heart and her sense of justice. Three others wanted to convict at the outset too, but as the hours wore on, and they reviewed the evidence, and the pro-acquittal jurors were so sure of themselves, Maddy felt defeated. She couldn't find the evidence, or the law, to show them that Zimmerman was guilty.

When she discusses deliberations, Maddy talks a lot about her heart. "I went in there wholehearted," she says, yet, "I listened to the lawyers when they said don't use your heart. That to me meant he was not guilty."

She admired the prosecutors for having a lot of heart and appearing to care deeply about Trayvon and his family, but "then they tell me to take the emotion out of it. Wow, that's all [they] gave me! That jacked me up!"

"The other women were talking a different language," Maddy explained. *Justifiable homicide, Stand Your Ground, manslaughter*— these legal terms were unclear to Maddy. "All their points were so educated. It didn't matter what I said."

"They knew I didn't know anything about the law," she said. What had been an advantage during jury selection—Maddy was the proverbial blank slate lawyers wanted, coming into the trial with almost zero knowledge of pretrial publicity or the rules of the game—now felt like a crushing disadvantage, as the other jurors insisted they knew aspects of the law or other important facts that had not come in at trial but that they'd seen on the news. Should she have studied for the trial beforehand?

As the hours went by, Maddy had the sinking feeling that the verdict she knew was right—guilty—was evaporating. The jurors fought. They wept. Maddy locked herself in the bathroom. She sat on the floor and cried. Another juror insisted she would fight for a conviction to the end. She could not let Zimmerman go without finding him guilty of *something.*

After ten hours of deliberation they took their first vote. Maddy, crushed, voted not guilty, along with another juror who'd initially wanted to convict. Two more continued to hold out for conviction, but Maddy knew it was hopeless. Eventually, after several more hours, the strong voices for acquittal had persuaded all the others. One "knew more than we knew," from the pretrial publicity, Maddy says. She knew that "Trayvon Martin was a bad kid," though no evidence of that had come into trial. She knew that Trayvon was "intentionally behind Zimmerman, that he knew he was going to hit him, and that he planned his own death." Maddy didn't know what to believe, or how to respond.

In the jury room, Maddy had been persuaded of several gravely incorrect understandings of the law as applied to the case. "They told me not to look at the beginning [where Zimmerman followed Trayvon], just the fight." She thought that "you are able to use force when force was used," and that "the law says that at the end of the day all that mattered is who was on top and who was on the bottom." (Actually, there is a great deal of legal significance attached to the run-up to the shooting. The rules for using *deadly* force are far more rigorous than that gross oversimplification, and all the circumstances should have been taken into account.)

Toward the end, the jury sent out a note to the judge asking for an explanation of one of the two charges against Zimmerman, manslaughter. The judge answered only that they needed to ask a more specific question. They were stumped and didn't want to embarrass themselves with another dumb question, so they didn't respond. Ultimately Maddy walked away with an outrageously incorrect view of the law, that manslaughter required that "when [Zimmerman] left home, he said, I'm gonna go kill Trayvon Martin."[10] (No, that would have been first-degree murder, which Zimmerman was never charged with.)

"I felt in my heart he was guilty to the end, but I couldn't prove it," Maddy said, dejected. Those weeks on the jury left her shattered. When she got home, she fell apart. "I literally fell on my knees and I broke down, my husband was holding me, I was screaming and crying and I kept saying to myself I feel like I killed him." Shortly after the trial, Maddy began psychotherapy for the first time in her life. "I feel that I was forcibly included in Trayvon Martin's death. I carry him on my back." Guilt consumed her. "I'm the only minority,[11] and I felt like I let a lot of people down."

But her faith centered her. "George Zimmerman got away with murder," Maddy said, "but you can't get away from God."

She tried to return to work at the nursing home, but her supervisor told her not to come in for a few weeks after the trial "to let things die down," and after that, no one there would return her calls. Unable to find another job, and with her husband out of work as well, Maddy and her family moved away from the warm Florida sunshine she had grown to love and back to inner-city Chicago. As this book went to press, Maddy and her family were homeless, staying temporarily with a friend.

Maddy tries to stay positive, but the experience scarred her. "I never experienced being treated as inferior before."

I WATCHED THE Zimmerman trial from a very different vantage point than Maddy. Having closely scrutinized many hundreds of high- and low-profile murder trials for Court TV, CNN, ABC, CBS, NBC, and other networks for nearly two decades, and having been a trial attorney since 1986 (I still maintain an active law practice), I understand how trials play out in American courtrooms. As a legal analyst, I'm interested almost exclusively in one thing: following the evidence. *All* of the evidence, to its own conclusion, whether that outcome is popular or unpopular.

Brought in to follow the Zimmerman trial intensively as a special project for NBC News and MSNBC, my assignment was to watch the entire proceeding, gavel-to-gavel, and to report fairly and accurately on what was going on in the courtroom. Watching sound bites or reading summaries would not cut it. In a case of this prominence, I wanted to

watch it all, every minute, and my networks agreed. I had no precon-
ceived notions as to who should win, and I went in with an aggressively open mind. I knew that a trial is an entirely different animal from
an arrest. Too many innocent people are convicted in this country. I
had previously written about our culture of mass incarceration, a social
evil fed by too many young men (often black or Hispanic) railroaded
by overzealous, overcharging prosecutors, unaided by overburdened
public defenders. Our harsh penal system devastates the lives of these
(predominately) young men as well as their families and communities,
as we continue to incarcerate more of our own people than any other
country on earth, or in human history. It's a subject I speak about often
on television and radio, most recently praising reforms of "mandatory
minimum" drug laws that impose long prison sentences on low-level,
nonviolent offenders. I did not want to see another of our citizens incarcerated unless he truly belonged behind bars, not in the Zimmerman
case, not in any case. Certainly those committing violent crimes like
murder or manslaughter should be locked up, but only if the evidence
conclusively establishes guilt. Our criminal justice system has its flaws,
but requiring proof beyond a reasonable doubt is not one of them.

Pretrial, I was uneasy that Zimmerman's arrest may have been made
solely on the basis of the massive community outcry that preceded it,
because a criminal trial is almost never the place for resolution of social
or political grievances. While many were gunning for a conviction before
the first witness testified, I found that unseemly, at odds with our obligation to find proof beyond a reasonable doubt or acquit. Racial profiling,
Stand Your Ground, our gun laws—these are all serious social issues,
crying out for public debate and reforms (as we shall see in Part Two).
But inside the courtroom, the case was about George Zimmerman and

Trayvon Martin and what happened during the few minutes of their encounter within the gates of the Retreat at Twin Lakes, where the incident occurred, when Trayvon was walking back to watch the All Star game with a seventh grader and Zimmerman was doing his Sunday grocery run to Target. Let me hear the witnesses. Show me the evidence. Let the chips fall where they may.

In the weeks before the trial began, I crammed, reading everything I could about the case: the news stories about "Witness 8," Trayvon's mystery "girlfriend" who we expected to be the star witness (later revealed to be the much-debated Rachel Jeantel, and simply a friend); the highly anticipated testimony of Trayvon's parents who would say it was their son screaming for his life on what would be known as the Lauer 911 call; the Sanford Police's alleged mishandling of the evidence and the investigation. I analyzed the map of the Retreat at Twin Lakes; I read Zimmerman's handwritten police statement; I listened to the audio of his interview with detectives; I watched his lengthy videotaped reenactment; I watched his television interview with Fox News anchor Sean Hannity; I put together a timeline.

After this initial review, it seemed to me the chips were falling almost entirely on the defense side of the case—that is, for Zimmerman. The prosecution faced a tough burden: they had to prove *beyond a reasonable doubt* that Zimmerman had *not* acted in self-defense. One might think that the defense, claiming that Zimmerman shot to save his own life, would have the obligation to prove that, but in forty-nine states, including Florida, it is the prosecution that must *disprove* self-defense once the defense raises a plausible argument for it.

Consider that challenge for a moment in a trivializing analogy that draws upon the common experience of parents: Your two kids skirmish in the backyard while you are inside, making dinner, listening to music. You didn't see or hear it. They both come running in, complaining of the other. You suspect one caused the fight and the other was the victim. But now imagine that you must decide if you can honestly say beyond and to the exclusion of any reasonable doubt that one did *not* act in self-defense while smacking the other. If you can't say that, you can't punish.

What would most of us say? *I don't know, I didn't see it.* In a criminal trial, that translates into reasonable doubt. An acquittal.

Zimmerman was the only surviving witness to the shooting, and he said he shot once to defend his own life, as Trayvon reached for Zimmerman's gun and threatened to kill him after pounding his head dozens of times on the concrete sidewalk. His calm, seemingly honest demeanor in telling his story (captured on audio and video); the internal logic of his story; the legal requirement (which most pundits were missing) that the jury focus less on what I call Phase 1 (his obnoxious profiling and following Trayvon—all perfectly legal) and more on Phase 2 (the "fight" and shooting); his full and open cooperation with the police, answering all their questions, submitting to every test; and his bloody head injuries all seemed to support his credibility.

Opening statements underscored my initial impression that this looked like a clear defense case—that is, that Zimmerman would walk. The media fixated on defense attorney Don West's dumb knock-knock joke.[12] His attempt at humor as he sat just a few feet away from the grieving parents of Trayvon Martin, who had fought for months to get law enforcement to prosecute their son's killer and then waited anxiously for the trial to begin, was grossly insensitive. It was also an easy sound bite and talking point, so most of the media focused on it rather than the remaining hour and a half of his opening statement and the large amount of evidence he methodically laid out for the jury, which was far more significant in previewing his side of the case. In contrast, the prosecution gave a widely lauded, passionate, short opening statement, which mentioned only a few pieces of hard evidence. Remember the profanity that startled Maddy? Drama only goes so far. In this murder case, the prosecution appeared to lack proof. In openings, the prosecution won on style, the defense won on content.

As the first week of witnesses played out, neighbors who heard or saw parts of the altercation and police responders testified. The defense undermined some of them by getting them to admit their memories were hazy, and they turned others in their favor, eliciting testimony that Zimmerman was well-liked, or that Trayvon was on top of Zimmerman in their encounter. Zimmerman seemed like a pleasant, reasonable guy— not a wild stalker and murderer—and very possibly the victim in the altercation. Even the cops liked him.

We were still in the prosecution's case—the beginning of the trial when the state puts on its witnesses—but the defense already seemed to be winning. Off camera, I spoke with my friends, top legal analysts from other networks, and we all saw it the same way. The case seemed grossly lopsided. The state was in trouble.

Watching every minute of the trial, analyzing and synthesizing the testimony with my producers, other attorneys, journalists, and academics, it was not until the Sunday of the July 4 holiday weekend that I had a moment to breathe. Two weeks into the three-week trial, I used the opportunity to take another look at the important evidence that had already been admitted in the trial, as I would if I were trying the case myself for either side.

That's when I noticed some critical evidence about the placement of Zimmerman's gun. That black KelTec 9mm PF-9 semiautomatic handgun was holstered not only inside his waistband (that is, inside his pants, concealed), but *behind* Zimmerman, on his backside.

That could not be right. Could it?

I learned this from Zimmerman himself, as I watched, and re-watched, and re-watched the videotaped reenactment of the incident with Zimmerman showing the police (I'm paraphrasing), *I was standing here, and he was there, and then he punched me, and then we were down, and then I took out my gun, like this.*

Stop. Rewind. Play.

Stop. Rewind. Play.

No matter how many times I rewound and replayed that video, there was Zimmerman, allowed to reenact the event in a standing position (did the police feel it would be too messy to ask a man who'd just killed a teenager to actually get down on the grass and reenact his story?), clearly demonstrating to the police that *his gun was holstered behind him.*

This had monumental implications for the case, as we shall see. Among other things, it completely contradicted and made virtually impossible Zimmerman's story about the most critical moment in the incident: that Zimmerman was pinned down on his back, Trayvon was on top, straddling him, punching him, and suddenly Trayvon *saw and reached for the gun*, leaving Zimmerman no choice but to draw his weapon and shoot.

On a very dark, rainy night, Trayvon *saw through Zimmerman's body* to a gun holstered behind him, concealed inside his pants? Did Trayvon have X-ray vision?

What shocked me most of all was that the prosecution had failed to raise this point at trial. Not in the opening statement. Not in the questioning of any of their witnesses. Not in cross-examination of defense witnesses.

If the state's attorneys missed this, what else had they overlooked?

I reviewed pictures of the crime scene again. I listened to Zimmerman's prior police calls about other suspicious people in the neighborhood. Astonishingly, the prosecution was missing or glossing over some of the most important evidence in the case—evidence that had been admitted at trial, but that for some reason they were not *using*.

My assignment had been to follow the evidence. But I never expected the proof to go in one direction and the prosecution to go in another. In nearly two decades of covering murder trials, this was a first. I had never seen prosecutors shy away from arguing their best evidence.

What, exactly, was going on here?

The final week of the trial, I appeared daily on several shows explaining not only what was going on in that Florida courtroom, but what wasn't: the many prosecution missteps, which were now leaping off the screen at me. Most of all, I talked about the gun-holstered-behind-Zimmerman issue, and others started talking about it too. It began to generate a lot of buzz in the on-air commentary about the case. "Someone needs to tell the prosecution about this," was a common refrain.

It appeared that may have happened. Four days later, in his closing argument, having missed many opportunities to argue this and other evidence in direct- and cross-examination of witnesses, prosecutor Bernie de la Rionda for the first time mentioned—*mentioned, briefly*—that Zimmerman's gun was holstered behind him. He did not slow down and emphasize the video. He did not begin or end with the point (the moments at which jurors would be most likely to remember it), did not reenact it with the gun and holster, did not use the courtroom dummy to drive home this point. He mentioned it, then moved on. Most of his closing was a rambling, disorganized presentation comprised of questions, *mights*, and *maybes*, telling the jury blithely that they knew the evidence, they could put it together.

The state was abrogating its responsibility to give the jurors a roadmap to conviction.

I started telling everyone, on and off air, to prepare for an acquittal. The prosecution and the defense both had doubt, not certainty. Given that, the jury could reach only one possible outcome.

With my MSNBC colleagues, I took the verdict on air live that Saturday night. When the words "not guilty" were pronounced, many were surprised. I was not.

Some analysts blamed the jury, some the laws. I continued to say what I'd said so many times before the verdict: the prosecution failed to aggressively argue their best evidence in the case, virtually guaranteeing this outcome.

I had a short break the next night, and I walked downtown to meet my daughter for dinner, trying to clear my head of this disturbing case. *Breathe*, I told myself. *Enjoy this summer night air*. Suddenly I heard a roar echoing down a Manhattan concrete canyon. "What do we want? JUSTICE!" "No justice, no peace!" Thousands of people marched down Second Avenue, holding pictures of Trayvon. Parents, kids, elderly folks, black, white, Hispanic, Asian.

I stared, speechless, stirred. This case, and its outcome, had deeply wounded so many people.

"Hey, Lisa Bloom!" a woman called out to me. I smiled weakly. "What happened?" she asked.

The evidence was there, I wanted to tell her. I can't explain why the prosecution missed it, or failed to bring it home. But I wanted to detail for her, for everyone with that question, everything that went wrong in this case. I couldn't do it in that instant, before she and the marchers marched on.

The next day, Monday, doing post-verdict wrap-ups, Tamron Hall, host of MSNBC's *NewsNation*, asked me the hardest question of all. "Lisa, did the prosecution blow it?"

I tried to hedge my answer on national television. I'd been critical of the prosecution, but up to a point. These were professionals, who presumably did their best. I did not want to so bluntly malign them. "Oh, there were a number of missteps . . . "

"So, that sounds like a yes. You're saying they blew it."

The *New York Times* asked me to write an opinion piece. I thought about it carefully, reviewing the evidence yet again. And in that op-ed,[13] for the first time in print, I pointed directly to some of the major prosecution blunders, including their decision to duck entirely the obvious racial issues in the case—the very issues that had propelled popular support for Zimmerman to be brought to trial.

I thought about Tamron's question in the days after the trial as the nation erupted in demonstrations, as President Obama himself spoke movingly of his own experience being racially profiled, as I was unable to close the door on this case and move on to the next.

The answer, to me, is unavoidable: Yes, the prosecution blew it. On a number of very significant points. Explaining how requires more than a brief TV appearance or a short op-ed. Though Zimmerman's story of the shooting was belied by the physical evidence, though he expressed overt hostility toward Trayvon from the moment he laid eyes on the minor, though he admitted to no remorse afterward and gloated months later that the killing was "God's plan," the defense won the trial by painting Trayvon just as Zimmerman had, as "a real suspicious guy." With his own voice silenced, and without any real courtroom advocates fighting for him, in a system coursing with racial biases, Trayvon never really stood a chance.

But it's not just about the state of Florida bungling the case. Because looking more deeply at the cultural context of this trial, the outcome was almost preordained. Our laws, beliefs, assumptions, and blind spots combined to create the conditions that led to the death of Trayvon and made Zimmerman's acquittal by far the most likely outcome. After all, those forces had created similar injustices many times before, and after this trial, innocent young African Americans continued to be gunned down by frightened white shooters claiming self-defense. Our cultural norms and implicit biases are the root causes of those tragedies, of the prosecution's failure to properly argue the case, of the judge's refusal to allow discussion of racial profiling in the courtroom, of the jury's attitudes about Trayvon and Maddy. The solution lies not only in reforming America's gun laws and eliminating Stand Your Ground laws, but also in owning up to and ultimately eradicating racial assumptions that continue to run deep in nearly all of us, poisoning every aspect of the criminal justice system.

Hence, this book. Many people feel in their gut that this trial was a miscarriage of justice, and they're often told to get over it because the jury heard all the evidence and reached a decision. I am here to say no, that in fact that gut feeling is correct, based on the evidence and the law as it should have been presented, as it would have been presented in most other murder trials in America.

Technically prosecutors represent the people of the state of Florida, not the victim, Trayvon Martin. But in a very real sense, they serve as his advocates in the courtroom, giving a voice to the silenced teenager. And Trayvon Martin did not get a fair trial. Not even close.

Can I say to a certainty that had the prosecution aggressively argued their best evidence, as I will outline it here, they would have won the case? I cannot. But we know that of the six jurors, four began jury deliberations wanting to convict (two would have convicted of the top charge of murder, two for the lesser charge of manslaughter) and two to acquit. We know that the pro-conviction jurors hungered for the facts and the law to be given to them in a way that could counter the strong voices for acquittal, and that, shamefully, that did not happen. Had the state of Florida done its job, this close case could well have gone the other way. The sympathies of most of the jurors, along with much of the nation, even the President, were on the side of the prosecution. I can now say with confidence, having analyzed every aspect of this trial, that this case was the prosecution's to lose. And lose it they did, by missing some critical evidence almost entirely, failing to emphasize other evidence, and making sure-to-fail choices contrary to what prosecutors in murder cases in American courtrooms do every day, such as failing to adequately prepare their key witnesses and never giving the jury their version of what happened that dark, wet night in that small Southern town.

Here's what happened.

# PART ONE

## A WINNABLE CASE IS LOST

# ONE

## *The People Demand an Arrest*

PROSECUTORS ARE THE most powerful players in our criminal justice system. Their day-to-day decisions can literally determine which Americans will lose their liberty, even their lives. In virtually every criminal case in America, prosecutors decide whether to file charges, and if they do, *which* charges to file—minor crimes (misdemeanors) or major ones (felonies)? Once a criminal defendant is charged, prosecutors choose whether to offer a plea bargain, and if so, what deal to offer (community service? A fine? One year behind bars? Twenty?) or whether to roll the dice and go to trial. Though they are public officials in our democracy, paid with our tax dollars, all of these decisions are made behind closed doors, without transparency or accountability, almost never subject to public review. If you and your friend are both involved in an incident, and you get charged and convicted and your friend does not, there's nothing you can do about it.

A great deal of the work prosecutors do is spent determining plea bargains. Limited resources drive them to make deals in most cases in order to avoid trial. Cases run the gamut from very strong (credible eyewitnesses, DNA evidence, a confession, a videotape) to very weak (defendant has a verifiable alibi, there's a lack of forensic evidence, witnesses don't exist or are not believable). Most fall somewhere in between, and prosecutors must sift through the evidence to decide if the case is strong enough for them to prove guilt to a jury beyond a reasonable doubt.

As many as 95 percent of cases[14] resolve by plea bargain,[15] where defendants give up their right to go to trial and gamble on the outcome in exchange for a lesser sentence offered to them by prosecutors and blessed by a judge. Courts across America, already budget-strapped, would be instantly crippled if every defendant insisted on a trial. And thus very weak cases do not get charged at all, even if law enforcement has a hunch that Defendant X is good for the crime. A gut feeling isn't enough. Cases rarely improve with the passage of time. If anything, they get worse. Witnesses get sick, die, disappear, forget, or pretend to forget what they saw or heard. So if the case isn't strong at the beginning, prosecutors leave it alone. (Which is as it should be. Those against whom a case cannot be proven beyond a reasonable doubt should remain at liberty.)

If significant weaknesses arise after an arrest—a witness recants, say, or a videotape shows the complainant to be lying—charges are dropped. (Again, this is as it should be.)

In middle-ground cases—not weak, not strong, cases with some evidence but that could go either way at trial—prosecutors offer a defendant a plea bargain, and those plea offers are accepted, after some back and forth, by most defendants, innocent or guilty, because the sentence is normally far less than the high stakes of losing at trial. If you're facing twenty years if convicted of the top charge at trial and the state offers you one year, unless you enjoy gambling with your freedom, you're probably going to take it.

This king- and queen-like power—*you* are free to go, *you* get charged with involuntary manslaughter, *you* get charged with murder and face life in prison—can almost never be challenged. Legal claims that prosecutors discriminated based on race in charging decisions have routinely failed, for example. The U.S. Supreme Court has deferred, allowing state attorneys to make these decisions without messy judicial oversight. Even the language prosecutors choose in their criminal complaints is hugely consequential, as Attorney General Eric Holder demonstrated in 2013 in directing his federal prosecutors to leave out specific drug quantities in low-level possession cases so as to avoid triggering draconian mandatory minimum laws. (Why not just change the laws? That would require acts of Congress. At the moment Congress is inert.) This one small change made by assistant U.S. attorneys means for potentially hundreds of thousands of drug offenders annually the difference between five or ten years in prison for a marijuana charge and no time at all. *You* (and your family) suffer the sucker-punch of a decade of incarceration; *you* just get probation. Who else in our legal system has that kind of power?

Most people think that judges wield the most authority in the system, but prosecutors are the gatekeepers who decide who even gets through the funnel to see a judge. Few do, because of all that plea bargaining, and so judges see only one in twenty offenders at trial. Even then, judges' hands are often tied by strict sentencing guidelines, and their decisions are subject to review by higher courts. Some high-profile judges have even resigned from their cushy lifetime appointments over the limits on their ability to rule in favor of what they think is right. Federal Judge Lawrence Irving said in frustration when he stepped down, "If I remain on the bench I have no choice but to follow the law. I just can't, in good conscience, continue to do this. I've had a problem with mandatory sentencing in almost every case that's come before me."[16]

I've never heard of a prosecutor resigning because he or she did not have enough power, or not enough discretion, and I probably never will.

As a result of the power to charge, to offer pleas, or to take cases to trial, most prosecutors have impressive-sounding trial records. In the Zimmerman case, assistant state attorney (as prosecutors are called in Florida) Bernie de la Rionda claimed to have an 80-1 win-loss record before the trial began. Wow! Wasn't the defense scared? No, probably not. While most prosecutors are good courtroom lawyers (as are most defense attorneys), that type of trial record is not unusual for state attorneys for two other reasons: because most juries will convict (who are you going to believe, that nice uniformed police officer or the sketchy looking guy who sits before you who's accused of assault?), and more importantly, *prosecutors generally only bring strong cases to trial—cases they feel confident they'll win.* (Defense attorneys, by contrast, are so used to losing that they consider a trial a win if their client is convicted of anything other than the top charge.)

Understanding the peculiarities of the Zimmerman murder trial requires grasping this key overarching fact: *The Zimmerman trial was an exception to this rule. Prosecutors did not choose it. They did not get to exercise their usual discretion.* In a very real sense, the case was foisted upon them. In fact, for the first forty-five days after the shooting, law enforcement refused to charge Zimmerman with any crime at all because prosecutors believed that they did not have the evidence to disprove Zimmerman's self-defense story. But then a groundswell of public protest and media attention changed all that, and it forced law enforcement to take an action it did not want to take: arresting George Zimmerman.

Here's the unusual way it all went down: Trayvon Martin was shot and killed at 7:17 PM on Sunday evening, February 26, 2012. We know the precise time because the fatal shot is heard on the Lauer 911 call (of the seven neighbors who called 911 before or after the shooting, Jenna Lauer's call captured screaming and the fatal gunshot.) Trayvon was not carrying identification, which makes sense for a kid just taking a walk to a nearby 7-Eleven. Disturbingly, after finding his body, police did not knock on doors in the neighborhood to see if anyone knew him. Did police assume Trayvon did not live in that gated suburban community? That he could not have been an invited guest there? First responders spoke to a few residents who gathered outside after the shooting but did not conduct a door-to-door search asking if anyone knew the teenager who'd just been shot and killed in the gated community. Had they gone a few hundred feet, knocking on less than a dozen doors, they would have come to the home of Brandy Green, where Brandy's fourteen-year-old son, Chad Joseph, who was waiting for Trayvon's return, would have identified the body. (Chad didn't hear the incident because he had headphones on and was playing Playstation 3 in an upstairs bedroom.) Trayvon's father, Tracy Martin, out to dinner with his fiancée, Brandy Green, would surely have been contacted right away. He would then have had the opportunity to raise questions about Zimmerman's self-defense story immediately. (Zimmerman said that Trayvon leaped out of the bushes in a homicidal rage? *Come on,* Tracy Martin would likely have said. *Trayvon was so quiet and mild-mannered that his nickname was Mouse.)*

Instead, Trayvon's body was taken to the morgue as a John Doe. His father assumed Trayvon had gone to a late-night movie with a friend and was not concerned about Trayvon's absence until Monday morning, when he reported him missing to the police. Once Tracy Martin made that call, law enforcement put together that the homicide victim was

Tracy Martin's son. Police came to Brandy Green's door that Monday morning and delivered to Tracy Martin the shattering news that his son had been fatally shot just down the walkway the night before.

By Wednesday morning, still in shock, Tracy Martin went to the Sanford Police Department looking for answers, and in particular, looking for an arrest. His son had been killed walking home from a 7-Eleven, armed only with candy and a fruit drink. Police knew who the shooter was. What was taking so long? Why was Zimmerman still free?

Getting nowhere with police, Martin turned in frustration to a family member who referred him to Tallahassee civil rights attorney Benjamin Crump. In 2006, Crump won a $7.2 million judgment against the state of Florida in a high-profile case on behalf of the family of Martin Lee Anderson, a black teenager who died in a boot-camp-style youth detention center. The case led to the closures of juvenile boot camps[17] in the state of Florida and local fame for Crump, especially in the African-American community.

Crump's practice is kept busy representing families of black Floridians killed under suspicious circumstances, usually by police. When he took Tracy Martin's call,[18] he was in court on behalf of the family of a black bail bondsman who had been shot and killed by a sheriff's deputy in Jacksonville, Florida, 125 miles north of Sanford.

Initially Crump did not take the Zimmerman case because he was confident that Zimmerman would be arrested in short order. *Patience*, Crump counseled. *It's only been two days*, he told Tracy Martin. *The system will work. Police are surely investigating the matter, and Zimmerman will be arrested soon.* "I believed in my heart of hearts they were going to arrest him," Crump told the Associated Press[19] a month later. "I said, 'Oh, they are going to arrest him. You don't need me on this.'"

But as days went by and no arrest was forthcoming, Crump knew something was wrong. The son of a soldier and a hotel maid, Crump, who is African American, had attended segregated schools until the fifth grade. He had a keen sense of civil rights injustices and understood that this was a case with monumental implications for the black community. And he began to see that his initial assessment was wrong. In fact, he was very much needed if an arrest was to happen.

Obtaining no resolution from the police, Crump made the fateful choice to take his case to the media.[20] He orchestrated a few press conferences with Trayvon's grieving parents speaking searingly of their loss. Initially only local media in Florida picked up the story. Then, Crump ratcheted up the pressure by enlisting U.S. Rep. Corrine Brown to help convince authorities to release the 911 tapes, recordings that brought the case to the attention of the national media. Working with civil rights activists, he organized a series of rallies demanding justice for Trayvon.

Crump contacted New York–based civil rights leader Reverend Al Sharpton ("Rev. Al"), head of the National Action Network, who in turn reached out to Pastor Ronald Durham of the Greater Friendship Baptist Church in Daytona Beach, Florida, a short drive from Sanford. Pastor Durham, a sixty-something local National Action Network leader with thirty-eight years in the ministry, who favors flashy gold and diamond rings and cufflinks, sprang into action. Together with other local clergy, he began to organize a rally. Immediately they realized that a church with a few hundred seats would not be big enough to contain the anger that was growing in central Florida over the unarmed black teenager who had been shot dead and the police's failure to arrest the known shooter. Working closely with city representatives, whom Pastor Durham calls "extremely, extremely cooperative," the local organizers reviewed every detail to be sure that community activities and traffic patterns would not be disrupted, assuring the city that the rally would be entirely law-abiding, which it was. (Later, in the pretrial jury selection phase, juror B37 would grossly mischaracterize this and related peaceful gatherings as "riots"—and though the prosecution had the opportunity to strike her from the jury panel, they did not.)

Pastor Durham called the rally a "star-studded event," featuring Rev. Al; TV's Judge Mathis; radio personality Michael Baisden; NAACP President Ben Jealous; Joe Madison, Sirius radio's "the Black Eagle"; and Marc Morial, CEO of the National Urban League, the nation's largest civil rights organization. Even more moving to Pastor Durham was that in just a few weeks' time, a passion for justice for Trayvon, a previously unknown high school student, had spread not only nationally but internationally. "People traveled to the rally from Hawaii, Australia, the UK, and France," he told me. Police estimated the crowd exceeded 30,000, he said. Spirited but peaceful demonstrations also occurred in New York, Washington, D.C., Los Angeles, and in other locations, demanding Zimmerman's arrest.

The first national media coverage of the case occurred on *CBS This Morning* on March 8, 2012. Websites, bloggers, and other national media quickly picked up the story. By the end of March 2012, nationally prominent black journalists took the lead in keeping the spotlight on. George Zimmerman's police call was made public, with the officer famously telling Zimmerman not to follow Trayvon. The Lauer 911 call was released, with the anguished, high-pitched screams followed by the gunshot that killed Trayvon. Sanford police chief Bill Lee[21] announced that he could not dispute Zimmerman's claim of self-defense. These and other new bits of information gave the story "legs"—news hooks that spurred on further broadcasts about the man who walked free after shooting an unarmed teenager. CNN's Don Lemon covered the story extensively on his weekend show. On MSNBC, Melissa Harris-Perry[22] said, "His name is Trayvon Martin. When innocent children are killed, when their parents are left to wonder if their children's lives matter at all, at least we can remember their names." Joy-Ann Reid, managing editor of TheGrio.com and MSNBC contributor, jumped on the story early, penning frequent in-depth pieces about the killing and its aftermath. The *New York Times'* columnist Charles M. Blow wrote about his personal fears for his black sons; Jonathan Capehart of the *Washington Post* said, "one of the burdens of being a black male is carrying the heavy weight of others' suspicions."[23] (These journalists and many others continued to cover the story extensively through the end of the trial.)

By the end of March, Rev. Al and civil rights activist Jesse Jackson had flown down to Florida to meet with Crump, discuss the case, and lead demonstrations. Rev. Al quickly became the leading national figure keeping attention on the case.

Worldwide press[24] covered the case as well. In the forty-five days between Trayvon's shooting and Zimmerman's indictment, France's leading news site *Le Monde* ran twelve news items on the story. The UK's *The Guardian* ran thirteen, outdone slightly by its domestic rival *The Sun*, which inked fifteen stories. Six pieces were published during this brief time period by Peru's *El Comercio,* ten from Peru's *La República,* and six by Cuba's *Granma.*

As Zimmerman remained a free man, international press zeroed in on the painful racial issues underlying the case. The Guardian led with Mamie Till's chilling warning to her fourteen-year-old son Emmett, as he headed south from Chicago to Mississippi for the summer of 1955:

"If you have to get on your knees and bow when a white person goes past," she told him, "Do it willingly." (It was no use. Three days after Emmett Till either said, "Bye, baby," or whistled at a white woman in a grocery store, his body was fished out of the Tallahatchie River with a bullet in his skull, an eye gouged out, and his forehead crushed. An all-white jury acquitted two men after just sixty-seven minutes of delibera-tion. "If we hadn't stopped to drink pop," said one juror, "it wouldn't have taken that long." Later the killers confessed to *Look* magazine, saying that they had only intended to scare Emmett, but when he refused to beg for mercy they "had to kill him.")

From the European perspective, little had changed in America.

*Le Monde* went after American Stand Your Ground laws, derisively calling the United States *"pays des homicide justifiable,"* "the land of justifiable homicides."[25] (Stand Your Ground and self-defense are a sub-set of justifiable homicides under American law.)

And everyone, it seemed, was appalled by America's lack of firearm restrictions. *Le Monde* played on Florida's official state nickname, The Sunshine State, calling it "The Gunshine State."[26] Many overseas pub-lications expressed horror at the sky-high numbers of American shoot-ing deaths annually. (This is not new. The rest of the world has been aghast at the U.S. gun death rate, the highest in the developed world,[27] for decades. Foreigners write polite, confused pieces[28] puzzling over why Americans own more guns per capita than any other country in the world, when their own countries figured out long ago that reducing the number of firearms reduces gun deaths.)

Alongside the world press, millions of individuals using social media, a powerful new global force, clamored for justice.[29] Kevin Cunningham, a Howard University law school graduate who heard about the story, launched a petition on Change.org on March 8, 2012, which Trayvon's parents then took over, called "Prosecute the Killer of Our Son, 17-year-old Trayvon Martin." The petition quickly broke all records on that website, garnering two million signatures by March 26, 2012. At times, 1,000 people were signing *per minute*. On Twitter, Spike Lee, Mia Farrow, Cher, and John Legend urged their followers to sign. By March 17, 2012, #Trayvon was trending on Twitter—meaning it was one of the top-ten topics Twitter's 500 million users were discussing. Later, #Justice4Trayvon became a popular hashtag, tweeted by Rihanna, will.i.am, Miley Cyrus, and dozens of other pop stars. The story of the unarmed kid walking down the street with Skittles and a soft drink, shot dead, the killer known but still at large, had caught fire as an obvious injustice crying out for an arrest.

Thus, by the end of March, one month after Trayvon was killed, Florida, the United States, and the world were watching. A teenager—whose mother was a county housing authority employee and whose father was a truck driver—was becoming a household name. A movement was afoot. Generous county employees including Miami-Dade's deputy mayor Jack Osterholt donated a total of eight months of paid vacation time[30] to Trayvon's mother, Sybrina Fulton, to enable her to pursue justice for her son. On March 23, 2012, the members of the Miami Heat basketball team all donned hoodies in support of Trayvon, and President Obama called Trayvon's death a national tragedy.[31]

Aided by celebrities and buoyed by a tidal wave of media attention, Trayvon's parents kept doing interviews and marching for justice. Indeed, key to fanning the flames of national attention was the united resolve of Sybrina Fulton and Tracy Martin to submit themselves to interview after interview, answering the same agonizing questions about the very recent death of their beloved son. News organizations always prefer to speak directly to "players"—people directly involved in a story—rather than advocates (like Crump) or legal analysts (like me). Fulton and Martin's willingness to endure so many interviews so shortly after Trayvon's death was instrumental in propelling the story to national and even international attention.

That old and new media firestorm quickly produced results. On March 22, 2012, Sanford police chief Bill Lee, who had become reviled for not arresting Zimmerman, was placed on paid leave. (Two months later, he was terminated "without cause.") State Attorney Angela Corey, designated by Governor Rick Scott as special prosecutor on March 23, was asked to review the case and make an independent determination as to whether Zimmerman should be charged and tried. Most observers, including me, expected her to submit the matter to a grand jury, a group of fifteen to twenty-one Floridians called upon to investigate legal matters as directed by a prosecutor and issue indictments (or not) and official reports of their findings. Grand juries almost always return the indictment (the legal charge) the prosecutor requests because grand jury proceedings are entirely one-sided: prosecutors present their case unburdened by the presence of any defense attorneys objecting, raising their own arguments, or otherwise participating in the proceeding in any way. "A grand jury will indict a ham sandwich," lawyers like to say. Still, submitting the matter to a group of individuals conscripted by the community means losing some control over the outcome. A grand jury was scheduled to convene on April 10, 2012, but was then cancelled. Corey, perhaps seeking to end the increasing media and public outcry, swiftly and decisively made the surprising move of choosing her other option: directly filing second-degree murder charges herself, which she did on April 11, 2012.

Many people who had signed petitions, spoken out, blogged, or demonstrated for the arrest of George Zimmerman rejoiced. At last, he would be brought to justice.

Corey then handed off the case to several prosecutors who had not exercised the prosecutorial discretion they would have in a typical case. Instead, the case was assigned to them. They did not choose whether to charge Zimmerman, and if so, what crime to charge him with. (Indeed, many criticized Corey for overcharging, arguing that she aimed too high and instead should have charged Zimmerman with the easier-to-prove crime of manslaughter.) They did not have the option to plea bargain the case to a lower-level crime with a lesser penalty, as the same public that demanded an arrest would have deafened them with its outcry if Zimmerman had been allowed to take a deal. And anyway, Zimmerman's attorneys[32] announced that they would not take a plea deal of any kind.

The prosecution's hands were tied.

Arrest George Zimmerman? On first pass, the State of Florida said no, but the public said yes, and the public prevailed. But the arrest, seen as a monumental victory by many, was only the beginning.

Down in central Florida, Pastor Durham told me that on April 11, 2012, when Zimmerman was arrested, he thought, "phew, *finally* we're going to get justice." He felt a tremendous satisfaction that Zimmerman had at last been officially charged. Though he was so loyal to his state that his blood had "turned to orange juice" (apparently this is a Florida-ism), he told me that the northerner in him was optimistic that Zimmerman would be convicted. If they didn't get him on that top charge of second-degree murder, then for *something*, surely. Zimmerman could not possibly escape entirely. Yet "an amazing number" of his congregants at the

Greater Friendship Baptist Church immediately tempered his optimism. "We know you're happy," they told him, "but it's not necessarily going to have the outcome you expect." Chilling words in that Florida heat.[33]

What these native southerners understood implicitly was that an arrest is merely an accusation that must be proven at trial through the introduction of admissible evidence—a job that would now be entirely within the control of the state attorneys' office. The groundswell that produced Zimmerman's arrest could not get into the courtroom and try the case for the State of Florida. World opinion that had shined a bright light on racial profiling could not teach its lawyers how to compellingly handle the sensitive subject of race in the courtroom. Community organizers could not review the evidence for the state attorneys and point to the "smoking gun," or intelligently prepare their witnesses, or choose experts for them, or work out a winning trial strategy for them.

Those jobs were for the state attorneys to do themselves, behind closed doors, as they prepared for trial, and as they presented the case in the courtroom over a year later. Handling the trial preparation and the trial itself was the one major piece of prosecutorial discretion that remained.

A prosecution team was assembled to try a case that virtually no one in law enforcement wanted to take to trial. The passion and mandate had come from the outside, not within. Police and prosecutors had believed Zimmerman's self-defense story, and neither the outside agitation nor the Special Prosecutor had changed their hearts and minds.

And that made all the difference. Because the overlooked evidence, lack of witness preparation, and poor strategic choices made by the state's attorneys were nothing short of astonishing.

TWO

## The State Misses Its Best Evidence

T HE INCIDENT THAT culminated in Trayvon's death on the night of February 26, 2012, divides into two phases. In Phase 1, Trayvon Martin walks back to the home of his father's fiancée, talking on his cell phone with his friend Rachel Jeantel, who is in Miami, 250 miles away. He is carrying candy for Chad Joseph and an Arizona watermelon drink for himself (often mistakenly referred to as an iced tea because the police logged it incorrectly in their crime scene records).

At the same time, a few minutes after 7 PM, Zimmerman is driving to Target in his SUV, looks out the window, and sees Trayvon. Immediately, he calls the police, identifying Trayvon as "a real suspicious guy," ostensibly because Trayvon is walking slowly in the rain. That four-minute phone call[34] records Zimmerman watching, following, and then apparently moving quickly on foot, breathing heavily, to catch Trayvon. "I don't know what his deal is," Zimmerman says. "Are you following him?" the police dispatcher asks Zimmerman. He admits he is. "We don't need you to do that," he's told. He continues following Trayvon anyway.

During Phase 1, the teenager and the twenty-eight-year-old man have not yet met. As each is talking on the phone during this time period, though, we do have a fairly good sense of their mindsets. Zimmerman believes Trayvon is a criminal ("there have been a lot of burglaries in the area . . . these assholes, they always get away"), and Trayvon, after observing Zimmerman following him, is fearful of Zimmerman, whom he calls, among other things, "creepy." Trayvon is concerned about the older man who is staring at him, following him, watching him. (On their phone call, the two teens warily discuss what might be happening. Jeantel tells Trayvon that she is afraid that the guy might be a rapist, and that he should run. At first Trayvon doesn't believe that is necessary, as he is almost home, and he thinks he's lost Zimmerman. When Zimmerman reappears, both sides agree, Trayvon does run.)

Though Zimmerman's behavior in Phase 1 is deeply disturbing (as we shall examine further in the next chapter) and relevant to the issue of intent, it is not illegal. It was not illegal for him to look out his car window and jump to insulting conclusions about a stranger. It was not illegal for him to say Trayvon was suspicious when he was just minding his own business because that was Zimmerman's opinion. As long as he wasn't lying to police, merely expressing his opinion to them was not illegal. It was not even illegal for Zimmerman to continue following Trayvon after the police dispatcher said, "We don't need you to do that," since that was merely a suggestion, which he was free to ignore. Some have suggested that Zimmerman "stalked" Trayvon. In the legal sense of that word, Zimmerman's behavior—spending a few minutes watching, then following, Trayvon—does not rise to the level of stalking.

Even racial profiling—making unfair assumptions about another in part on account of race—by a private citizen is not illegal in and of itself. If Trayvon had made it home that night, and only Phase 1 had transpired, no crime would have been committed.

From the standpoint of the criminal trial, Phase 2, when the two met, interacted, and became physical, was the core of the case. According to one of Zimmerman's versions of the evening, Trayvon "jumped out of the bushes" and sucker punched him in the face.[35] From the force of the blow, Zimmerman then fell down on his back onto the grass, he says, and Trayvon mounted him, Trayvon's knees to Zimmerman's armpits, and then pounded Zimmerman's head onto the concrete.[36] Critically—this is the most important part of his self-defense story—Zimmerman claimed that as he was being assaulted in this position, Trayvon saw Zimmerman's gun and reached for it, saying, "You're gonna die tonight, motherfucker." Zimmerman says at that life-or-death moment, he drew his gun first and fired it once at Trayvon's heart, to save his own life.[37]

An important legal decision flowed from the defense's decision to stick with this story. Because Zimmerman claimed he was pinned down, the defense opted not to argue a "Stand Your Ground" defense. Stand Your Ground was a relatively recent Florida law that eliminated the old requirement that a combatant retreat from violence if an escape is possible. Since Zimmerman maintained that Trayvon was restraining him, and retreat was therefore impossible, the defense acknowledged early on that Stand Your Ground was inapplicable to the case. Before trial, the defense explicitly waived Zimmerman's right to a pretrial Stand Your Ground hearing which, had the defense prevailed there, could have exonerated him entirely without the need for a full-blown trial. They gave up this opportunity for an early win because they knew they didn't have the facts to support a Stand Your Ground defense. (Yet Stand Your Ground language seeped into the jury instructions and into at least one juror's decision to acquit, as we'll see.)

We don't have Trayvon's account of what happened in Phase 2. His call with Jeantel dropped just as the first words were spoken between Zimmerman and Trayvon (according to Jeantel, Trayvon said, "Why are you following me?" and Zimmerman said, "What are you doing around here?") Minutes later, the first police officer arrived, and Trayvon was already dead.

No one witnessed the moment of the shooting. Some neighbors saw or heard some portions of the altercation. One saw two men on their feet, moving across the grass (inconsistent with Zimmerman's story). One saw Zimmerman on top, Trayvon on the bottom (inconsistent with Zimmerman's story). One saw Trayvon on top, Zimmerman on the bottom (consistent with Zimmerman's story). No one could confirm Zimmerman's critically important details: (i) that Trayvon was banging Zimmerman's head on the concrete in the final moments before Zimmerman killed him; (ii) that Trayvon saw and reached for the gun; and (iii) that at that moment, Zimmerman pulled the gun and fired.

In the courtroom, Phase 2 was key, both from the legal and common-sense angles. It was obvious from the outset that if the jury believed that Zimmerman was down on his back, pinned, his head getting painfully banged on the concrete, his gun visible to Trayvon, and Trayvon reached for the weapon, menacing him, that that situation would be so terrifying that *of course* he would take out his weapon and shoot to defend himself. Wouldn't any of us do that? We wouldn't be required to wait another second. Kill or be killed. If Zimmerman's story about those final few seconds was true, the case was over, and he would walk. And he should.

Thus, if they believed in their case, it was absolutely essential that the prosecution focus on and disprove these three allegations. Instead, remarkably, the prosecution essentially *conceded* Zimmerman's version of what happened, so that by the end of the trial, the jury saw both sides reenacting the defense scenario.

Shrewdly driving home to the jury the life-or-death nature of the altercation according to Zimmerman, the defense reenacted the scene in the courtroom, with lanky defense attorney Mark O'Mara (playing the role of Trayvon) straddling a life-sized mannequin (representing Zimmerman) in a vivid, live demonstration. O'Mara, an effective trial showman, grabbed the mannequin's torso and pounded its head on the floor, *BAM BAM BAM*, as the jury looked on, transfixed. By the end of the trial, the prosecution had accepted this picture and joined the defense in straddling the mannequin, arguing mainly about the details, reinforcing the terrifying image of a man down, pinned, beaten nearly to death before he managed to unholster his gun and fire it to save his life.

We know now that the jury believed that Trayvon had Zimmerman down, was assaulting him and reaching for his gun, and because they understood the law allowed him to "meet force with force," they acquitted Zimmerman. This visual demonstration was important to them in reaching that understanding.

Unfortunately, that conclusion was based on a misapprehension of both the law and the evidence, both of which were poorly presented to them in the courtroom. Because the prosecution did not walk the jury through the three simple, essential elements of the law of self-defense, and because the state failed to give the jury a realistic reenactment that incorporated *all* the known evidence, they were left with the oversimplified, erroneous impression that Zimmerman simply met force with force once he was down, which was permitted.

Saving one's own life is a natural, normal human instinct, and the law, as it should, permits us all to do that, even if it requires taking the life of another. *But only when absolutely necessary, under real, honest-to-God life-or-death circumstances.* Because under our laws, human life is paramount. In a classic law school example, one may not set up a spring-loaded device to kill a burglar entering one's empty home. Why not? Because human life has a higher value than property. Human life has a higher value than anything else (or at least, it used to. More on this in Chapter Eleven). Thus it is not permissible in an ordinary fistfight, say, to take out a gun and kill the other guy. Two men wrestling on the ground should not result in one of them losing his life. We are not barbarians.

Legally, in fact, this case was relatively simple. There was no doubt whatsoever that Zimmerman shot and killed Trayvon, and that he did so intentionally. He admitted he did that—he took out the gun on purpose, pointed it at Trayvon, and pulled the trigger, *intending to shoot him.* "I took my gun, aimed it at him, and fired,"[38] Zimmerman told police. There was no accident. Not a case of, "I took the gun out just to scare him and—oops—it went off!" He didn't unholster the gun to clean it. He didn't intend to shoot someone else. No, this was always an intentional homicide. (If he killed with hatred, malice, or ill will, then the crime is second-degree murder, the top charge. Was it an intentional killing without those factors? Then the crime is manslaughter.)

The only real question for the jury in the trial was whether Zimmerman killed in self-defense, as he claimed immediately that night and throughout the trial. If he truly shot Trayvon in self-defense, he must be found not guilty. Because an intentional killing is perfectly legal if all the elements of self-defense are met.

When may a person kill in self-defense, then?

Florida law is brief and clear on this point. The entire relevant portion of the law[39] as applied to this case is:

[A] person is justified in the use of deadly force and does not have a duty to retreat if:

(1) He or she reasonably believes that such force is necessary to prevent imminent death or great bodily harm to himself or herself.

Three important concepts jump out of this one sentence. Zimmerman's shooting of Trayvon was in self-defense if he (i) *reasonably* believed he had to shoot to prevent (ii) *imminent (iii) death or great bodily harm*. All three of these factors had to be present. If the prosecution disproved one or more of them, Zimmerman did not act in self-defense. Then we are back to the fact that he intentionally shot Trayvon, and the only options would be manslaughter (intentional killing) or murder (intentional killing with hatred, ill will, or spite).

First, a quick look at *reasonableness*—a common phrase that sweeps through so much of American law. We are almost always required to behave rationally, sensibly, fairly. In our civil and criminal courts, the law does not reward extremists, whack jobs, people who fly off the handle. In sexual harassment cases, for example, juries deciding whether workplace misconduct is bad enough to constitute a hostile environment are instructed to evaluate the facts from the objective standpoint of a "reasonable person." (This used to be the "reasonable *man*" test, which, especially in sexual harassment law, was a mess. We've evolved.) Civil rights law does not serve "as a vehicle for vindicating the petty slights suffered by the hypersensitive."[40] On the criminal side, a shooter's fear of his victim must be reasonable. We will not reward someone, smoking gun in hand, who says, "I feared him because he looked at me sideways. Maybe you wouldn't shoot for that reason, but that just bugs me. It freaks me out." Nope, not reasonable. (Law students! When in doubt on your law school exams, apply a reasonableness test. Odds are high you'll be at least partially right.)

Therefore, Zimmerman could not shoot even if he really and truly feared death if his fear was *unreasonable*—he misread the situation, he panicked, he lost it. Thus the jury was required to review all the evidence to determine whether Zimmerman's assessment of the situation was levelheaded or exaggerated.

Second, *imminence*. He could shoot if he feared death, but only if that threat was upon him at that very moment. If the concern was that he could be killed some time in the future—in five or ten minutes, say—the element of imminence would not be met. Similarly, if he feared death based on events of minutes earlier, the threat from which had now dissipated, that would not be *imminent* danger.

Third, *death or great bodily harm*. We may kill in self-defense only to save our own lives, or to save ourselves from major, horrible, crippling injury. Zimmerman could not shoot if he feared only bruises, scrapes, or humiliation. Minor injuries are part of the rough and tumble of life we are all expected to endure stoically—*reasonably*—and are insufficient to justify taking the life of another.

All these restrictions on self-defense should have been important at the trial, but one barely heard a word about them from the prosecution team, who left the jury with the false impression that if Zimmerman was getting assaulted, he could shoot to kill, or "meet force with force," as the jury incorrectly understood it.

With these three elements firmly in mind, let's examine the evidence. In this and every murder case, we are short one witness. We know that we are only hearing the killer's side of the story, and the deceased cannot speak, so we must be vigilant in analyzing the shooter's story. Since most people know that killing in self-defense is not a crime—and Zimmerman, for sure, knew this because his criminal justice professor testified at trial that he'd been taught the law of self-defense and had even received an A in the class—the killer's account of what happened must be approached skeptically, lined up with any and all available evidence and the self-defense statute, to ascertain whether it holds together or whether the shooter is lying to avoid life in prison. Not all shooters are liars, but they all have a powerful motive to lie: to avoid incarceration.

Thus all aspects of Zimmerman's story, like that of anyone who has killed another human being, should have been combed over again and again by law enforcement and the state's attorneys. His version should not have been taken with a grain of salt. It should have been taken with the entire Pacific Ocean's supply of salt.

Consider Zimmerman's holster. Admitted into evidence, we know to a certainty that it was a matte (i.e. not shiny) black "inside-waistband holster." Zimmerman's best friend, Mark Osterman, who persuaded Zimmerman to purchase and carry a hidden weapon, confirmed in his trial testimony that the entire purpose of this type of holster is conceal-ment.[41] Zimmerman's choice of gun, a KelTec 9mm PF-9 semiautomatic handgun, is a popular choice for concealed carry. And Zimmerman had obtained a concealed carry permit. So there is little doubt that Zimmerman's gun and holster were hidden from view, as intended by the manufacturers.

But wait—if the gun was *concealed*, how could Trayvon have seen it? Because, remember, the most critical moment in Zimmerman's narrative was deep into Phase 2, when Trayvon supposedly saw the gun and reached for it, allegedly saying, "You're gonna die tonight, motherfucker." If he didn't see the gun, he didn't take the actions that flowed from it—the alleged reaching, the alleged threat to kill.

There's no question that Zimmerman wore his gun hidden inside his pants. The first police officer on the scene, Tim Smith, noted in his police report[42] that *"Located on the inside of Zimmerman's waistband, I removed a black KelTec 9mm PF-9 semiauto handgun and holster."* (My emphasis.)

But a waistband on any pair of pants goes all the way around, front to back to front again. Where exactly on his waistband was Zimmerman's pistol holstered?

This is how a gun is often holstered in an inside-waistband holster.

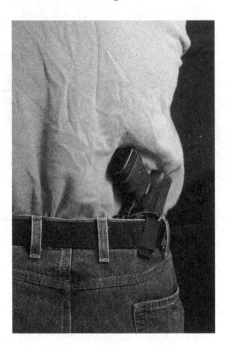

But is that how Zimmerman wore his? The day after the shooting, police walked with Zimmerman through the Retreat at Twin Lakes with a videographer recording Zimmerman's play-by-play as to what had happened the night before. On that video, Zimmerman demonstrates that the gun was holstered *behind* him, over his buttocks, in this very position. Thus all but the grip (handle) of the gun would have been covered by the seat of his pants. That grip would have extended diagonally to Zimmerman's center back, as in the photo above. While the grip would not be covered by his pants, Zimmerman was also wearing a T-shirt and a jacket during the incident, which would have covered the gun if he was in virtually any position other than standing on his head.

Not just once, but three times, in three different ways, on that video, plain as day, Zimmerman showed the police that his gun was concealed inside his pants, and on his backside. He patted his rear end to show where his gun was. In demonstrating how Trayvon supposedly reached for the gun, he reaches across his chest toward his backside. Finally, he reached back behind him one more time to reenact pulling the gun and shooting it.

Zimmerman was not asked to lie supine in his reenactment, a significant lapse in the police investigation. Less than twenty-four hours before, he had killed an unarmed teenager. Did they not want to subject him to the inconvenience of showing exactly how the shooting happened?

Putting together just these two simple, irrefutable pieces of evidence—that Zimmerman's gun was holstered *inside* his pants, and that it was located *behind* him—proves the falsity of Zimmerman's story. If Trayvon truly had Zimmerman down on his back, he could not have seen the gun, because Zimmerman would have been lying on top of it. Add in a few other facts agreed to by the neighborhood witnesses: it was a very dark night, and it was raining. Many witnesses talked about how visibility was extremely poor in that area, and that unless one stood directly under a townhouse porch light, there was really no light at all. Add that the altercation ended on the grass, which would also obscure even a sideways glance at an object affixed to someone's backside as he was lying down on the ground.

And yet Trayvon, somehow, on that wet, black, low-visibility night, saw through the grassy ground cover, through the bulk of Zimmerman's body, through Zimmerman's shirt, and through his jacket to a matte black gun concealed in a matte black holster clipped inside Zimmerman's waistband.

Can anyone possibly believe this story?

And if Zimmerman had been punched in the face and fallen backward, as he claims, he would have landed hard onto his back, on that solid metal object holstered inside his pants—ow, sounds painful, right?—and yet there was no evidence at trial that he had a bruise, an abrasion, a cut, or even redness from the gun pressing into his backside after he supposedly fell on it. Every nick and scrape Zimmerman experienced was carefully catalogued and reviewed at the trial. Nothing on his back.

Somehow, during the presentation of the evidence at Zimmerman's trial, the prosecution was unaware of the vitally important fact that

Zimmerman's gun was holstered on his backside. At various points, both the prosecution and the defense attorneys demonstrated the position of the gun by patting the front of their waistbands, as in the photo below, giving the jury the false impression that that's where Zimmerman carried his weapon, in that far-more visible location. No one in the courtroom corrected that misperception. The state was in possession of Zimmerman's videotaped demonstration for over a year, as well as Zimmerman's gun, holster, and all the information about the dark, rainy night, and the grass, which came from their own witnesses.

But disturbingly, they failed to put the evidence together, or to use it. With their own neighborhood witnesses, the prosecution could have emphasized how very dark that suburban neighborhood gets at night, connecting it to this issue. They could have asked questions like this:

PROSECUTION: How dark was it that night?

RESIDENT: Oh, very dark.

PROSECUTION: Can you describe it?

RESIDENT: Once I step off my porch, away from my porch light, I need a flashlight to walk around.

PROSECUTION: And how about the rain? Did that make it easier or harder to see things?

RESIDENT *(laughing)*: Well of course, harder. It's tough to see through the rain, especially at night.

PROSECUTION *(holding up the holster)*: Would you have been able to see this?

RESIDENT: On that night? No.

PROSECUTION *(putting the holster inside his pants, behind him, then lying down on the floor)*: How about like this? Would you have been able to see it?

RESIDENT: You've got to be kidding. No way.

PROSECUTION: How about the grass? Would it be easy to see a small black item like this with the grass in the area all around me?

RESIDENT: The grass would make it harder to see, I'd say.

Oh sure, the defense might start objecting. But the prosecution would have made its point. Lest you think I am being overly dramatic suggesting that the prosecution put the holster in his pants and lie on the courtroom floor (I'd add the gun too, if the court would let me), attorneys for both sides were down on that very floor, or using their own bodies to demonstrate their version of events, at many points throughout the trial. But just as the police never required Zimmerman to put all the parts of his story together and truly reenact it, so too the state's attorneys never synthesized the evidence before them, never demonstrated to the jury that the most important life-or-death moment of Zimmerman's story could not be true.

And if the point could not be made through a lay (nonexpert) witness like a neighbor, it certainly could have been made later on in the trial, on cross-examination of the defense's expert on fighting, Dennis Root, who was called to say that Zimmerman's story of the altercation all made sense to him and was consistent with the evidence he'd reviewed.

With expert witnesses, attorneys are given wider latitude on cross-examination. Expert witnesses are professionals who sign up to testify at trials, and they are paid for their time doing so. Everyone understands that attorneys will challenge their credentials, their methodology, their opinions, and their findings, from every angle possible, aggressively (though respectfully).

The prosecution missed its opportunity to push back at Root with questions like this:

PROSECUTOR: Your testimony is that Mr. Zimmerman's account of his altercation with Trayvon is consistent with normal fighting tactics as you know them?

ROOT: Based on my experience, yes.

PROSECUTOR: Would you be willing to step down off the witness stand, Mr. Root?

ROOT: Certainly. (*Stands in the well of the courtroom, before the jury.*)

PROSECUTOR: Here is the gun Mr. Zimmerman used that night. Don't worry, it's been secured by the officers and it's not loaded. Would you hold it please?

ROOT: Yes. (*Holds gun.*)

PROSECUTOR: Here is the holster that Zimmerman was wearing that night. Would you please put the defendant's gun in the holster?

(*Root does so. Starts to get anxious.*)

PROSECUTOR: Incidentally, are you familiar with this gun and holster?

ROOT: Not really. I'm an expert on fighting tactics, not guns and holsters.

PROSECUTOR: Well, according to the defendant, this was a fight that ended with a shooting. Isn't that correct?

ROOT: Yes, it is.

PROSECUTOR: And you were called upon to analyze the entire incident, weren't you?

ROOT: I was.

PROSECUTOR: But in doing so, you didn't look at the actual gun and holster, or copies of them?

ROOT: Just in the photographs.

PROSECUTOR: Now I am putting on the holster the way Mr. Zimmerman wore it that night. You've seen the reenactment video, where the defendant partially reenacted the shooting, haven't you?

ROOT: Yes, I watched the video.

PROSECUTOR: But he didn't really reenact the final moments just before he killed Trayvon, did he?

ROOT: Well, he demonstrated as best he could.

PROSECUTOR: He demonstrated from a standing position, didn't he?

ROOT: Yes.

PROSECUTOR: But in fact, he says he and Trayvon were both on the ground at the time of the shooting, right?

ROOT: He does say that.

PROSECUTOR: Any reason why he couldn't get down on the ground and show the police what he says happened?

ROOT: Not that I know of.

PROSECUTOR: On that video, the defendant made it clear that the gun was concealed and holstered behind him, didn't he?

ROOT: Uh . . . if you say so.

PROSECUTOR: You didn't notice that?

ROOT: I don't remember that specifically.

PROSECUTOR: Oh, well then let's take a look. (*Shows thirty-second clip where Zimmerman indicates three times that the gun was holstered behind him.*)

ROOT: Oh. OK. Yes, I see that.

(*Prosecutor gives jury a meaningful look.*)

PROSECUTOR: So let's put it all together and do a real reenactment for this jury right now, OK?

ROOT: If you say so.

PROSECUTOR: (*securing the gun in the holster, putting the holster inside his pants, on his backside, jacket over the gun*): I'm the defendant, and my firearm is concealed and secured by the holster, behind me. That's how Mr. Zimmerman had it, right?

ROOT: I believe that's right.

PROSECUTOR: Well, we all just watched the reenactment video to refresh our recollections. Do you need to see it again, Mr. Root?

ROOT: No, I don't need to see it again.

PROSECUTOR: All righty. Now I'm going to lie down, and you straddle me, the way Mr. Zimmerman says Trayvon Martin did.

DEFENSE: Objection!

JUDGE: He's a fighting expert, and this is his area of testimony and expertise. I'll allow it.

**PROSECUTOR** (*now supine*): Do you remember how the defendant said Trayvon Martin was straddling him?

**ROOT**: Knees to armpits?

**PROSECUTOR**: Exactly. Go ahead.

At this point the jury would be rapt. They'd all be leaning forward in their seats. What an exciting part of the trial was now playing out before them! Two grown men, one on top of the other, recreating the final, dramatic moments of Trayvon Martin's life. Now that the prosecutor pointed it out, this had not been demonstrated accurately on that Zimmerman police video! Where was the prosecution going with this? The anticipation would be high. This demonstration would not require understanding any confusing legal concepts, nor would it make them sit through hours of boring testimony before the lawyer got to the point, both of which happened far too often at this trial (and happen at most trials). If a picture is worth a thousand words, a live demonstration is worth a million.

And what would they see? That even in the bright, dry courtroom, Zimmerman's gun was not visible. Not to the defense expert atop the prosecutor, not to the jurors, not to anyone.

Bringing in a patch of fake grass the same length as the grass at the crime scene would have been helpful too, to show its obscuring effect. Ever lose an object in grass? On a dark night? Most of us would not even start looking until the next morning. Prosecutors could have even gone so far as to dim or turn off the lights in the courtroom to remind the jurors of the darkness on the night of the shooting.

The prosecutor could then put it all together, right before the jury's eyes:

PROSECUTOR *(down on the floor, on his back)*: Now, you remember how the defendant said that Trayvon Martin saw and reached for the gun?

ROOT: I do remember that part of his story.

PROSECUTOR: Can you see the gun right now, Mr. Root?

ROOT: No, but . . .

PROSECUTOR: But what? Do I not have the gun and holster on my person the way the defendant indicated? Am I not in the position he said he was in just before he shot Trayvon Martin?

ROOT: You are. But a fight is dynamic. They were moving around. Maybe Trayvon saw the gun at a different point in the fight.

PROSECUTOR: You've reviewed all of the defendant's stories as to what happened?

ROOT: I have.

PROSECUTOR: And in which one of those stories did he say that Trayvon Martin saw the gun at some other moment that night?

ROOT: I don't know.

PROSECUTOR: Would you like to review your notes?

ROOT: Yes, I would. (*Root returns to the witness stand. Minutes tick by silently as he flips through his pages of notes. The prosecutor knows there is no version of Zimmerman's story where he says Trayvon saw the gun while the two were upright, or in any other position.*)

Finally . . .

ROOT: I can't find that. Perhaps Zimmerman was mistaken when he said that Trayvon saw the gun at that point in the fight.

PROSECUTOR: Mistaken. Mistaken? Let me give you some other possibilities. The defendant was exaggerating when he said Trayvon saw and reached for the gun just before the defendant shot and killed him?

ROOT: That is possible.

PROSECUTOR: The defendant was lying when he said Trayvon saw and reached for the gun just before he shot him?

ROOT *(squirming in his seat)*: That is possible.

Had the state attorneys put this all together before the trial, as they should have, they could have called their own fighting expert to make the point clearly for them. They failed to do so. But even if they didn't figure this out until the trial was already underway, they could have made the point effectively during direct examination of their own lay witnesses, or during cross-examination of the defense expert, Dennis Root. The fact that none of this happened leads inescapably to one conclusion: no one in the state attorneys' office noticed the best evidence, the "smoking gun" evidence, that was right under their noses.

If the prosecution had done its job and hit hard on this issue, one wonders what the defense could have come up with in response. *Maybe Zimmerman was wrong about Trayvon seeing and reaching for the gun. The fight all happened so quickly, and the two men were moving around a lot.* That would have been a devastating admission, because, remember, to prevail on his self-defense theory, Zimmerman was required to show that he was in *reasonable* fear of *imminent* great bodily injury or death. *Imminent.* Meaning, he was about to die, in a matter of moments. He could not legally take out his gun and end the fight by killing Trayvon Martin without immediate impending life-threatening (or at least, great-bodily-injury-threatening) harm.

*Maybe Zimmerman was wrong?* He cannot be wrong about this and hang on to his credibility, his *reasonableness*—that all-important self-defense factor. If Zimmerman was wrong, he was lying (and now jurors have no basis to believe he killed in self-defense) or he was exaggerating (which is really just another word for lying, and at best indicates he panicked, which means he was not *behaving reasonably*, as the law requires.)

If Trayvon was not about to take Zimmerman's life, the shooting was not justified. If the shooting was not justified, Zimmerman is guilty of either manslaughter or murder.

*But he was pounding my head on the concrete too!* Zimmerman said in several of his statements. Defense attorney O'Mara even hauled in a heavy chunk of concrete in his closing argument (a nice move on his part—the defense understood the power of visual aids) to show the jury that the sidewalk could be a deadly weapon. And indeed it could. If the incident ended on the sidewalk. Which it didn't. Trayvon's body was found on wet grass, a substantial distance from any concrete. And Zimmerman said he didn't move Trayvon's body—that he merely slid out from under it. Thus we can conclude the altercation ended there, on soft, wet grass. Unless Zimmerman's neck extended eight or ten feet at a time like a Pez dispenser, his statement that Trayvon was banging his head on the concrete was false. Exaggerated. A lie. (Zimmerman's attorney conceded in closing argument that given Zimmerman's minor injuries, his head was probably not banged dozens of times on the concrete, as Zimmerman told police. This was a major concession that the prosecution should have capitalized upon, but they failed to. It was an admission to another exaggeration, another example of panicked overreaction—of Zimmerman not meeting his legal obligation of *reasonableness*.)

The physical evidence disproved the core of Zimmerman's self-defense story. Without Zimmerman's statements that Trayvon saw and reached for the gun (enhanced by the gangster-movie-sounding threat he attributed to Trayvon while Trayvon was supposedly reaching for Zimmerman's not-visible gun: "You're gonna die tonight, mother-fucker") and his allegation that Trayvon was pounding his head on concrete too far away to be reached, Zimmerman had nothing left to meet the legal requirement that he *reasonably* believed he was in *imminent* risk of *great bodily injury or death*.

All this the prosecution failed to mention in opening statements, or on direct or cross-examination of any witness day after day, week after week, for three weeks, missing one opportunity after another to drive this essential point home to the jury. At the very end of the case, after we'd been hammering this point on television all week, miraculously, in closing argument, prosecutor de la Rionda *for the first time* mentioned his brand-new observation that Zimmerman holstered his gun behind him. Mentioned, only briefly. He didn't show the jurors the portion of the video where Zimmerman himself pats his backside to indicate his gun's placement. He didn't point out that Zimmerman had failed to truly reenact the final moments of the altercation. Was it because Zimmerman knew he'd be found out if he actually lay down on the ground with his gun behind him? The prosecutor didn't put the gun and holster on himself, or on the dummy, and lie down to show the invisibility of the pistol in that position. He didn't connect any of the evidence up with the three important elements of the law of self-defense. He did ask the question, in showing a clip of another video, how Trayvon could have seen the gun. But it wasn't a *question*, by the end of trial. The point required an aggressive, declarative statement from the man asking the jury to find Zimmerman guilty of murder, that Zimmerman's story was now proven to be impossible, a lie, and therefore his self-defense claim was disproved, beyond a reasonable doubt. It required a prosecutor's fire-in-the-belly belief in his own case. The prosecutor should have explained that Trayvon was killed intentionally, without any legal justification; that Zimmerman came up with a self-defense story, a story that may have been believable at first, but once all the evidence was put together, could now be seen as a fabrication. Self-defense, then, would no longer be a part of this case. It would be out. And without it, what's left is an intentional shooting without justification—with manslaughter or murder the only remaining options.

# THREE

## *Too Squeamish to Talk About Race*

A GROUNDSWELL OF AFRICAN-AMERICAN grassroots activism, rising up through the churches, civil rights organizations, social media, as well as persistent and powerful commentary by leading black journalists, pushed the state to arrest and try Zimmerman, as we've seen. Yet from the beginning, Zimmerman's defenders pushed back, denying that the case was "about" race, insisting it was a straightforward case of self-defense. Throughout the trial, commentators posed the question "Do you think Zimmerman racially profiled Trayvon?" In online polls, cable news reports, on talk radio, Facebook, and Twitter, opinions swung back and forth. *Zimmerman has African-American friends, family members!* his supporters said. *He's a racist!* a mysterious family member anonymously phoned in to the police shortly after the shooting. *He did racially profile! He didn't!* The debate raged, unresolved.

The divide did not always neatly line up along racial lines. Prominent black commentators Juan Williams and Larry Elder flatly refused to see racial profiling in the case. Trayvon's black stepmother,[43] speaking emotionally about the young man she helped raise (she said Trayvon lived 85-90 percent of the time with her, her two daughters, and his father, Tracy Martin, for fourteen of his seventeen years), said she did *not* think

Zimmerman followed Trayvon because he was black. An anonymous African-American neighbor of the Zimmermans was quoted by Reuters as wanting to "talk about the elephant in the room. I'm black, OK?" the woman said. "There were black boys robbing houses in this neighborhood," she said. "That's why George was suspicious of Trayvon Martin."[44]

Others presented more muddled views on the subject. Members of Trayvon's immediate family and their legal representatives struggled with the question to such an extent that one wonders whether the prosecutors instructed them to tone down the racial aspect of the case in their public statements. Benjamin Crump, the Martin family lawyer, said in September 2012 that the case "shouldn't be about race," though if the roles of the two young men were reversed, he said, an arrest would have occurred quickly. (Crump had concluded with "that's why race is involved in this case.")[45]

And after Rachel Jeantel testified to the only racial epithets uttered in the courtroom, including Trayvon's characterization of Zimmerman as a "creepy-ass cracka," another family attorney stood alongside Trayvon's parents at a news conference and said, "To this family, race is not a part of this process. Anybody who tries to inject race into it is wrong."

Yet Trayvon's parents had traveled to Washington to attend a Congressional forum[46] on racial profiling and hate crimes on March 27, 2012, which resulted in the Congressional Black Caucus's describing the killing as one of "racial bias." And earlier that month Tracy Martin had said, "For the Sanford Police Department to feel as though they were going to sweep another young black minority death under the rug, it's an atrocity." Central Florida, the United States, and much of the world had organized and focused on the case because the racial implications seemed clear, especially to African Americans who saw this as the latest in a sad long line of unarmed black men killed based on unfounded suspicions, with police slow to arrest and prosecutors unenthusiastic about prosecuting. The NAACP, the Urban League, and the National Action Network spoke out loudly and often about the shooting, the perceived cover-up, the insensitivity—and the case was *not* about race?

Ultimately, all the chatter about whether observers thought the case involved racial profiling or not was entirely irrelevant. Because the topic was not a matter of personal belief or disbelief. One may as well ask, "What is your opinion: was it 55 degrees at 3 PM today, or not?" That is verifiable information, and so is the fact—the *fact*—that Zimmerman followed Trayvon in substantial part on account of his race.

How can we be so sure? Because of this much overlooked point: *the defense conceded the point at trial, unapologetically.*

When asked to explain his killing of Trayvon, Zimmerman always began the same way he had begun his police call when he first spotted Trayvon walking through the neighborhood: "Hey, we've had some break-ins in my neighborhood and there's a real suspicious guy . . . " After the shooting, he was taken into police custody. He was read his Miranda rights, he waived his right to remain silent and to have an attorney present, and he answered the detective's open-ended "tell me what happened that night" in the same vein: "This neighborhood has had a lot of crimes. My wife saw our neighbors get broken into . . . "

*There's been a lot of crime around here—burglaries—we've had some break-ins.* The shooting was framed by that context, each time Zimmerman told it, just as Trayvon might have begun, "I was walking back from 7-Eleven when a creepy guy started following me" or a neighbor would begin, "I heard screaming outside my window." Zimmerman provided a handwritten statement[47] to the police that night as well, starting the story at the same point in time, providing more detail: "In August of 2011 my neighbor's house was broken into while she was home with her infant son. The intruders attempted to attack her and her child; however, SPD [the Sanford Police Department] reported to the scene and the robbers fled."

For him, the story did not begin where one might expect, with his seeing Trayvon walking down the street on that late-February night. It began months earlier, with intruders who were strangers to Trayvon, and, the jury would quickly learn, who shared his skin color. It was in that context that Zimmerman saw Trayvon, as he explained each time. And his defense attorneys hewed to that script throughout the trial, reminding jurors whenever possible that crime, and especially burglaries by African Americans, had been a problem for various residents of the Retreat at Twin Lakes.

That's why Zimmerman had organized a neighborhood-watch program and appointed himself its leader, which some community members appreciated, though the president of the homeowners' association testified that he didn't think it was particularly necessary. (Perhaps that's because Zimmerman himself caused the worst outcome—a fatal shooting—far more serious than any of the more minor crimes he was ostensibly out to prevent).

Lawyers like to begin and end with their most powerful witnesses, because the communication theory of "primacy and recency" teaches that an audience is most likely to remember one's first and last points. All that stuff in the middle tends to mush together. And so Zimmerman's highly skilled defense attorneys saved until almost the very end the young white mother Zimmerman had mentioned at the beginning of his written statement, Olivia Bertalan. Bertalan's neighborhood house had been robbed six months before the Trayvon Martin shooting. Testifying about her frightening experience, she said she'd cowered in her child's upstairs bedroom, baby in her arms, as one or two African-American males entered and burglarized her home. (She did not, however, testify to Zimmerman's even scarier rendition of the story, that "the intruders attempted to attack her and her child." She said instead that they never entered the room she was in, as the police arrived and they ran off. In this and in his own story of his altercation with Trayvon Martin, we know that Zimmerman tends to exaggerate threats.)

While the defense comfortably handled the race issue straightfor-wardly (if illogically, as we'll see), the prosecution and the judge seemed to want to stay a million miles away from it. In an incomprehensible ruling just before opening statements were set to begin, Judge Debra Nelson decided that the word "profiling"—but not the phrase "racial profiling"—could be used in opening statements. But what other kind of profiling could possibly have been involved here? Could jurors seriously imagine that Zimmerman considered Trayvon a criminal solely because he was walking slowly in the rain as he chatted on the phone? Lawyers were free to use the profanity involved in the case over and over again, but initially the "r" word was off limits, as if its very mention would blow the roof right off the courthouse. More incomprehensibly still, the prosecution didn't push back on this ruling, for example by asking that it be lifted once evidence of racial profiling came in, apparently because they had already made a decision that they were *not going there.*

Either the prosecutors themselves did not believe that racial profiling was a part of the case even though the defense conceded that it was, or they did not trust the jury to handle the hot topic. Prosecutors trusted jurors to dispassionately evaluate photos of a dead teenager's remains and of the bullet hole through his heart as well as photos of blood dripping from George Zimmerman's head. But the state was too squeamish to put the touchy issue of race squarely before the six-woman jury.

Bertalan's entire testimony could have been neutralized with one polite but searing line of cross-examination questions:

PROSECUTOR: Ms. Bertalan, I'm sorry about your experience. But did Trayvon Martin have anything to do with it?

BERTALAN: Uh . . . no, of course not.

PROSECUTOR: Was he one of the burglars?

BERTALAN: I don't think so, no.

PROSECUTOR: You don't think so? Are you suggesting to this jury, sitting here today, that you think there's any possibility Trayvon Martin had something to do with your house being broken into?

BERTALAN: No! No, I am not suggesting that at all.

PROSECUTOR: Other than skin color, did Trayvon Martin have anything in common with the guys who robbed you?

BERTALAN: No.

The prosecution never asked these questions, nor objected to evidence about the Bertalan burglary in open court. To Zimmerman, and the defense team, Trayvon was inherently suspicious because he was of the same race as the burglars. It was the prosecution's responsibility to undermine this outrageous association of Trayvon with two burglars he'd never met, if for no other reason than as a matter of trial strategy, and they entirely failed to do it. To attribute the wrongs of two

African-American men to all African Americans is the very definition of racism. But the prosecutor never said so in court or called the jury's attention to this fact, thereby missing one of the core issues in the case.

In his closing argument, defense attorney O'Mara drove home the idea that Zimmerman's profane police call was reasonable, arguing that Trayvon "did match the description [of the Bertalan burglars], unfortunately, and that's just maybe happenstance."

But other than race and youth, no other description of the burglars was admitted into evidence. Race and youth were the sole basis of what defense lawyers deemed "a match."

The state did not question any of this, much less point out that racial profiling was not happenstance—something that just rains down upon some of us, unfortunately!—but a choice to focus almost entirely on race to the exclusion of all other, nonracial, identifying factors.

The prosecution could have continued the cross-examination of Olivia Bertalan:

PROSECUTOR: Ms. Bertalan, how tall were the burglars who came to your house that day?

BERTALAN: I didn't get a good look at them, so I can't say.

PROSECUTOR: What did they look like, other than being black?

BERTALAN: I'm not sure I understand what you mean. They were black males.

PROSECUTOR: Did they have any noticeable tattoos?

BERTALAN: I didn't see any. But they could have had tattoos, who knows?

PROSECUTOR: How about facial features? Big nose, squinty eyes? Anything you can describe for us?

BERTALAN: I don't know.

PROSECUTOR: What kind of haircuts did they have?

BERTALAN: Short hair, I think.

PROSECUTOR: Did you hear them talking? Did they have low voices, high voices, or something else?

BERTALAN: I don't remember.

PROSECUTOR: Any unusual gait? For example, the night they burglarized you, had they been seen walking slowly in the rain?

BERTALAN: I don't think so. I didn't see that.

PROSECUTOR: Were they talking on the phone before they came to your house?

BERTALAN: Not that I know of.

PROSECUTOR: Were they carrying candy and fruit punch?

BERTALAN: I don't think so.

PROSECUTOR: As far as you know, did they have anything whatsoever in common with Trayvon Martin besides skin color?

BERTALAN (*uncomfortable*): Not that I know of. But I never said they looked like Trayvon Martin!

A witness spontaneously uttering words like that is rare, and if she did, the prosecutor should pause, let that all sink in, and slowly make his way back to his seat. Otherwise, he might have finished by pointing out that all African Americans do not look alike, not even by skin color:

PROSECUTOR: Were the burglars dark-, medium-, or light-skinned African Americans?

BERTALAN: Um, medium-skinned, I guess.

The prosecution didn't go near this fertile ground for cross-examination, accepting the defense premise that shared skin color justified suspicion. The burglars' and Trayvon's mutual blackness obscured all else.

By the defense logic, all young African-American males in the neighborhood would warrant a call to the police simply for walking while black—this in a racially diverse, middle-class community that is 20 percent African American.

BOILED DOWN TO its essence, here was the defense's simple syllogism, which, unfortunately, went entirely unchallenged in the courtroom:

1. Two black burglars had robbed a house in the neighborhood.

2. Trayvon was black.

3. Therefore, Zimmerman was suspicious of Trayvon, and that suspicion was reasonable.

Though this deductive reasoning seems sensible to many people, even intelligent lawyers, commentators, and thinkers, *it is entirely specious.*

The ancient Greeks, who developed the syllogism, are turning in their graves. Because it is wrong. False. If you took Logic 101 and wrote this on your final exam, you would get an F.

Let's examine this illogic, taking the hot-button issue of race out of it. Consider this similar logical fallacy:

1. Ninety-five percent of housekeepers are female.

2. Susan is female.

3. Therefore, when Susan comes to my home, it's fair for me to hand her a mop.

*I'm not sexist, it's just happenstance that's she's female!*

Or this one:

1. Nine out of ten child molesters are male.

2. Eduardo is male.

3. Therefore, Child Protective Services should take his kids away.

*Unfortunately, he's a match!*

Last one:

1. Nearly every alligator wrestler in America lives in Florida.

2. Rick Scott is the governor of Florida.

3. Therefore, he likely keeps his crocodilians locked up in the governor's mansion.

*I'm just trying to protect the community!*

The fallacy is the flipping of the syllogism, which should be deducing from the larger group to the smaller, not the other way around. Proper reasoning goes this way:

1.  All nuns are Catholic. (Big, all-inclusive statement.)

2.  In-Hei is a nun. (She fits within the subset of the big, all-inclusive statement.)

3.  Therefore, In-Hei is Catholic. (Therefore, she fits into the bigger group.)

The Zimmerman logic incorrectly extrapolates *backward* from a limited subset (burglars) to a much larger group of people (black males), as in the other fallacious examples. The population of housekeepers, child molesters, or alligator wrestlers is extremely small. To generalize from a tiny sample to a much greater one, such as the population of women, men, or Floridians, sweeps in a lot of people who have nothing to do with the smaller group, which is the flaw in the deductive reasoning. Most women are not housekeepers, most men are not child abusers, and most Floridians are not alligator wrestlers (thankfully for the poor reptiles).

Neither are most (nor even many) black males burglars.

In fact, the defense logic, seeing Trayvon as suspicious because of the Bertalan burglars, as a matter of pure deductive reasoning, is far worse than my examples. Each false syllogism above involved a smaller group (housekeepers) that was more than 90 percent comprised of the larger group (women). There is considerable debate over how much crime is attributable to African Americans, as we shall see in Part II, but no one claims it's anywhere near 90 percent, or even over 50 percent. So the defense syllogism could not even begin with "*most* crimes are committed by blacks," but at best, "*a few* crimes in the neighborhood were committed by blacks" (as we'll see in a moment), weakening the connection between the two groups. If you fear all black males because of two black burglars, then by the same logic, you would believe that all men are child molesters.

Even if African Americans committed a hugely disproportionate amount of crimes, even if *all* burglaries at the Retreat at Twin Lakes in the year before Trayvon went out for a walk were committed by black males, it would still be illogical to assume that Trayvon was a burglar. *Even though all nuns are Catholic, most Catholics are not nuns, so it would be silly to assume a random Catholic woman is a nun. Even if all burglaries were committed by black males, most black males are not burglars, and it's equally foolish to assume that a random black male is a burglar.*

Why is it so easy for us to understand the former but not the latter? The nuns but not the burglars? The fact that the defense's logic seemed intuitively right to so many people, yet my nonracial examples are so obviously ridiculous, is a testament to the pernicious "black men are suspicious" stereotype that has long attached itself to the American psyche like a virulent tick.

Lumping Trayvon Martin in with the Bertalan burglars seemed so logical, so rational, so fair that nearly everyone—including the prosecution—just accepted it. *Oh, there were some black burglars in the neighborhood? Well, then, we can't blame Zimmerman for being suspicious when he saw Trayvon.*

Oh, yes we can. And much more significantly, we can blame the professionals for failing to object loudly to the racial profiling that was being accepted by everyone in the courtroom about a dead teenager who could not speak for himself.

The prosecution could and should have gone after and dismantled each of the wrongheaded assumptions being fed to the jury about race. One of the first suppositions made by Zimmerman and repeated by the defense at trial that could have been easily destroyed was that many—or most—or at least, a lot (this was never nailed down)—of the neighborhood crimes were committed by African-American males. One got the impression that the neighborhood was overrun by black males breaking and entering homes.

In fact, there is no evidence of that whatsoever. At trial, we only heard about the two Bertalan burglars and then some generalized statements about there being a lot of other crime—but committed by whom? We never learned.

According to an exhaustive review by Reuters,[48] in the fourteen months prior to Trayvon's death, there were eight burglaries and "dozens" of attempted break-ins and "would-be burglars casing homes" at the Retreat at Twin Lakes. (Already the data is getting soft, since some of these may have been ill-founded suspicions, as in the case of Trayvon. But we'll go with these numbers.)

"Dozens" is vague, but let's pick a low "dozens" number of three, for thirty-six attempted or suspected break-ins, plus the eight actual burglaries, for a total of forty-four crimes at the Retreat at Twin Lakes. Three were committed or attempted by black males, says Reuters, the Bertalan burglars plus one more. So, three out of forty-four in our local crime sample were known to be African American. That number would be significantly less than the 20 percent of the population blacks comprised of the Retreat at Twin Lakes, and far less than the 40 percent African American composition of the area surrounding Sanford.

If that's all there were, one could say that blacks would be *less* likely to break and enter than members of other races.

But we can't assume all the unknown-race thieves were white, any more than we could assume the remaining forty-one were black, or Hispanic, or Asian American, or anything else. Most burglars are not known to their victims, as they operate stealthily, arriving and leaving unseen. (The Bertalan burglars, for example, rang the doorbell first, probably preferring to rob an unoccupied home.)

There is no evidence that the neighborhood was awash in black criminality, or even that African Americans were committing crimes there in numbers greater than their proportion of the population. Zimmerman's fears were not well founded—not *reasonable*. Wouldn't that have been worth mentioning?

Squarely addressing the race issue would have meant not only attacking the defense's fatally flawed reasoning (via cross-examination of witnesses where the race issue was raised, and certainly in closing arguments), but also using the state's own strong evidence that Zimmerman had a clear pattern of improperly racially profiling African Americans. Because his call to police that night about Trayvon looking like "a real suspicious guy" was not Zimmerman's first, or second, or third. As the self-appointed neighborhood-watch coordinator, he had called many times before about suspicious-looking men in his community. Guess what percentage of them were African American? Since the population was 20 percent African-American, 40 or 50 percent would be a lot, wouldn't it?

All of them. One hundred percent of Zimmerman's calls admitted into evidence about suspicious persons involved African Americans. (Zimmerman had even called the police about a seven- to nine-year-old black boy walking down the street alone, ostensibly concerned for his well-being, even though he was walking toward an elementary school.)

In the first week of trial, the state fought hard outside the jury's presence to enter into evidence police calls Zimmerman had made in the months before the shooting. Though the judge ultimately granted the state's request and admitted recordings of these calls into evidence, strangely the prosecution did not use the evidence and remained silent on Zimmerman's pattern of racial profiling throughout the trial.

Let's take a look at those calls. Over the eight years he'd lived in the community, the hyper-vigilant Zimmerman made forty-six police calls[49] (some were to 911 and some to a nonemergency police line). Audio of only the most recent six were preserved, and five of those were calls about people in the neighborhood he deemed suspicious. (The sixth involved no humans—simply a garage door left open.)

In addition to the April 22, 2011, call about the little African-American boy, Zimmerman contacted the police about these individuals:

- On August 3, 2011, **a black male** wearing a white tank top and black shorts, walking in the neighborhood, whom he called a "match" to a recent burglar, according to his wife's description. Zimmerman became agitated that the man walked away from him while he was on the call. At the end of the call, he indicated he was going to follow the man, and a woman, probably Zimmerman's wife Shellie, said, "Don't go."

- On August 6, 2011, **two black teenaged males** he said matched the description he'd heard from his wife of burglars in the neighborhood, wearing tank tops, shorts, and jeans, walking near the back gate of the community. Zimmerman told the dispatcher "they typically run away quickly."

• On October 1, 2011, **two black males** who were "suspicious characters" in a white Impala, mid-twenties to early thirties, at the gate to the community. Zimmerman did not recognize them. He was concerned they were connected with recent burglaries.

• On February 2, 2012, **a black male** in a black leather jacket, black bomber hat, and flannel pajama pants who was walking near the house of a neighbor. "I know the resident, he's Caucasian," Zimmerman said.

In a rare moment of a police officer on the case actually investigating Zimmerman's motives, the lead detective on the case, Chris Serino, noticed Zimmerman's pattern of racial suspicions. In his formal request to the state that Zimmerman be charged with manslaughter, signed March 13, 2012, Detective Serino noted that "All of Zimmerman's suspicious person calls while residing in the Retreat neighborhood have identified Black males as the subjects."[50]

Detective Serino, a sixteen-year veteran of the Sanford Police Department, was authoritative and credible, an appealing witness whom jurors later praised. He testified at length about his investigation, putting together the jigsaw pieces for the jury as a seasoned homicide detective.

Yet in court, he was not asked a single question about this keen observation he'd made early in the case. The prosecution avoided it like it was radioactive. They did not even let Serino discuss Zimmerman's racial profiling as one piece of the puzzle. The state's other major blunder with Detective Serino was allowing the defense to elicit from him his opinion that he found Zimmerman's self-defense story truthful. The lead detective believes Zimmerman! That was a big moment in the courtroom. The next day, the prosecution woke up and objected retroactively, as witnesses are not permitted to opine on credibility of other witnesses, which is the province of the jury. The judge agreed, and told the jury to strike that powerful testimony from their minds. They didn't. Juror B37 relied on it in reaching her verdict, she later told CNN's Anderson Cooper. A better strategy would have been for the prosecution, on redirect (their next chance to question Serino), to show the detective his request that Zimmerman be charged with manslaughter, which demonstrates clearly that he thought Zimmerman should be held accountable for the killing. In other words, he may have initially found Zimmerman credible, but once he'd had an opportunity to review all the evidence in the case, including the strong evidence of Zimmerman's racial profiling, he wanted Zimmerman arrested. That would have cleared up the issue. But it never happened.

Though the prosecution failed to use the evidence of Zimmerman's recent police calls about supposedly suspicious African-American men (none of whom were actually doing anything criminal), though they failed to ask a single witness about it, though they stayed away from the subject in closing arguments, a courtroom amateur picked up on Zimmerman's pattern of racial profiling: Maddy, the juror. The jurors listened to those audio recordings during deliberations, Maddy explained, and she said, "I noticed that all the prior calls about suspicious people were about black guys." She put together evidence that the prosecution had not put together for her. "Yeah, he profiled him from the beginning," Maddy said. "The evidence is there. He profiled him because he was black, but the law says that at the end of the day, all that mattered was who was on the top and who was on the bottom." She didn't mention the subject in deliberations because she'd been told race was not part of the case. If anyone else noticed it, they didn't speak up about it either, she says.[51]

As we saw in Chapter Two, the jury was hopelessly confused about the law of self-defense, which definitely does *not* state that in a physical altercation, the person on the bottom can take out a gun and shoot to kill the guy on top.

Here, had the dots been connected for the jury as they should have been in closing arguments, they would have understood that racial profiling was relevant to two key issues in the case. First, did Zimmerman *reasonably* fear that Trayvon was going to kill him, as he claimed? Recall that reasonableness is an essential element of Zimmerman's self-defense case. One who jumps to panicky conclusions every time a black male walks down the street is not reasonable. Zimmerman was not reasonable when he instantly concluded that Trayvon was "up to no good," a criminal, an *asshole*. Racial profiling is, to put it mildly, *unreasonable*. In this case, it was deadly.

Second, one of the elements of the top charge, second-degree murder, was intent. That is, that Zimmerman *intentionally* killed Trayvon with hatred, spite, or ill will. One who assumes a stranger, even a minor, is a "fucking punk," a criminal who "always gets away" simply because the stranger is African-American is certainly not behaving with goodwill.

The state fumbled the race issue throughout the trial, most noticeably in prosecutor John Guy's rebuttal closing argument, the state's last chance to drive its points home with the jury. Guy insisted forcefully that the case was not about race. Relying on a strategy reminiscent of the film *A Time to Kill*, Guy asked the jury to consider a role reversal: would Trayvon be convicted if he had followed and then shot Zimmerman? After this obvious, if implicit, reference to race, Guy finished up by reminding the jury that the case was not about race.

Huh?

One of the final photos the defense showed to the jury was a 7-Eleven surveillance camera image of Trayvon an hour before his death, the kind of blurry photo one sees on the local news when the police are searching for a holdup suspect. *This* was the person Zimmerman encountered, defense counsel insisted.

By the following night, Zimmerman was acquitted. Afterward, smiling broadly after her team had just lost the case, Angela Corey, the special prosecutor, said, "This case has never been about race. But Trayvon Martin was profiled. There is no doubt that he was profiled to be a criminal. And if race was one of the aspects in George Zimmerman's mind, then we believe we put out the proof necessary to show that Zimmerman did profile Trayvon Martin."[52] It was the same confused babbling about race the state had engaged in during the trial, the same incomprehensible mixed message.

# FOUR

## *Bungling the Science*

W ITH THE TELEVISION show *CSI* and its spinoffs, *CSI: Miami* and *CSI: NY*, as well as popular crime shows like *NCIS* and *Forensic Files*, the crime show juggernaut has taught the public that science—precise, verifiable, dazzling—can solve cases a heck of a lot better than human witnesses. Bestselling author and forensic anthropologist Kathy Reichs has written nineteen popular novels in her Temperance Brennan series, translated into thirty languages, about how forensic science cracks cases and conclusively proves the guilt or innocence of accused rapists and murderers. (The hit TV show *Bones* is based on her books.) The original in this genre was the bestselling Kay Scarpetta series by Patricia Cornwell, with its female heroine, a smart chief medical examiner for Richmond, Virginia.

And like the television and reading audience, jurors respect forensic evidence, often to the point of awe. What's not to love? Eyewitnesses err, innocently or intentionally. Science doesn't lie, right?

While we love shows and books based on crime scene forensics, most Americans' scientific knowledge comes woefully short. Only 21 percent[53] of us can explain what it means to study something scientifically, and the vast majority of Americans are unable to read the science section of a newspaper, which is written for a lay audience.

Into that chasm between reverence for scientific evidence and our own ignorance of the field come expert witnesses, who bridge the gap by using their years of study and experience to explain key aspects of a case to jurors. The right medical expert can make or break a case because the jurors may simply cede the decision to him or her. *Ah, the doctor says so, and that settles it. Who am I to say otherwise?*

In a 2009 Emory University experiment,[54] a group of adults was asked to make a decision while contemplating an expert's claims, in this case, a financial expert. An M.R.I. scanner gauged their brain activity as they did so. The results: when confronted with the expert, it was as if the independent decision-making parts of many subjects' brains switched off. They shut down and went with the professional's recommendation, even if the advice was bad.

Thus, we expect jurors to lean forward in their seats when scientific professionals take the stand, bringing their medical degrees and credibility, their lab reports, their jargon-heavy opinions, their expert analysis that pulls together the facts into one neat explanation of what happened.

But scientific opinion is only as good as the fallible humans presenting it to the jury.

REMEMBER PRIMACY AND recency? Just as movies want to start and end with a bang, lawyers usually want to put their strongest witnesses on first and last, to seal them in the jurors' memories. The prosecution chose to call its medical examiner as its final witness in its case-in-chief (its primary case; after the defense's case, a brief opportunity for rebut-tal remained). Dr. Shiping Bao, with his twenty-four years of experience in forensic pathology (the study of corpses to determine cause of death), performed the autopsy on Trayvon Martin the day after his death, February 27, 2012. He was there to explain to the jury what his medical review of Trayvon's remains showed—to speak for Trayvon, in a sense, beyond the grave.

The jury remembered him all right. Months after the trial, at the very mention of Dr. Bao's name, Maddy laughed: "Oh my God, that man was a hot mess!" At the time he testified, commentators across the spectrum at last found something to agree upon in the controversial case. The medical examiner's testimony in no way advanced the state's case against Zimmerman, scored at least one real point for the defense, and was, overall, a fiasco.

To begin with, there was a bit of a language problem. Dr. Bao, a Chinese national who immigrated to the United States at age twenty-nine for the "American dream," spoke with a thick accent, which was some-times difficult to decipher. But he was aware of it, and so on the stand he overcame that moderate hurdle by speaking slowly, as clearly as he could, and spelling words that he knew might not be properly understood. (Language problems are surmountable. Another Chinese American, Dr. Henry Lee, also speaks with a noticeable accent, is considered one of America's foremost forensic scientists, and is a celebrity expert witness.)

The bigger problem was that Dr. Bao often appeared unwilling or unable to answer the prosecutor's questions, preferring to veer off into subject matters that were not being asked of him. By the time of his testimony, at the end of the second week of trial, the jury had become accustomed to the basic rhythm of witness testimony: the lawyer asks the question, the witness answers it. Repeat. Repeat. Repeat. No veering off onto tangents, no rambling, no challenging the lawyers. Yet there was Dr. Bao, the state's own professional witness, who one assumes has done this once or twice, being admonished by Judge Nelson several times to *please just answer the questions*, and *only* the questions posed. Dr. Bao came across as unfamiliar with the court rules and at odds with the prosecutor, de la Rionda, who was asking him questions.

Why so much friction between two people ostensibly on the same side of the case—the state's attorney and the state's medical examiner? Did they not communicate before Dr. Bao took the stand?

Now we know. A month after the trial, Dr. Bao was fired by the Volusia County Medical Examiner's Office for his poor performance in the Zimmerman trial. He promptly hired flashy local attorney Willie Gary, whose website's home page leads with photos of Gary in his white Bentley and seated in a private plane, set to the tune of the theme song from *Rocky*. A voiceover modeled on "let's get ready to ruuuumble!" announces that Gary, a personal injury attorney, calls himself "the giant killer" and proclaims that he has won over 150 settlements and verdicts over $1 million. Rather than file suit, Gary promptly took Dr. Bao on a media tour, in which they threatened to sue the county "shortly"[55] for $100 million—a headline-generating, astonishing demand in the context of a wrongful termination case, where the typical recovery for a successful complainant is a few years' pay. (Dr. Bao earned less than $200,000 annually; punitive damages are not available in an action against a government entity, like a county.) At the time this book went to press, no lawsuit had been filed.

With Gary at his side, Dr. Bao claimed that the state intentionally threw the case and would not allow him to introduce medical evidence he wanted to discuss, which would have helped the state's case. Dr. Bao did not elaborate on what this evidence would have been. Insisting that an attitude of hostility or indifference toward the case permeated the medical examiner's office, as well as the team of police and prosecutors, Dr. Bao said that behind the scenes, many thought that "Trayvon was a criminal and he was on drugs." For example, Dr. Bao noted that it was customary for police investigators to attend his autopsies, so they could ask questions and interact with him as he examined the deceased's remains. No one showed up for Trayvon's examination. (Through a spokesperson, police investigators said that they were busy trying to identify the remains[56] at that time.)

His testimony was treated as so unimportant, Dr. Bao said, that the prosecutors did not do basic pretrial preparation with him. For example, Dr. Bao's prior sworn testimony in his pretrial deposition was not sent to him until just a few days before his trial testimony, and then only after Dr. Bao made repeated requests for it, he says. (A spokesperson for the state attorneys' office[57] says that Dr. Bao indicated he did not need to review his prior statement before trial.) And the state attorneys only met with Dr. Bao the day before his trial testimony, on a holiday, July 4, 2013, to go over what he would say—after Dr. Bao insisted that some preparation had to happen. It is not only customary that lawyers meet with witnesses to review their testimony well in advance; for key witnesses and scientific experts—Dr. Bao was both—preparation is essential.

That lack of planning made for a stunningly poor performance in the state's presentation of medical evidence. First, Dr. Bao did not remember a single moment from the autopsy he performed on Trayvon, and, worse, he seemed to delight in pointing out that deficiency, with frequent comments like: "I do not have any recall. I do not have any memory of the day of autopsy. I do not remember anything. Zero,"[58] he said. (One imagines the prosecutor thinking, *Got it. Stop. Please.*) To be fair, Dr. Bao performed autopsies daily, sometimes several times a day, week in and week out, as that was his job. Who could possibly recall them all? At the time he analyzed Trayvon's remains, it was just another day in the coroner's office, and his examination was not particularly memorable. In this case and in every case, however, Dr. Bao took notes to record his findings and relied upon those notes in the trial.

Still, a more polished Q and A on this point would have been:

PROSECUTOR: Do you have an independent recollection of this autopsy, which you conducted sixteen months ago, Dr. Bao?

DR. BAO: I do not.

PROSECUTOR: Is it customary for you to rely upon your notes, then?

DR. BAO: Yes.

PROSECUTOR: Thank you, Dr. Bao. Please feel free to do so when necessary in answering my questions.

Appearing entirely unfamiliar with court rules, Dr. Bao wanted to simply read his notes aloud on the stand, rather than answer the prosecution's questions—a sign of inexperience, and, again, lack of preparation.

And those were just style points. On substance, Dr. Bao had some entirely new theories to offer on the stand—scientific opinions that surprised the prosecutors, the defense, and everyone else in the courtroom. He went off script. Sure, he'd come to some conclusions eight months earlier when he testified under oath in his deposition, but at trial, the critical moment in the case, he changed his mind. At his November 2012 deposition, Dr. Bao had said that Trayvon could have survived the gunshot wound to his heart for one to three minutes. Now, based on a different case he'd been involved with three weeks before the trial, Dr. Bao had a new opinion—that Trayvon could have lived from one to *ten* minutes. Caught flat footed, de la Rionda tried to limit the impact of this change, and Dr. Bao, defensively, repeatedly explained that facts don't change, but opinions can, and that there was nothing wrong with an expert changing his opinions. In a heated exchange with de la Rionda, Dr. Bao blurted out that only "mentally retarded" people never change their opinion, and that as an expert he was entitled to change his opinion every day if he liked.

Well, theoretically, yes, in the lab or classroom, but Dr. Bao seemed painfully unaware that changing one's testimony damaged one's credibility at trial, since the facts had remained the same—only Dr. Bao's interpretation as to what they meant had changed. Next week, might he change his mind again? If so, how could the jury possibly rely on his testimony and convict a man of murder?

And springing this on the state at trial left the prosecutors gobsmacked and scrambling to improvise with these new opinions from their own expert. Was Dr. Bao actively trying to stick it to the state attorneys?

Outside the presence of the jury, the court conducted a hearing on this surprise change of heart by Dr. Bao. The issue was whether the state knew about Dr. Bao's new positions, because if so, they'd have been required under the discovery rules to disclose them to the defense, so that they too could be prepared. De la Rionda showed the judge his notes, essentially saying, *hey, we didn't know about this, don't blame us*—as if the state's lack of preparation was something to be proud of. The prosecution was off the hook on the alleged discovery violation—but their much bigger problem, failing to prepare one of their most critical witnesses, festered.

The number of minutes that Trayvon may have remained alive after the shooting was, ultimately, not all that significant in the case because the most important facts were those leading up to the gunshot, not what happened afterward. Whether Trayvon lived for one minute, three minutes, or ten minutes more, there was no question that Zimmerman's bullet to the heart took the teenager's life. The only minor relevance of this time period is that Zimmerman had said that after he shot Trayvon, he'd turned Trayvon onto his stomach and spread his arms to prevent him from getting to his imagined weapon, and left him in that position. Yet when the first responders arrived, Trayvon's arms were found tucked *under* him, probably in a heartbreaking attempt to press on the painful bullet wound as he lay dying. This position is inconsistent with Zimmerman's statement of how he left his shooting victim, unless in the minutes after Zimmerman got off Trayvon, Trayvon was still alive and able to move.

The prosecution wanted to argue that Zimmerman's statement that he'd left Trayvon with his arms spread was another lie, because Trayvon's arms were found under him. But this knee-jerk approach to calling any inconsistency a lie missed the point: Why would Zimmerman lie about this? How would it help his story? It wouldn't. So focusing on Dr. Bao's estimate of the number of minutes that Trayvon survived was a distraction that did not advance their case and undermined their own forensic pathologist's testimony and credibility.

More significant was the testimony Dr. Bao now wanted to give about the trace amounts of marijuana found in Trayvon's system— his second changed opinion. At his deposition, Dr. Bao had said that Trayvon would have been unaffected by the small amounts of THC, the active ingredient in marijuana, found in his body. Since then, he said he had done additional research into the toxicology. As a result, Dr. Bao wanted to testify at trial that the presence of THC in Trayvon Martin's system could have decreased aggression and made him more relaxed— the commonly understood mellowing effect of marijuana.

Again due to a lack of communication between the state and Dr. Bao prior to his testimony, the prosecution was caught off guard by this new position. After a hearing outside the jury's presence, Judge Nelson reversed an earlier ruling and held that given Dr. Bao's new opinion, she would have to allow testimony about THC in Trayvon's system. Ultimately the defense, after winning that ruling, did an about-face and decided *against* letting the jury know about the marijuana after all. Of course they did. Because while they could have introduced evidence that in a tiny number of cases THC has the opposite effect, the science is clear that marijuana is overwhelmingly a relaxant. If the jury knew that Trayvon had THC in his system, they might conclude he was less likely to have been the homicidal, enraged attacker Zimmerman described. (Zimmerman himself was never given an alcohol or drug test after the shooting because the police did not have probable cause to believe he was under the influence. His medical records revealed that he had been prescribed the stimulant Adderall, commonly used to treat attention deficit disorder, and Temazepam, a drug used for insomnia and anxiety, but the judge did not allow this information to reach the jury.)

The prosecution too stayed away from the marijuana evidence, perhaps concerned about the image of Trayvon Martin as a pot-smoking thug, an unfounded, ugly image that had widely circulated online. But in today's America, 35 percent of us have tried cannabis, and half favor legalization,[59] according to Gallup. A few months before the trial began, a solid 70 percent of Floridians[60] favored legalizing medical marijuana in the state. Most people understand that THC has a calming effect, rendering its users far more likely to be lazy than violent.

Nevertheless, like race, the prosecution did not want to touch this issue. And because the amounts of THC in Trayvon's system were so minute—he could have ingested it days or even weeks earlier—testimony on its effects on him on the night of February 26, 2012, would have been highly speculative.

And so Dr. Bao did not testify about his view that marijuana would have reduced any aggressiveness on Trayvon Martin's part because neither side wanted to bring in that testimony. Nor did he tell the jury any other medical theories he had about the shooting because he was not asked, and he'd already been warned by the judge not to volunteer information.

I reached Dr. Bao three months after the trial and asked him specifically what additional scientific theories he'd wanted to explain to the jury. First, he said that while everyone understood that the bullet to the heart killed Trayvon, no one had talked about his *lung injuries*, which had some significance. Two bullet fragments, he said, punctured Trayvon's lung, as he had noted in his autopsy report.[61] Those fragments caused hemorrhaging and a condition called pneumothorax, which is air in the pleural space that separates the lung from the chest wall and which interferes with normal breathing. "His lung would have been squeezed like a balloon and would not have been able to expand," Dr. Bao said, "therefore, Trayvon would not have been able to speak, not at all." Zimmerman had claimed that Trayvon said, "You got me," immediately upon being shot, another gangster-movie-sounding line. The medical evidence shows that to be an impossibility, Dr. Bao said.

Dr. Bao tried to tell the prosecutors this in their very brief, perfunctory preparation of him, he says, but they brushed it off. "They didn't want to hear it," he says. They didn't want to hear about medical evidence that contradicted Zimmerman's story? "I tried to tell them, but they didn't listen."

A spokesperson for the prosecutor's office[62] called Dr. Bao's claims about their alleged shortcomings in the case "unconscionable," without specifically responding to the allegations that the state's lawyers had been lax in preparing him to testify.

It was clear by the end of the trial that the prosecutors had had it with their own medical expert. In closing argument, John Guy distanced himself from his forensic pathologist, asking the jury: "If you don't like . . . Shiping Bao, ask yourself, who produced this trial? Who made up the witness list?" Yes, Zimmerman's shooting caused the trial to happen, but, hey, the prosecution makes up its own witness list, the state of Florida chooses its own medical examiners, and the state attorneys' office chooses to prepare its witnesses, or to let them flounder on their own.

The only reference to his own expert was a negative one, validating the jury's presumed dislike for Dr. Bao and offering no defense of his own witness.

IN CONTRAST TO Dr. Bao, far and away the defense's best witness was Dr. Vincent DiMaio, an amiable "hired gun" medical examiner who examined the scientific and medical evidence in the case and testified in a clear, compelling manner that Zimmerman's story was consistent with all the forensic evidence in the case. His testimony focused on the gunshot residue (also called stippling or powder tattooing), which are tiny particles emitted from a fired gun, which can be measured in close-range shootings to determine the distance between the gunman and the victim. Dr. DiMaio said that here, the gunshot residue around the bullet wound on Trayvon's chest established that the shot had been fired two to four inches from Trayvon's skin, and that the gunshot residue around the bullet hole in Trayvon's outer sweatshirt showed that Zimmerman's gun had been fired while pressed directly against it. Thus, a gap of a few inches existed between Trayvon's hoodie and his skin at the time he was shot. And therefore, Dr. DiMaio testified emphatically, at the moment he was shot, Trayvon was crouched above Zimmerman, with gravity pulling Trayvon's shirt away from his body, just in the way Zimmerman claimed it happened.

A perfect scientific fit with Zimmerman's self-defense story! At least, that's how this evidence went to the jury. Because while this testimony could have easily been undermined and countered on cross-examination, the state punted. And while the prosecution knew about this witness in advance, it failed to secure its own expert to respond to Dr. DiMaio.

The prosecution's rebuttal case is its chance to bring forth one of its witnesses already called (like Dr. Bao) or a new witness to counter the defense's best witnesses. The state called no one to answer Dr. DiMaio. Because of these two choices—a very soft cross-examination and not calling anyone to present the other side—Dr. DiMaio's strong presentation went to the jury unchallenged.

Jurors, we know now, saw Dr. DiMaio's testimony as a breath of fresh air. Maddy praised him, appreciating that "he made connections on things that I was confused about," precisely the role of a good expert witness. Even before he took the stand, jurors heard his name, as Dr. Bao conceded on cross-examination that he had reviewed Dr. DiMaio's book on gunshot wounds, thereby strengthening Dr. DiMaio's credibility as the preeminent expert in his field. In marked contrast to the prosecution's presentation of its forensic expert, there was no tension between the defense expert and the attorneys for his side. He'd obviously been carefully prepared, so the questions posed to him and his answers on direct examination flowed smoothly. He smiled, sat back in his chair, and explained medical concepts in plain English for the jurors like a wise, kindly grandfather. His primary point—that the two- to four-inch gap between Trayvon's shirt and his skin at the time of the shooting was consistent with Zimmerman's story that Trayvon was crouched over Zimmerman—was communicated clearly and unambiguously—and consistently with his prior deposition testimony. A home run for the defense.

The state needed to come back aggressively to undermine Dr. DiMaio. By this point in the trial, jurors understood that this was a murder trial, not a tea party. The attorneys' job is to ask impertinent questions on cross-examination, to see whether the witness's story holds up. This is especially true for expert witnesses. While trial lawyers can turn jurors off with overly tough questioning of regular folks on the stand, for whom we may have sympathy as they were thrust unwillingly into a high-profile case, experts like Dr. DiMaio are highly educated and richly compensated to be there ($400 an hour in this case, he told the jury), and as forensic professionals who signed up for this line of work, they should be able to withstand the most aggressive cross-examinations allowable in criminal trials. Withering cross-examination of paid experts is fair game.

Instead, prosecutor Bernie de la Rionda chose to bolster Dr. DiMaio's credibility and get chummy with him. Rather than approach him with the outraged attitude of "I'm here to lock up a murderer and your bogus science seeks to free him," de la Rionda seemed to want to be Dr. DiMaio's new best friend. Beginning with a joke about how they both have loud voices and they are both balding, de la Rionda seemed to be bonding with the witness. Later in the cross-examination, de la Rionda joked that they are also both hard of hearing (a third attribute they shared!). Dr. DiMaio suggested they discuss which ear to see how close the similarity was. The jury had to notice, *what a likeable guy this Dr. DiMaio is! Even the prosecutor is charmed by him.*

Equally disturbing, on cross-examination of Dr. DiMaio,[63] the state chose to repeatedly reinforce the expert's credibility by reminding the jury that Dr. DiMaio was "head of the medical examiner's office in Bexar County, Texas," for twenty-five years. This experience dwarfed Dr. Bao's two years in Volusia County, where he was not the head of the office, but merely an associate medical examiner. And Dr. DiMaio was the "head of the ME's office in that beautiful city of San Antonio," de la Rionda mused. Dr. DiMaio agreed that his city's famed River Walk, in particular, was lovely.

Is this a murder trial, or a first date? Is the prosecutor there to avenge the unlawful taking of an innocent teenager's life, or to schmooze with a celebrity?

"You also mentioned that you testified all over the world," de la Rionda continued, further underscoring Dr. DiMaio's authority. Well, in some cities around the world, Dr. DiMaio responded with faux modesty.

What a waste of time. Instead, the prosecutor could have pointed out that Dr. DiMaio had spoken about the case on television—a tactic the defense had used to undermine a number of the prosecution witnesses, who had gone on TV talk shows about the case. While there is nothing illegal or immoral about witnesses submitting to media interviews during high-profile trials, jurors often feel those who do so lack credibility, as they may have been simply seeking their "fifteen minutes of fame." The prosecution missed an opportunity to tell the jury that Dr. DiMaio had done his own media interview, just like some of their witnesses.

A more significant credibility issue is at stake when witnesses deviate in their trial testimony from recorded interviews. Those inconsistencies can be fatal before a jury, so bringing them up on cross-examination is Lawyering 101. Dr. DiMaio had appeared on NBC's *Today Show* on May 13, 2012,[64] discussing the autopsy results after they had been leaked. At that time, Dr. DiMaio said only that the stippling (gunshot residue) around the bullet hole in Trayvon's body showed that "the range was most likely between two and four inches." Dr. DiMaio did not in that interview say that the gunshot wound confirmed Zimmerman's story, that Trayvon was on top, Zimmerman on the bottom, at the time of the shooting—his ultimate conclusion now at trial.

This was the big, important opinion he offered to the jury, one that he emphasized was so easy to reach. "This is not exactly a complicated case forensically," he told the jurors. He hadn't been required to put a lot of hours into the case because this conclusion was so obvious to him, he told them.

Then why hadn't he breathed a word of it on the *Today Show*, after he'd reviewed the same autopsy results he was now testifying about? Why hadn't he even suggested that this conclusion was *possible*? The prosecution never asked. When did this conclusion become so obvious to him? Was it only after he was offered $400 an hour to testify on Zimmerman's side?

While we're on the subject of the witness's credibility—a standard cross-examination topic—the jury learned that Dr. DiMaio had testified in recent years in two other high-profile murder cases, the Drew Peterson case (the Illinois police officer accused of drowning his third wife Kathleen Savio in the bathtub, and who is a suspect in the disappearance of his fourth wife, Stacy Peterson) and the Phil Spector case (the music producer accused of fatally shooting a woman, Lana Clarkson, in his Los Angeles mansion).

On this subject, the cross-examination went like this:

PROSECUTOR: You've testified in other high-profile cases?

DR. DIMAIO: Yes.

PROSECUTOR: You testified in the Phil Spector case? And Drew Peterson?

DR. DIMAIO: Yes, I did.

And that was it on this subject. Nothing more. This only bolstered his image as an important expert called upon to give his opinion in high-profile murder cases. But cross-examination seeks to discredit a witness, to expose the weaknesses in his credibility or testimony.

Here's how it *should have* happened, if it were done by an aggressive prosecutor who set out to undermine the opposing side's best witness:

PROSECUTOR: You enjoy testifying in high-profile cases, don't you?

DR. DIMAIO: Well, I don't know if I enjoy it. Maybe I do.

PROSECUTOR: Well, you've testified recently in two other murder cases that got a lot of media attention, didn't you?

DR. DIMAIO: I suppose I did.

PROSECUTOR: You testified in the Phil Spector murder case, right?

DR. DIMAIO: Yes.

PROSECUTOR: And in that case you were retained by the defense?

DR. DIMAIO: Yes.

PROSECUTOR: In other words, you were testifying on the side of the accused murderer, Phil Spector?

DR. DIMAIO: Yes.

PROSECUTOR: And just briefly, in that case he was accused of intentionally shooting a young woman, Lana Clarkson? And you testified that the science proved that he didn't do it, but in fact that she killed herself?

DR. DIMAIO: I believed it was a suicide, yes.

PROSECUTOR: And you lined up all the medical and scientific testimony in that case, and told the jury it all added up to suicide, right?

DR. DIMAIO: It was consistent with suicide, yes.

PROSECUTOR: And what was the outcome of that case?

DR. DIMAIO: He was convicted.

PROSECUTOR: Convicted of murder and sentenced to nineteen years to life in prison?

DR. DIMAIO: Yes.

PROSECUTOR: So the jury didn't believe your testimony in that case? They rejected it?

DR. DIMAIO: They convicted him.

PROSECUTOR: Now let's just quickly talk about the Drew Peterson case. This was the infamous Illinois cop whose fourth wife, Stacy, went missing and was never found? And his third wife also died under mysterious circumstances, and he was on trial for her murder?

DR. DIMAIO: That's the case.

PROSECUTOR: And you testified on behalf of the accused murderer in that case too, just like you did in the Phil Spector case, just like you're doing here?

DR. DIMAIO: Each case is different, but yes, I testified for the defense.

DEFENSE ATTORNEY: Objection, Your Honor, relevance.

PROSECUTOR: His credibility is at issue, Your Honor. And I just have a few more questions in this line.

JUDGE: Finish up, counsel.

PROSECUTOR: Yes, Your Honor. And in the Drew Peterson case, you testified that the scientific and medical testimony was consistent with the defense theory of that case, which was that Kathleen Savio had an accident alone in her bathtub, while she was in the middle of a contentious divorce with Drew Peterson? That she caused her own death?

DR. DIMAIO: I believed the evidence pointed to that, yes. I still believe that.

PROSECUTOR: How did that case turn out?

DR. DIMAIO: He was convicted.

PROSECUTOR: Of murder?

DR. DIMAIO: That's what he was convicted of, yes.

PROSECUTOR: So the jury rejected your testimony in that case, too?

DR. DIMAIO: You could look at it that way. There was a lot of other evidence in the case, too.

PROSECUTOR: If the jury believes you in this case, then, gosh, I guess it would be the first time a jury believed you in a high-profile murder case in the last decade, wouldn't it?

The jury would then be primed for cross-examination of Dr. DiMaio on the facts of this case, which could have begun with the highly unscientific manner in which he'd demonstrated the key issue of Trayvon's sweatshirts separating from his body. In explaining his theory to the jury, Dr. DiMaio had often used his own fitted men's dress shirt that he happened to be wearing that day, leaning forward, leaning back, pulling his shirt away from his body. This was fertile ground for cross-examination, though the state failed to explore it.

What actually happened was that Dr. DiMaio admitted a lack of familiarity with hoodies, laughing along with the prosecutor, suggesting that they were both old men who don't wear that type of thing, ha ha. Not funny. He is testifying on behalf of an accused murderer, trying to use science to acquit him, softening up the jury with each bit of laughter he can share with them.

Another missed opportunity. Science demands testing, experimentation, replication. And using the right sample to begin with. De la Rionda mentioned only that hoodies are worn big, emphasizing that they "hang down." He went on to state that "something in it"—the Arizona fruit drink—made Trayvon's shirt a little tighter. It was entirely unclear what the point was here, and as so often happened during this trial, one could even forget which side the prosecutors were on.

The state *should* have explained that in normal wear, a hoodie—this hoodie—is worn baggy and loose, and would have ballooned out from Trayvon's body.

It could have gone this way:

PROSECUTOR: Dr. DiMaio, when you have been using your own shirt to demonstrate your theory of the case to this jury, that's not scientific, is it?

DR. DIMAIO: No, not really. I'm just using my own shirt to give them the idea.

PROSECUTOR: In fact, it's highly unscientific to use your own men's dress shirt that you're wearing today under your suit jacket to demonstrate anything about Trayvon Martin's hoodie, isn't it? Because it's an entirely different kind of shirt? Different fabric, different cut, different size and style—as different as two shirts can be, really, aren't they?

DR. DIMAIO: It's just a visual aid. I'm not saying it's scientific.

PROSECUTOR: You testified that you shot bullets into the heads of live animals to prove your gunshot residue theories?

DR. DIMAIO: Yes, ha ha. [In fact, Dr. DiMaio had giggled when discussing his animal experiments, probably unaware that two of the six jurors rescued animals.] It was the only way to scientifically substantiate my hypothesis about powder tattooing.

PROSECUTOR: Why is that funny? [Allow for uncomfortable pause.]

DR. DIMAIO: Oh, it's not. I apologize. But animal experiments are done by many scientists, not just me.

PROSECUTOR: So it's that important to you as a scientist—it's important to all scientists—to test your hypotheses with conditions as close to the actual conditions at issue as possible?

DR. DIMAIO: Yes, certainly.

PROSECUTOR: So important that you're willing to take the lives of animals?

DR. DIMAIO: When necessary, yes.

PROSECUTOR: And so in this case, since you're testifying on behalf of an accused murderer that the science is consistent with his theory of self-defense, it was important to you to conduct an experiment, using conditions as close to those involved here, to prove your theory is correct, right?

DR. DIMAIO: Well, I couldn't shoot a person, counsel.

PROSECUTOR: Of course not. But you could do better than demonstrating with your own fitted dress shirt, couldn't you?

DR. DIMAIO: I'm not sure what you mean.

PROSECUTOR: Trayvon Martin was wearing two sweatshirts on the night of February 26, 2012, wasn't he?

DR. DIMAIO: Yes.

PROSECUTOR: Did you make any attempt to go online and purchase replicas of those shirts so that you could experiment on them?

DR. DIMAIO: No, that wasn't necessary. I had photos of them.

PROSECUTOR: Photos? That's what you worked with? Let's take a look at the real thing. Here's Trayvon Martin's first layer, his inner shirt. At the bottom of that sweatshirt, there is a band of fabric that's tighter than the material above it. Do you see that?

DR. DIMAIO: Yes.

PROSECUTOR: And do you see those lines extending up diagonally like a sunrise from the band at the bottom of the shirt, even when the shirt is pulled flat onto the exhibit?

DR. DIMAIO: Yes, I see them.

PROSECUTOR: That band at the bottom, and the extra fabric pulled into it, causes the sweatshirt to billow or bag out above the band when worn, doesn't it?

DR. DIMAIO: I suppose so.

PROSECUTOR: That's kind of the whole point, isn't it? Kids don't walk around in men's dress shirts. The style is to wear these sweatshirts loose and baggy, right? That's why this band is there around the bottom, to increase the bagginess of the shirt?

DR. DIMAIO: I would assume so. I'm not a fashion expert, ha ha.

PROSECUTOR (*not laughing*): But you're testifying as an expert witness in this case, aren't you? And key to your testimony is how this sweatshirt separated from Trayvon Martin's body at the moment the defendant shot him, isn't it?

DR. DIMAIO: That is part of my testimony, yes.

PROSECUTOR: And you never examined the actual shirts, did you?

DR. DIMAIO: I looked at the pictures.

PROSECUTOR: Now let's examine Trayvon Martin's outer sweatshirt, his hoodie.

DR. DIMAIO: OK. I've seen the picture of it.

PROSECUTOR: Well, then, let's look at the actual shirt Trayvon Martin was wearing when he was killed. If the inner shirt is baggy, what happens to the outer sweatshirt?

DR. DIMAIO: It would be baggy too.

PROSECUTOR: And this one has a fabric band around the bottom as well, doesn't it?

DR. DIMAIO: It does.

PROSECUTOR: So even without a shirt underneath it, it would bag out, away from the wearer's body, wouldn't it?

DR. DIMAIO: That's possible.

PROSECUTOR: Would this hoodie have been worn tight fitting or loosely by Trayvon Martin?

DR. DIMAIO: I don't know. I didn't see him wearing it.

PROSECUTOR: And you didn't purchase replicas of the shirts yourself, did you?

DR. DIMAIO: I did not.

PROSECUTOR: Did you find a mannequin the height and weight of Trayvon Martin, put both sweatshirts on that model, to see whether or not they pressed against the wearer's body in a standing position?

DR. DIMAIO: No, I didn't.

PROSECUTOR: Did you have a person the height, weight, and build of Trayvon Martin walk, turn, move, and run in those same two sweatshirts to see if they would be pressed against the wearer's body in positions other than straddling and crouching?

DR. DIMAIO: I did not.

PROSECUTOR: Why not?

DR. DIMAIO: It wasn't necessary.

PROSECUTOR: As a scientist, wouldn't you agree that replication is an important part of the scientific method?

DR. DIMAIO: Certainly.

PROSECUTOR: And replication simply means that a scientist tests his or her theories to see whether they can be reproduced?

DR. DIMAIO: That's what it means.

PROSECUTOR: And you never did that for your theory here?

DR. DIMAIO: I did not.

PROSECUTOR: Wouldn't that have been a more scientific way to substantiate your theory?

DR. DIMAIO: I only said that the evidence was consistent with the defense's narrative, counsel. It could be consistent with other versions too.

PROSECUTOR: It could? All right. So the gunshot residue could be consistent with Trayvon Martin standing at the time the defendant shot him?

DR. DIMAIO: Possibly.

PROSECUTOR: You don't know, because you didn't work with the actual sweatshirts? Or a mannequin or model wearing them?

DR. DIMAIO: I didn't.

PROSECUTOR: And Trayvon Martin could have been moving, causing the outer sweatshirt to separate a few inches from his body? He could have hunched his shoulders, as many teenagers do? He could have moved quickly backward, causing the sweatshirts to billow forward?

DR. DIMAIO: He could have.

PROSECUTOR: You don't know, because you didn't test your theory?

DR. DIMAIO: I didn't.

PROSECUTOR: And because you didn't, you can't say, sitting here today, that Mr. Zimmerman's story that Trayvon Martin was straddled over him is any more likely than Trayvon Martin standing, backing away, hunching, or moving at the time he was shot, can you?

DR. DIMAIO: They are all possible. I only said that the forensic evidence was consistent with Mr. Zimmerman's account.

PROSECUTOR: And that same forensic evidence is equally consistent with many other scenarios, too, isn't it?

DR. DIMAIO: It could be.

In closing argument, the state could have then taken this and run with it, reminding the jury that Dr. DiMaio was willing to put bullets into the heads of innocent animals to be sure about some of his other scientific theories but couldn't be bothered to buy a few sweatshirts to test his theories in this case. Maybe he didn't think of it. Maybe he didn't want to know how those tests would turn out. Maybe that would defeat his ability to earn the hefty expert witness fees and national fame by testifying so conclusively for the defense in this high-profile case.

To further drive home the point, the prosecution could have called its own expert witness who had done such experiments with two sweatshirts the size and make of Trayvon's, on a person or mannequin his height and weight, demonstrating that a few-inch gap between his hoodie and skin meant nothing, nothing at all. That gap could be found with Trayvon standing, hunching, walking, or in any one of myriad situations of dynamic movement of a physical altercation. Zimmerman could have been holding Trayvon's shirt to prevent him from escaping ("they always get away"). Trayvon could have been quickly backing away from the guy with the gun, causing the can of fruit drink in his hoodie's front center pocket to swing away from his body, creating a few inches of space. The possibilities are endless.

In short, the state missed its chance to destroy Dr. DiMaio's testimony.

Other prosecutors, in other high-profile cases, have effectively dismantled Dr. DiMaio for similar shoddy methodology. As we've seen, the jury convicted music mogul Phil Spector for the murder of Lana Clarkson notwithstanding Dr. DiMaio's expert testimony on behalf of the murderer that the evidence was "consistent with" suicide. (The defense claimed that Clarkson, having just met Spector at a Hollywood nightclub, went home with him, found Spector's gun, positioned herself in a chair next to the front door, purse over her shoulder, and killed herself. A slew of other women testified that when they tried to leave Spector's home on prior occasions, he'd threatened them with guns.) In that case, Dr. DiMaio hid behind the very same "consistent with" language he used in the Zimmerman case, in an effort to position himself on the defense side of the case, even though the evidence could be readily interpreted several ways.

Here's how the very effective Los Angeles prosecutor Alan Jackson handled the cross-examination in the Spector case (I've edited the conversation for brevity):

JACKSON: You testified yesterday and today . . . that the GSR [gunshot residue] is consistent with Miss Clarkson having fired the gun? You testified to that, correct?

DR. DIMAIO: Which means I'm consistent with what I said in the first place, and I'm consistent when I publish, and that's what I said it's consistent with.

JACKSON: And you didn't say . . . it's also consistent with Miss Clarkson not firing the gun, did you?

DR. DIMAIO: No.

JACKSON: Is there any reason you left that out of your testimony, Dr. DiMaio?

DR. DIMAIO: Because that's how you testify, consistent with. I mean, you know it's just—never mind.

JACKSON: Actually, you told the jury a half-truth. You didn't indicate the second half of that statement, which the entire scientific community agrees with, Dr. DiMaio, which is gunshot residue will not tell you who fired a weapon, correct?

DR. DIMAIO: Right, sir.

JACKSON: And it's also the GSR that appears on Mr. Spector's hands are also consistent with him having fired a weapon; isn't that true?

DR. DIMAIO: Sure. You can argue it that way if you want.

JACKSON: But you didn't tell this jury that in your direct testimony either, did you?

DR. DIMAIO: (No audible response.)

JACKSON: Yes or no?

DR. DIMAIO: No, sir, I did not.

JACKSON: All right, thank you.[65]

Stick a fork in him, he's done. At that point, it was over for Dr. DiMaio in the Phil Spector case. No such moment came in the Zimmerman case because the prosecutors did not go for the jugular, and did not point out the same half-truths Dr. DiMaio was peddling to the jury on behalf of yet another killer.

Dr. Bao told me that he very much wanted to be called back to the stand to respond to Dr. DiMaio's testimony, which he found absurd and refutable. "No one could tell who was on top and who was on the bottom at the time of the shooting" based on the stippling or any other medical evidence, he felt strongly. "We just don't know." From the standpoint of science, not knowing is a valid opinion, not one to be laughed off, he insisted. Where there is a lack of evidence, certainty is what's foolish. In other words, the gunshot residue was *consistent with* any number of scenarios. He asked the prosecution to call him as a rebuttal witness so that he could respond to Dr. DiMaio's misstatements of the forensic evidence in the case. They refused to do so.

In closing, the defense, predictably, asked the jury to consider the absence of such a rebuttal witness, asking why the state didn't have one.

The state never answered that question.

# FIVE

## *The State's Star Witness, Rachel Jeantel, Is Neutralized*

ONLY TWO WITNESSES in the trial could be said to give voice to Trayvon's side of the story. The first was the medical examiner, who typically becomes the voice of the silenced victim's body based on a careful review of the deceased's remains. *He shot me here*, the bullet wound cries out, *and then I couldn't move. I wasn't drunk*, the toxicology reports say. *I didn't have my hands on his throat*, Trayvon's blood-free hands, had they been properly bagged on that rainy night, might have said on his behalf. *I couldn't speak, I couldn't breathe*, his lung wounds proclaim. And so on. As we've seen, the state and Dr. Bao, in concert, lost that opportunity.

The second witness who could speak not for Trayvon's physical body but for his all-important state of mind was his nineteen-year-old friend, Rachel Jeantel, who had spent five hours in a series of telephone calls with him on the day he was killed, including the final minutes when, she says, Trayvon saw Zimmerman, feared him, ran from him, lost him, and then was confronted by Zimmerman, who reappeared and initiated the physical altercation. She was the state's most important fact witness at trial and the only one who could come close to presenting

Trayvon's version of what happened that night. Yet like Dr. Bao, she was ill-prepared to testify, spoke in diction that was at times difficult for many to understand, and was all but abandoned by prosecutors, depriving the jury of the essential information she had to offer.

Every trial lawyer knows that a witness this important requires special attention before and during her testimony. People aren't just flung into courtrooms, tongue-tied and apprehensive about what they're supposed to do and say. Witnesses in general require trial preparation, and extra time and patience is needed with those who have never previously testified in court, those who are young, anxious, or reluctant, or who have shown previous problems in testifying (such as at pretrial depositions). Jeantel was all of these. And as the key witness for the state, she should have been prepared energetically and meticulously.

Prosecutors like to say, "We don't go down to central casting to choose our witnesses," a truism through which they hope to separate themselves from witnesses who come across poorly on the stand, embarrassing them. (Though making such a statement in closing arguments is an insult to one's own witnesses, as we shall see.) But every day in America, prosecutors put drug dealers, gang members, jailhouse snitches, and shackled prison inmates on the stand because their testimony, while imperfect, is crucial to locking up someone else. And they get convictions based on the words of those unsavory characters by preparing the witnesses to testify, educating them on how to put the clearest testimony straightforwardly before the jury, and then getting them off the stand as soon as possible.

Rachel Jeantel, of course, was none of these. She was simply a fish out of water, an awkward rising high school senior removed from her Miami family and friends to the bewildering world of a distant courthouse, with a sea of satellite news trucks parked outside and police and lawyers and judges and headache-inducing questions and questions and more questions posed to her, leaving her defensive. The whole experience was a nightmare for her. In part, that's due to the fact that she had no native guide to walk her through the unfamiliar terrain.

In many cultures, direct questions are perceived as rude and confrontational. To many of us, conversations are most pleasant and natural when they are indirect and roundabout, when each speaker has the chance to chime in with her thoughts on the subject, or on another subject that may strike her fancy at the moment, related or not. If your friend doesn't want to discuss an unpleasant topic, you'd be impolite to press her on it.

Legal proceedings are the polar opposite of these social norms. Attorneys, usually strangers to the witnesses, pose blunt, personal, brazen questions ("Why didn't you go to Trayvon's funeral?"), and witnesses are expected to answer them clearly, directly, and fully, without any emotional reaction. If they don't, the attorney repeats the inquiry, perhaps verbatim, perhaps changing a detail, honing in on the omission. The attorney knows all the tricks. The hapless witness must answer, answer, answer according to unfamiliar rules, and if she doesn't, she's in contempt of court.

In my decades of experience examining and cross-examining witnesses, very few people are capable of responding directly to lawyer questioning. They're not trying to be evasive, they are just being asked to speak a foreign tongue. Highly educated CEOs, doctors, and even lawyers who don't practice litigation get stumped, their words twisted (in their view), annoyed at what they perceive as the hostile tone of the interrogation, being asked over and over again questions they are sure they've answered. Witnesses commonly cry, yell, spew profanity, run out of the room, or become enraged. Trial lawyers often consider it a victory to "break" a witness in this way because their emotional outbursts appear to undercut their credibility, and credibility is what it's all about for any witness.

Consider normal human conversation:

DAVID: Hey honey, what's for dinner?

CARLOS: Something good! How was your day?

DAVID: Oh, you know, a little of this, a little of that.

CARLOS: Hey, after dinner, want to watch a movie?

DAVID: Sure, whatever.

David and Carlos hug. They are so happy together.

Consider normal courtroom questioning:

LAWYER: What did you have for dinner last night?

FATIMA: Oh, it was pretty good.

LAWYER: Objection, nonresponsive. (*Sighs heavily.*) Can the witness be instructed to answer the question?

JUDGE: Please answer the question.

FATIMA: I thought I did.

LAWYER: Motion to strike that last answer.

FATIMA: Oh, geez. I had lasagna, okay?

LAWYER: What were the ingredients? What was in it?

OPPOSING COUNSEL: Objection, compound.

FATIMA: Wha—?

JUDGE: Sustained.

FATIMA: So should I answer . . . ? I'm confused.

LAWYER: Please list everything that went into the lasagna.

FATIMA: You know, a little of this, a little of that, whatever I had around, I guess.

LAWYER: Don't guess! Your Honor, the witness is not answering my questions! She's obfuscating!

FATIMA: I'm—What?

JUDGE: Ma'am, please focus on the precise questions being asked of you.

FATIMA (*exasperated*): Whatever.

JUDGE: Please wait for the question.

Fatima is confused. Why is everyone jumping all over her? Over *lasagna*? Are these people nuts? The lawyers and judge are frustrated too. Recalcitrant witnesses just waste everyone's time. Fatima obviously has something to hide, and lacks credibility, they think. The jury will never believe her story now.

Now imagine that instead of that insignificant conversation about a meal, the lawyer is grilling you about the most horrific and shocking experience of your life. Sixteen months after her friend Trayvon was killed,

Jeantel remained traumatized and emotional about the day that she'd been bantering on the phone with her friend, only to learn days later that he had been shot dead minutes after her call with him ended. She was not capable of processing it. (After the trial she said, "Death creeped me out. I don't do death at all." [66]) People had the nerve to ask her why she didn't go to his funeral. ("I didn't put him at that funeral," she pointed out later.)

The unsettling point she repeated often, trying to get the lawyers to listen to her, was: *I was the last one to speak to him.* This fact spooked her. She didn't know what to do with it. "You. Got. To. Un. Der. Stand," she said in the courtroom, dragging out each syllable for emphasis. "I'm the last person. You don't know how I felt." Normal, decent Homo sapiens would respond to that with, "How awful. I am so sorry." But in the courtroom, the grueling questioning continued. Later, she said to defense attorney Don West, who'd turned his back on her, "Are you listening?" Because it appeared that no one was. [67]

She'd already endured her pretrial deposition, a legal proceeding months before the trial began, where she'd been required to make the five-hour drive from her home in Miami Gardens to Jacksonville, Florida, only to wait and wait as other matters were argued between counsel, such as whether her deposition would be videotaped. (Lawyers are used to delays of hours, days, weeks, or months in legal proceedings. The "hurry up and wait" pace drives witnesses crazy.) Finally she left, telling the attorneys that if they wanted her deposition, they could get a court order. A month later, she made the trip back up to Jacksonville for her deposition. There, she'd been rattled by Don West's seven hours of questions, and she'd lost her cool with him on a few occasions. This was the man who was defending her friend's killer, she bore in mind. The experience was unbearable.

So she had a sense of what to expect at trial—more of the same, only this time, she wouldn't be in a small conference room with a few lawyers and a videographer. She'd face a packed courtroom, her image broadcast live nationwide.

With the trial date approaching, two women from Jeantel's church, knowing that she needed help, purchased some clothing for her that would be appropriate for the solemnity of the Sanford murder trial. Less than a week before the trial was to begin, they reached out to Miami attorney Rod Vereen, telling him, "This young lady needs help." No one from the prosecutor's office had contacted her; she was apprehensive and needed someone to guide her through. Vereen had grown up with the women and immediately agreed to jump in. Then a police officer who was to transport Jeantel and protect her during the trial told Vereen the same thing. "It felt like divine intervention," Vereen told me. She had no funds to pay Vereen, but he assisted her pro bono—without compensation.

While Vereen took Jeantel under his wing, he wasn't in the position the prosecutors were. He didn't have their voluminous files. He wasn't privy to their trial strategy, or the mountain of pretrial discovery that had been exchanged in the case. What questions did they intend to ask Jeantel? What were the most important areas of questioning? Where were the pitfalls?

Without this information and short on time, Vereen did what he could. He introduced himself to Jeantel the day before the trial began, and he went to court with her the next day. He told her to answer questions yes or no whenever possible, and to be respectful.

Vereen bumped into the prosecutors in the elevator on Monday, June 24, 2013, the first day of trial. Optimistically, he told them that they were doing a great job, and that he represented Jeantel. He gave them his business card and asked if there was anything he could do to help them vis-à-vis Jeantel. They accepted his card, shook his hand. "They never called me," he said.

In the fall of 2013, I spoke with Jeantel herself.[68] What, exactly, did the state attorneys' office do to ready her to take the stand and provide the best possible testimony for the state?

She appeared in court Monday morning, the first day of trial, she said. She then spent the entire Monday, she said, sitting in a small room in the courthouse, mostly alone. She knew that at any time a deputy could walk in and tell her it was her turn, and she'd be required to walk into the courtroom and in front of a room full of strangers and television cameras transmitting her words and image to millions and have to talk about the most painful event of her life. She'd previously been identified in court papers only as "Witness 8," but now she'd have to speak her real name, and the world would be watching her.

She wasn't called to testify on Monday after all. On Tuesday morning, June 25, 2013, she returned, fatigued by the tension of the day before. Again, she was told she could be called to testify at any point that day. Each of those days she was given the video recordings of her deposition. Jeantel told me five DVDs were given to her to watch, each several hours long. Much of these "long, boring" recordings consisted of defense attorney West repeating the same questions to her. "I couldn't pay attention," she said. She tried hard not to fall asleep watching them, hour after hour. She was not given any instruction as to what to look for on the videos, no analysis of what she'd done right or wrong, no coaching on how to improve from her pretrial performance.

By Wednesday, Jeantel was worn out by two days of stressful waiting, feeling defeated by her inability to focus on all those video recordings of herself being questioned by West. In total, she told me, she had approximately twenty minutes of real live preparation with the assistant state attorney, Bernie de la Rionda. He told her to just "tell your story, who you are, how you knew Trayvon, stay calm, be respectful." He didn't mention particulars of the points to be covered—neither the key points of his direct examination of her, nor anticipated cross-examination by West, were reviewed. "Your testimony should last about an hour," he advised. *An hour*, Jeantel thought. *Oh, sure.*

Some prosecutors prepare the young, the aged, or the frightened by going to their homes before trial, sitting in their living rooms or taking a walk with them, just visiting and establishing a comfort level. Later, once a working relationship has developed, the lawyer returns and goes over the relevant questions and answers, allowing the witness to speak in whatever manner is comfortable for her. This allows the witness the comfort of knowing the lawyer, so that when she testifies on direct examination she looks into the eyes of a friend, whom she trusts to guide her. And it allows the prosecutor to know what the pitfalls are—where he needs to slow her down, allow her to explain or define terms. And it would not be uncommon, especially in a case of this magnitude, to bring a witness like Jeantel into an empty courtroom before the trial begins, sit her up on the witness stand, and allow her a little practice with speaking clearly into microphones, which can be intimidating to the uninitiated. All of this is not only humane, relaxing the witness, but it's strategically prudent, as the clarity, flow, and presentation of the witness's testimony is greatly improved.

None of this happened for Jeantel. Almost completely unprepared, then, Wednesday afternoon, Jeantel took the stand, the most important fact witness for the state in the highest profile murder case in America in years.

EVEN ON DIRECT examination[69]—the easier, friendlier first round of questions propounded to her by the lawyer for her side (the prosecution)—Jeantel fared poorly. In that thirty-minute examination, Jeantel's speech was difficult for many to decipher. She was at times inaudible, and her grammar and diction could be hard to interpret. The jurors protested aloud that they could not hear or understand her—many times. In response, Judge Nelson repeatedly told her to slow down, speak clearly, and speak up. Objecting constantly, sometimes every question or two, West successfully broke up any flow of the testimony by making it impossible to get a clear sense of her story. The two microphones in front of Jeantel were fussed with and moved. West complained his view of the witness was obstructed—unfair! He couldn't see! The judge invited him to move his seat.

Who could follow this young woman's testimony with all those interruptions and distractions?

At the time of trial, Jeantel had an underbite—a bone condition that required surgery. As a result, she had a speech impediment, which caused some of what came across as mumbling and slurred words. The prosecutors' failure to bring that information out, so the jurors would understand that she had a simple medical problem, was a major oversight. Dental work has nothing to do with credibility.

In addition, Jeantel spoke an urban teenaged lingo that was an alien tongue to most of the white, suburban, middle-aged jurors. She answered some questions this way:

"I axed him how the man looked like."

"I told him OK, why he keep looking at you for?"

"I told him to run. He say, naw, he almost by his daddy fiancée house."

What no one pointed out was that Jeantel spoke a common vernacular. While one might think that American English is American English and that's that, in fact hundreds of dialects are analyzed by linguists, reflecting regionalisms and language patterns of various ethnic groups. My grandmother, who grew up in West Virginia, would warn away my suspected misbehavior with, "You better hadn't!" If she was considering an action, she'd say, "I might could." We considered this charming, not a sign that she was not trustworthy.

Yet Jeantel's speech patterns, because they are associated with poor African Americans, were perceived by many, including the people who mattered most, the jurors, as unintelligent, and worse, evidence that she was not credible. In fact, she used a common dialect spoken by millions of Americans, with its own intricate rules of grammar and pronunciation. When young people like Jeantel grow up in communities where this dialect is spoken, they are told in school to "speak properly," belittling their community's tongue and pressing them to learn a second set of grammar and vocabulary rules, at least in school, which many do. (Most of Jeantel's testimony was in "proper" American English, so she was capable of switching back and forth.)

Linguist John McWhorter defended Jeantel's speech:[70] "It's Black English, which has rules as complex as the mainstream English of William F. Buckley. They're just different rules. If she says to the defense lawyer interrogating her, 'I had told you,' instead of, 'I told you,'" it's because "black people around the country use what is called the preterite 'had.'"

Intelligence had nothing to do with it. She was able to easily and accurately identify names and complex relationships (Chad Joseph was Trayvon's future stepbrother; Trayvon was staying in the home of his father's fiancée). Dates and times were readily available to her—unusual for most witnesses, who couldn't possibly tell you the date something happened more than a year before, much less the precise time. Handed a page of phone records, she immediately corrected the exhibit, saying that she had spoken to Trayvon beginning at noon on February 26, 2012, yet the records showed that her first call was at 5:09 PM. She recalled the exact date she and Trayvon had begun texting and speaking on the phone frequently, February 1, 2012, and that March 17, 2012, was a Saturday. In each of these statements, remarkably, she was correct. In addition, we learned later that she was trilingual, speaking Haitian Creole and Spanish. She was fluent in more languages and dialects, then, than 90 percent of Americans.

But none of that came out clearly because her dialect and diction were difficult for the jury to understand. Worst of all, the jury heard from her for the first time in the trial, without explanation, two loaded racial terms— and they were attributed to Trayvon Martin. Jeantel said that when she asked him to describe the man who was following him, Trayvon said he looked like a "creepy-ass cracka." "What?" said some of the jurors. "Creepy-ass cracka." She was made to repeat the phrase several times so the court reporter could get it down, defense could hear, judge could get it, etc. A few minutes later, describing Trayvon's reaction when he thought he'd lost Zimmerman, only to have him reappear, Jeantel quoted Trayvon: "The nigga is still following me." *WHAT? WE CAN'T HEAR. WE CAN'T UNDERSTAND*, clamored the jurors, in a rare moment of speaking aloud in the courtroom from the jury box. She said it again.

"Forgive me—nigger? The N word?" Bernie de la Rionda gingerly offered. "That's slang," Jeantel began to explain, but she wasn't given the opportunity to say more, as the prosecutor was eager to move on.

Sitting in the jury box, Maddy felt bad for Jeantel, having to repeat her testimony so many times. Her language didn't faze Maddy a bit. She'd heard it all before. Some of Maddy's kids were teenagers close in age to Trayvon and Jeantel. "I hang with a young crew," she told me. "When you do, you learn slang."

All the other jurors, though, were offended by "creepy-ass cracka," Maddy said, and they were *done* with Jeantel once they heard that. When Jeantel used the word "nigga," other jurors turned to Maddy, asking her, "What did she say? *Nigger*? Isn't that a racist word?" *Why are they asking me?* Maddy wondered. *Because I'm black?*

Maddy had an entirely different view. "Nigga," she knew, was different from "nigger," the former being a slang word among some minority youth comparable to "dude," a word that can apply to anyone of any race. The latter is a highly offensive word when uttered by non–African Americans. "How is she racist?" Maddy said to me later, "She's black, and she's using the word 'nigga' about a white man." In the jury box, Maddy thought, *here we go again*, feeling marginalized, her community misunderstood.

"I love Rachel Jeantel!" Maddy told me later. "I love her because I understood her. I understood what she was saying." But the other jurors did not.

To understand Jeantel's testimony, one must perform an exercise not available to the jury: sit in a quiet room, watch the video of her answering the courtroom questions multiple times, translate some of her dialect for those not familiar with it, eliminate the large amount of repetition, and cut

out the constant stream of objections, comments, and courtroom distractions, which Jeantel was bombarded with far more than any other witness
at the trial. The jury even had to be admonished to *stop speaking aloud
during her testimony*, but instead to raise their hands if they had a problem.

That exercise reveals the essence of what Jeantel was trying so hard
to say about her final phone call with her friend Trayvon, which the jury
never got to hear with any clarity:

> He kept complaining that a man was watching him. He said the
> man looked like a creepy-ass cracka.
>
> I told him the man might be a rapist.
>
> Trayvon said, "Stop playing with me."
>
> I told him OK, then why does he keep looking at you?
>
> Trayvon said he'd try to lose him, and then he calmed down a
> little bit.
>
> Then he told me the man was following him.
>
> He started walking home. He said he was leaving the mailing
> area, which is where he was.
>
> Then we started talking about the All Star game. He told me to
> go check for him if it was on.
>
> Then Trayvon said, "The nigga is still following me."
>
> I told him to run.
>
> Trayvon said, no, he's almost by his daddy's fiancée's house.

Trayvon said he was almost there, but he was complaining that the man was still following him. Then he told me that he was going to run from the back. Then I heard wind, and the phone shut off. I called back, he answered.

I asked him where he was.

He told me he was in the back by his daddy's fiancée's house. He said he lost him.

I told him keep running.

A second later, Trayvon said, "Oh shit, the nigga behind me." I told him he better run. He was almost by his daddy's fiancée's house.

Then I heard Trayvon say, "Why are you following me for?" Then I heard a man, breathing hard, say, "What are you doing around here?"

I started saying, "Trayvon," then I heard a bump, which was his headset. Then I heard wet grass sounds. I was calling, "Trayvon, Trayvon." I kind of heard Trayvon say, "Get off, get off."

The phone then shut off. I called him back. He didn't answer, and I never spoke to him again.

The poor presentation of Jeantel's testimony meant the jury missed the fact that Trayvon was in fear of Zimmerman throughout, repeatedly tried to lose him, and was running back home to escape Zimmerman, trying to get away from him. At one point, he thought he'd lost Zimmerman, and he returned to talking about the basketball game—not, "I'm going to find and kill that guy," not, "I'm going to hide in the

bushes, Rachel, and then jump out at him," but, "Hey, go check and
see if the game has started yet, I don't want to miss it." Jeantel's story
directly contradicts much of Zimmerman's, but so little of it got to the
jury in any understandable way.

Jeantel also said that it was Trayvon's voice screaming on the Lauer
911 call, without elaboration. None was asked of her by the prosecution. (Later on cross-examination, we learned from Jeantel that Trayvon
sometimes had a "baby" voice. The man's screaming on the call was
high-pitched. Only lack of preparation by the prosecution would have
left this corroborative detail out of her direct examination.)

After the trial, speaking to CNN's Piers Morgan, Jeantel was permitted to explain those explosive terms she said Trayvon had used about
Zimmerman. "Cracka" was the word, not "cracker," she said, and it
means a cop or security guard and is not racial in her view. (And indeed
the term "cracker," according to UrbanDictionary.com,[71] originates
from slave owners "cracking the whip." The first definition, however, is
"a term used to insult white people.")

Because the prosecution did not understand Jeantel's dialect, and
was too afraid to linger on anything related to race in the case, it missed
an opportunity to diffuse these terms for the jury, who predictably were
surprised and affronted by them. In this racially charged trial, the prosecutor should have neutralized the language on direct examination.

This is how the practice should have gone, during witness preparation:

PROSECUTOR: What did he say next, Ms. Jeantel?

JEANTEL: He said nigga following me.

PROSECUTOR: He said what?

JEANTEL: Nigga following me.

PROSECUTOR: You mean, the N word? Trayvon said that about Zimmerman? But Zimmerman's white, so I don't get it.

JEANTEL: Oh, the way we use that word isn't the way you use it.

PROSECUTOR: I don't use it at all!

JEANTEL: Okay, chill. I just mean, it's not racial. "Nigga" is just a guy, like "homie" or "dude." "Nigga following me" just means the guy [Zimmerman] was back, following him.

PROSECUTOR: So it's not a racial slur?

JEANTEL: Naw, he was talking about a white man so how could it be? How could he be both a "cracka" and a "nigga" if both the terms are racial? That doesn't make any sense. It's just how we talk. Like in our music and movies. Trayvon didn't know his name, so he's just "nigga." Maybe you would say "the guy."

PROSECUTOR: I think I understand. So when you testify, when we get to this part, please, Rachel, say it slowly and clearly, because that's going to freak some people out who aren't used to hearing the word the way you use it. And then I'm going to ask you what that word meant as you understood it in your conversation with Trayvon, and you explain it as you just did. OK?

JEANTEL: Yeah, if that's what you want.

PROSECUTOR: Trust me, this is important. Now let's go back and go over it again so that when you speak to the jury your testimony will be clear. Let's take it from the top.

JEANTEL: Aw, do we have to?

PROSECUTOR: Yes, Rachel, we do. We are going to go over this until your testimony is clear, so that the jury can understand it when you get up on the witness stand. Can you do that for Trayvon?

JEANTEL: Well, when you put it that way, yes. Okay, let's practice again.


They go over it again. And if necessary, again and again.

AFTER HALF AN hour on the stand being questioned by Bernie de la Rionda, Jeantel was not done. Not even close. To her horror, she then endured five hours (over two days) of cross-examination questions from West. He went over her entire story again, in painstaking detail, as well as the lie she'd admitted to on direct—to get out of going to Trayvon's funeral she'd told his family she was in the hospital—and several others, all of which were lies about herself in clumsy attempts to get out of being involved in the case. She'd said she was sixteen, rather than her true age at the time, eighteen, when initially contacted about the case. She'd given nicknames, Dee Dee and Diamond, rather than her real name, in an effort to protect her privacy. None of that worked, of course, and here she was, on the stand, being interrogated, analyzed, and judged by the nation.

The prosecution badly misstepped by not bringing out all of Jeantel's fibs on direct, allowing her to explain them with a friendly questioner.

Instead, on West's cross-examination, Jeantel came across like a patho-
logical liar, one false statement after another being thrown at her. A jury
might understand making up a story to get out of a funeral ("I didn't
want to see the body," Jeantel said on the stand, wiping her eyes), but
the others, piling up, began to sound like a pattern.

Throughout the trial Judge Nelson indicated a willingness to move
the testimony along whenever attorneys were long-winded, repetitive in
their questioning, or prone to going off on tangents. While West was
all of these during his cross-examination of Jeantel, de la Rionda rarely
objected, leaving Jeantel on her own to handle West, a man who'd been
cross-examining witnesses longer than she had been alive. Nitpicky
questions on irrelevant topics—such as detailing how her meeting with
attorney Crump was set up, or texts leading up to a media interview,
or the scheduling and rescheduling of her deposition—went nowhere,
but Jeantel had to wrack her brain, stay calm, and try to answer, as the
prosecution sat mutely by. Despite Jeantel's clear testimony that she was
not Trayvon's girlfriend but just his friend, West asked her many questions, without objection, as to whether that was *really* the case. (She
maintained her position throughout and he never got anywhere with it.)
Judge Nelson surely would have instructed West firmly, in front of the
jury (as she did on other occasions) to *move it along*, if only the state
attorneys had risen to their feet.

After several hours on the stand and the seemingly endless, repetitive
questions from West, Jeantel, feeling disrespected, got testy. She mut-
tered that she was leaving at the end of the day and not returning the
next. Despite seeing that the teenager's nerves were frayed, the prosecution did not offer her a break nor ask the court for one. They let her twist
in the wind.

False bravado notwithstanding, she did return, and on the next day, she arrived preternaturally calm, adding "sir" to her answers to boot. Trial watchers speculated that the prosecutors must have sat her down and explained to her that her demeanor needed to change, shoring her up for her second day to come. But that would be giving the state attorneys too much credit. Left on her own after her first day of testimony, what actually happened, Jeantel says, is "I went to my room, said my prayers, said, OK, this is for you, Trayvon."[72] She resolved to keep going, for him. On a more practical note, her attorney, Vereen, told me that he decided to get her out of the painful, pinching high heels she'd been wearing on the first day, and he purchased a better pair of shoes for her second day, so she could be more comfortable. (Now *that's* a full-service attorney.)

Jeantel told me that contrary to popular belief, no one spoke to her about her demeanor that night. "I was just so tired, worn out," she said, after spending the day being cross-examined by the man defending her friend's killer. She went back to her hotel room, "no cell phone, no TV, oh my God!" she said in teenaged disbelief, and went to sleep. Clearly the good night's rest improved her testimony, as she was markedly calmer, more relaxed, and more respectful the next day. Unfortunately, though, much of the damage had already been done.

ON CROSS-EXAMINATION, WEST went after Jeantel for varying her account of what happened in different statements she'd given. By the time of trial, Jeantel had given a dizzying number of pretrial statements to different people in different contexts: among others, to Tracy Martin, who first contacted her, to Sybrina Fulton, to Crump, to the police, and to the lawyers present during her deposition. This was not a problem created by Jeantel, who at all times was trying to extricate herself from having to give statements, but rather by the police's failure to contact her immediately in their investigation of Trayvon's shooting, their failure to discover the important testimony she had to offer, their failure to get one clear pretrial statement from Jeantel and then direct her to give no others. Though phone records would have quickly revealed that she was speaking with Trayvon in the minutes before his death, inexplicably, police did not contact her, leading them to initially conclude that Zimmerman's statement was consistent with all the evidence. Thus Trayvon's family had to pick up the ball, contact Jeantel, and plead with her to share the information she had.

These multiple interviews contained some inconsistencies, as nearly always happens when a witness tells and retells her account. (This is why lawyers favor long, detailed depositions of opposition witnesses, to undermine their credibility.) In her case, that was especially true as she was traumatized by her teenaged friend's death and was trying to be polite to his grieving parents, which meant leaving out some details in an effort to spare them more pain. In addition, in early accounts Jeantel gave quick summaries of what she knew, in order to minimize her role in the situation, which was then emerging as a high-profile matter that she wanted nothing to do with. As she was asked later exactly what Trayvon said and what she said on the call, more details in her story emerged. The defense called this embellishing, but her story overall remained consistent.

The defense also grilled Jeantel about her view that the altercation between Zimmerman and Trayvon was "just a fight" and not "deadly serious"—which was her initial opinion after hearing the sounds of wet grass and then her call dropping. But the opinions of fact witnesses are not admissible—especially when she's speculating what happened after her connection with Trayvon failed. The prosecution failed to object to this, so it came in.

However, on redirect examination, when they had a chance to question her again, the prosecution could have exploited this topic by allowing her to explain: Trayvon didn't express anything to her about planning to attack, much less kill, Zimmerman. He wanted to go home and watch the All Star game and get away from Zimmerman. So the sounds she heard at the end of the call with him—words exchanged, Trayvon's headset getting bumped, the sounds of wet grass—sounded to her like the beginning of a fight, not something deadly. Her testimony on that point was entirely consistent with the state's position that Trayvon did not intend to assault or kill Zimmerman. Put another way, if Trayvon had told her, "I'm going to kill that guy," she would have been alarmed when the call dropped. She wasn't, because it sounded to her like at most, "just a fight."

And that should have been the essence of Jeantel's testimony to the jury: that Trayvon was doing the opposite of what Zimmerman claimed. He wasn't gunning for a fight. I asked Jeantel what kind of mood Trayvon was in on that phone call. "He was *funny*," she told me. "He was cracking me up most of the call." Trayvon's sense of humor was one of her favorite things about him—that and his loyalty to his friends. She was doing her hair at home while Trayvon was walking through the Retreat at Twin Lakes, and he was teasing her about her hair obsession: "You're gonna die with those hot rollers on, Rachel!" She laughed, he laughed. He asked her to check on whether the All Star Game had started yet, and she did. The prosecution was so stuck in the weeds (*He said what? And then you said what?*) that they missed the overarching theme Jeantel could have described for the jury: these were two high school kids having a lighthearted, jokey chat, even *after* Trayvon saw Zimmerman staring at him. Far from lying in wait for him and jumping out of the bushes to sucker punch him (as Zimmerman described in one of his versions of what happened), Trayvon wanted to get away from the "creepy" guy and go back home to catch the game and continue teasing Jeantel.

Finally, while the prosecution quickly shied away from "creepy-ass cracka" and "nigga," the defense, naturally, seized on them, getting her to repeat the terms again for the jury to hear. West then asked several times whether Jeantel thought the case was "a *racial* thing," with a slight emphasis on the word that implied bringing such a topic into the trial was distasteful.

"Yes, it is racial," Jeantel said bravely, staring at the white-majority jury. She knew they wouldn't understand, but she stuck to it. (As soon as she saw the jury composition, Jeantel told me, "I knew it would be a waste of my time.") Jeantel was the only voice in that courtroom ever to say that Trayvon was racially profiled, something she understood implicitly, but was not ready to defend in depth. "Why is that?" West wanted to know. She murmured that Trayvon described being stalked, that Zimmerman was watching and following him. "Why is that *racial*?" West pressed. She didn't have an answer.

Ah, if only she'd been prepared, what a powerful moment it could have been in that courtroom:

WEST: Do you think this trial is a racial thing?

JEANTEL: I think Zimmerman's killing of Trayvon is racial, yes.

WEST: Why is it racial?

JEANTEL: Because he targeted and followed Trayvon, who was a young black kid, for no good reason. A teenager. Who was just minding his own business, not bothering him or anybody. Who was unarmed, and who has the same right to walk down the street as you and your kids do, Mr. West. This happens to unarmed black men in America every day.

WEST: That's what makes it racial? How do you know what was in Zimmerman's mind?

JEANTEL: Aren't you the ones saying there were black burglars in the neighborhood? They got nothing to do with Trayvon. Why do you keep bringing up the black burglars if it's not racial?

WEST: Objection, Your Honor, the witness is argumentative.

JUDGE: You asked the questions, counsel. She's just answering them.

WEST: I'll move on.

JEANTEL: And I heard that all his police calls about suspicious people were about black men. Is that true? Come on, Mr. West.

WEST: Let's move on.

She had the moxie and the brains to pull this off, if she'd had a chance to practice it beforehand. But without preparation, she didn't have the backup to defend her position. And without the prosecution's advocacy that of course this case was about racial profiling, as outlined in Chapter Four, she was hung out to dry alone on the subject.

Lacking that support, the defense painted her as improperly playing the race card (as if anything about this trial was a game) instead of a young woman who perceptively understood the obvious, a view shared by millions.

After the trial, she stuck to her position. "It was racial. Let's be honest, racial," she said in a post-verdict interview.[73]

At the end of a case, normally state attorneys explain to the jury all the ways their witnesses got the facts right, why they should be seen as reliable, why they should be believed. Here, incredibly, both prosecutors distanced themselves from their star witness in closing arguments. De la Rionda, clumsily invoking Martin Luther King, Jr., said he had a dream that Jeantel would be judged not on the "color of her personality" (what color would that be, exactly?) but on the "content of her testimony" (which few had been able to follow, and which he did not clarify for them). Translation: nobody, including us, likes her, but please believe her testimony anyway, if you can figure it out. He said that "Rachel Jeantel may not be sophisticated"—how sophisticated are most high school students?—"but she is a human being." Was that really the best he could say about her? Was there a lack of clarity as to what type of mammal she was? John Guy[74] said, "There are no Rachel Jeantels on CSI." Translation: so disfavored are plump dark-skinned women in our culture that they are rarely seen on TV, but please try to relate to her anyway, somehow.

That "damning by faint praise" was only the culmination of the state's ineffective handling of Jeantel from the beginning. Having failed to interview her immediately after the shooting, having failed to prepare her to testify in any meaningful way, having failed to conduct her examination in a manner in which the jury could follow and understand her

testimony, having failed to object to the defense's overlong cross-examination of her, the state effectively washed its hands of Rachel Jeantel in
their final summations.

In the first interview after Zimmerman was found not guilty, juror
B37 said she had found Jeantel not credible, largely because of her poor
communication skills, and that she "felt sorry for her." Maddy told
me that no one mentioned Jeantel in jury deliberations. Her testimony
played no role whatsoever in their decision. The state's star witness had
been entirely neutralized.

I SPOKE WITH Jeantel three months after the verdict. Bubbly, upbeat,
and relaxed, she had found her voice and was easy to understand. She
laughed at herself often during the interview, a robust, infectious laugh.

With the trial behind her, she had much to be happy about. Radio
host Tom Joyner, watching Jeantel on a post-trial television interview,
sensitively noticed that when she said she and Trayvon had talked about
their futures, the interviewer failed to ask her what lay ahead for her.
What were her goals, her hopes and dreams? Trayvon would have no
future. But Jeantel still could, perhaps with a little help and incentiviz-
ing. Shortly thereafter, Joyner publicly offered[75] Jeantel a full scholarship
to any one of America's one hundred historically black colleges, if she
could graduate high school and get accepted. He even sprung for tutors
to help her through her senior year of high school.

Attorney Vereen stuck with Jeantel months after the trial ended,
watching out for her as well. "I'm a whip cracker," he says. "No Ebonics,
no slang, don't talk to me about the underbite. I don't want to hear it.

No excuses. Don't be lazy." She respects him as her mentor, he says. When making life choices she'll think, "What would Rod say?"

All that community support was paying off. The teenager who admitted at trial that she couldn't read cursive was achieving nearly straight A's in her first semester of senior year in high school, looking forward to graduating in June 2014 and attending college thereafter. While she'd briefly flirted with the idea of studying law, with some distance from the trial she realized it was not for her and had returned to her original goal, a career in fashion design. How'd she feel about the prospect of college? "Excited!"

If only that help had come just a few months sooner, and she'd had that confidence, pleasant attitude, and those improved communication skills at trial. The support of a few adults had made such a difference in her life.

I brought the conversation back to her friend Trayvon. What did she want us to know about him? "He could be one of you, your child. Forget his race, color. He's one of us. He's not an animal."

*She's a human being,* de la Rionda had said of Jeantel.

*He's not an animal,* Jeantel says of Trayvon.

And Jeantel has not forgotten his sense of humor. A year and a half after his death, she still smiled broadly thinking about Trayvon, speaking of him, as always, in the present tense: "He is a funny person."

# SIX

## Mishandling the 911 Call

N o v i d e o t a p e o f the shooting of Trayvon exists, but the killing was captured on audiotape. Neighborhood resident Jenna Lauer, hearing the altercation, called 911, and the police recording of that call captured not only Lauer's and the dispatcher's conversation but the background sounds of one person yelling "aaah!" intermittently over a period of about forty seconds. The gunshot then unmistakably rings out, and the cries go silent. But was it Trayvon or Zimmerman who was calling out?

More witnesses were asked about this than anything else, as it became one of the most litigated issues at the trial. If Zimmerman was the screamer, his self-defense story is plausible and corroborated—*He was banging my head on the concrete, trying to suffocate me, threatening to kill me. I called for help, but no one came. So I had to shoot him to save my own life.*

If Trayvon was screaming, another narrative would apply, such as: Zimmerman was pointing a gun at Trayvon, cursing him and threatening to kill him if he tried to escape ("these assholes, they always get away.") Zimmerman was scary, brandishing the gun, indicating that he meant those threats (months later, that chilling attitude came through in Zimmerman's interview with Sean Hannity, when he said he had no regrets and the killing was "God's plan"). Trayvon was terrified and yelled urgently for help. *BANG!* The fatal shot to Trayvon's heart silences him.

The jury heard the Lauer 911 recording many times in the courtroom, as both sides played it with various witnesses who testified as to who they believed was yelling out for help. The prosecution called three witnesses (Jeantel and Trayvon Martin's brother and mother) to say it was Trayvon's voice. The defense had nine family members and friends to say it was Zimmerman.

Once again, the state failed to effectively put together the pieces of evidence it had, all of which pointed to Trayvon Martin as the screamer. The state glossed over the issue with its witnesses, asking the question briefly (whose voice is that?), getting the answer (Trayvon Martin), and then moving on. But of course Trayvon's friends and family would want to believe it was Trayvon, just as Zimmerman's would want to believe it was Zimmerman. The state's attitude appeared to be, *We'll put the witnesses on, but we know we can't prove this.*

The defense, on the other hand, understood that the issue could make or break the case. And so they hit hard, not only by calling a much larger number of witnesses, all of whom seemed to fervently believe Zimmerman was the one crying out, but by breathing color and credibility into their witnesses' accounts.

For example, one of the defense witnesses, retired physician's assistant John Donnelly, forty years earlier had worked in the battlefields of the Vietnam War. A pleasant, likeable older man who now worked in litigation support, he said that "George Zimmerman is a very good friend of mine." Zimmerman had hung around his office, wanting to learn about business, and Donnelly had advised him on matters large and small, including how to tie a Windsor knot. The clincher in Donnelly's testimony was his description of working in combat conditions, where, he said, he would hear hysterical cries of wounded soldiers, identify them, and run out to treat their injuries. In the midst of combat, there are a lot of people yelling and screaming for help. "You can distinguish the screams for a medic, you go where they're at, but because you know the men you eat and sleep with, you know who it's going to be before you get there."[76] Donnelly appeared to suppress some emotion recalling the anguish of the Vietnam battlefields. Dabbing at his eyes and nose with tissues, he then said it was his friend Zimmerman on the Lauer 911 call.

Juror B37 said later that Donnelly was one of the most credible witnesses in the entire trial. She incorrectly thought he was a doctor.

While a witness like Donnelly should be treated with respect and sensitivity, his Vietnam story is entirely uncorroborated. War stories, by their very nature, can be subject to embellishment. Did Donnelly truly have an uncanny ability to know who was yelling out in wounded distress before he got to them, or was that exaggerated, even fabricated? There's no way to know. We have to take his word for it. Because when any of the men of his company would call out, injured, for a medic, wouldn't he have gone? In other words, *did it matter which of his men was calling out*? Wasn't it his job to render aid regardless?

Second, the conditions in Vietnam are entirely different than those found in the Zimmerman case. Even assuming Donnelly's testimony was true, that he could identify a man crying out in anguish after being injured in combat before seeing him, the army setting was obviously dissimilar to the Retreat at Twin Lakes. Donnelly had said that as a medic, he ate, slept, and spent all his time with the men in his company, with whom he lived daily in perilous conditions. In other words, he was extremely familiar with them. While Donnelly said that he'd been Zimmerman's friend for some time, their relationship was not analogous to those he'd had with soldiers in Vietnam.

And most importantly, he'd never heard Trayvon's voice. How could he be sure without knowing both voices?

The question was never asked. None of these points were raised.

Additionally, none of the nine defense witnesses could say they'd ever heard Zimmerman screaming hysterically for his life, so how could they be sure how he would sound when his life was, allegedly, threatened? There would only be one way. They could ask Zimmerman to scream again, in the privacy of their homes, to see if it sounded like the Lauer 911 call. The prosecutors couldn't make Zimmerman do this in the courtroom, as he invoked his Fifth Amendment right against self-incrimination when he elected not to testify. But his friends could have asked over the previous year. Of course, no one did this. Why not? Didn't they want to be sure? Or were they afraid they'd be wrong?

They were not asked.

Zimmerman himself said to the detectives who played the tape for him the first time, "That doesn't even sound like me."[77] The prosecution failed to run with this critical piece of evidence. He didn't say, "That's funny, I was definitely screaming, but that doesn't sound like me." He didn't say, "It was me, though it doesn't sound like it now." Just, "That doesn't sound like me." Isn't Zimmerman in the best position to know who was screaming? Shouldn't that be case closed on the subject once he'd said that?

Most importantly, the state failed to drive home the significance of the fact that *the screaming stops instantly with the gunshot*. (This was mentioned, but not elaborated upon.) That makes it far more likely that the shooting victim was the screamer. The defense argued that Zimmerman stopped screaming because the threat was then removed—he no longer needed help, as he'd shot Trayvon. But once again, the prosecution failed to argue the evidence—that Zimmerman himself admitted in his police statements just the opposite, that he *didn't think the threat was over* once he pulled the trigger. He didn't think his bullet hit Trayvon, he said. He was *still afraid* that Trayvon had a weapon or was otherwise going to harm him. Recall his fear minutes earlier, telling the police dispatcher: "He's got his hand in his waistband [pause] and he's a black male." (On that call, he'd already been asked Trayvon's race, and given it, so why repeat it when mentioning the hand in the waistband, if not for dramatic effect?) Trayvon remained a threat after the shooting, according to Zimmerman, which is why he asked neighbor John Good, the first to come outside after the gunshot, to "help me"; why he says he extended Trayvon's arms out as he lay dying (because he thought he might be armed). By his own words and actions, Zimmerman was still scared.

So why would he stop screaming? He wouldn't.

The screamer was almost certainly the unarmed kid who was being threatened by the man with the gun, the man who had followed him and was angry at him, and who, more than anything, didn't want him to get away. Shot directly in the heart, he fell silent instantly. If Dr. Bao had been allowed to testify that the bullet fragments in Trayvon's right lung would have prevented him from speaking immediately upon impact, due to pneumothorax, the jury would have understood even more clearly why Trayvon's screams stopped precisely at the moment he was shot.

The state's failure to properly argue this evidence meant they lost their best proof that Trayvon was the victim, not the aggressor, in the final seconds before the shooting.

# SEVEN

# Closing Arguments: A Disaster
# for the Prosecution

CLOSING ARGUMENTS (ALSO called summations) are most attorneys' favorite part of the trial. All other stages of the trial are so tightly constrained. In opening statements, attorneys may only lay out what the evidence will show, without arguing what it all means. During the presentation of witnesses, trial lawyers may only ask permissible questions or raise brief objections. Though it would be helpful, we can't say to the jury, "Hey, before I put this guy on the stand, let me explain to you why he's important." Question, answer, question, answer—that's all that's allowed. After a particularly good bit of testimony, we can't turn to the jury box and say, "Did you catch that? Remember the witness who testified the day before yesterday? This supports what she said!" Not allowed.

But once all the evidence is in, attorneys get their one and only chance to pull it all together for the jury in closing arguments. With the rules loosened, trial lawyers can and often do quote the founding fathers, poetry, movie lines—whatever may sway the jury's hearts and minds. Now inferences may be drawn from the evidence—reasonable interpretations that each side argues supports its position. Attorneys hold up physical evidence, they replay audio and video evidence, they create charts and graphs and timelines to synthesize the facts. *At last, most lawyers think, a chance to connect all the evidence with the law and argue in the most forceful possible terms that the jury should vote my way. Finally, I can respond to those ridiculous arguments made by the other side.*

In criminal trials, prosecutors and defense attorneys have very different jobs. Prosecutors in every case must prove all the elements of the crime beyond a reasonable doubt. The defense, on the other hand, raises doubt wherever possible. Thus in closing, prosecutors typically explain to the jury what the elements of the crime are, since this is new, foreign legal language to jurors, and then connect the dots to show that their evidence has proved each and every one of those elements. Defense attorneys chip away at that evidence, arguing that the jurors really can't be sure, and if even one element of the crime is in doubt, the verdict must be "not guilty." Prosecutors want the jurors to join them in reaching definitive conclusions. Defense attorneys want them to question, to wonder, to be uncertain.

In the Zimmerman case, because they had the burden of proof, the state got to give two closings, their initial closing argument, and then, after the defense's closing, a rebuttal closing argument. (This is common.) Two chances, sandwiching the defense's argument. First and last, primacy and recency. From a rhetorical standpoint, a huge advantage.

But both of the prosecution's final arguments were disasters.

First, the state's summations were haphazard and disorganized. Instead of going through the elements of the crimes Zimmerman was charged with, second-degree murder and manslaughter, prosecutors did an odd hop, skip, and a jump through the evidence, going witness by witness, reminding the jury of a few points about each. But the jury had already sat through the trial, hearing each witness in order. They needed the salient points from each connected with the elements of the crimes alleged if they were to convict, and the prosecution did not give them that. As a result, though the elements of the homicide Zimmerman was charged with were simple, the jury wound up hopelessly confused about the law, walking away from the trial with wrongheaded interpretations of what they had to find in order to convict. Though de la Rionda briefly put up the law of manslaughter and murder an hour into his rambling, disjointed presentation, he raced through it, leaving the jury bewildered rather than enlightened on the rules they'd be required to follow to convict.

Second, for reasons only they can possibly explain, the state attorneys asked a series of questions in closing rather than using declarative statements to drive their case home. Far from demonstrating their own authoritative grasp of the evidence, the state seemed confused by the facts, resorting to telling the jury that they, the jurors, knew the trial, so hey, they could put it all together. For example, regarding the scratches on the back of Zimmerman's head, de la Rionda said:

> How small were they? You recall the testimony of the witness Miss Folgate. I think I had her tell me how big it was. I think she was . . . I mean it was hard to keep . . . anyway, you remember it.[78]

Had that stumble happened only once, one might chalk it up to a small mistake that could happen to anyone in a live trial. But over and over again, the prosecutor appeared not to have reviewed the evidence, and so he asked the jury to work it out themselves. Regarding the all-important crime scene map and time line, the prosecutor said:

You can see the map, you can track down the time line and see
does it match up in terms of when he's talking. I would submit
to you again it doesn't, but you rely on what the evidence shows.

After an exhausting three-week trial and sequestration, the jury is
expected to go into the deliberation room and "track down" evidence
and piece it together, when the state's detectives and attorneys could not
or did not? And what are they looking for, exactly? What supposedly
doesn't match up? And if it doesn't, what does that mean? Reasonable
doubt or a conviction? The message was hopelessly confused.

It's the prosecutor's *job* to fit all the puzzle pieces together for the
jury in summation, to lead them smoothly along the primrose path to
a guilty verdict. This isn't just a style point. The message that shone
through the state's closing here was, *If there is proof to support conviction, we don't know where it is. Maybe you can find it. Good luck.*
This is unbelievably poor courtroom strategy, if it was an actual strategy
rather than simple carelessness. I know of no other lawyers who have
ever effectively handled a closing argument this way.

Issues big and small were handled with questions, not answers. On
what should have been the biggest issue in the case, the prosecutor for
the first time in the trial pointed out that Zimmerman's gun was concealed behind him but then asked only, "How could the victim have seen
the gun in the darkness?" First, calling Trayvon the "victim" throughout
dehumanized him. He should have been called by his name. Second,
questions invite speculation and multiple possible answers. Several
spring immediately to mind. Since he'd been walking around for a while,
his eyes had adjusted to the darkness? The fight was dynamic and he saw
it when Zimmerman moved? Zimmerman's jacket had ridden up, as he

said? He saw the gun earlier in the fight, when they were close to the light? *Questions imply reasonable doubt.* Thus questions are a far weaker method of making a point than a definitive statement, like "Trayvon Martin could not have seen the gun. It would have been impossible. The gun was behind him and he was on his back, Mr. Zimmerman said. Mr. Zimmerman's story is a lie. We now know this not only beyond a reasonable doubt, but beyond a shadow of a doubt." If the state isn't sure, how can the jurors be? If both sides are arguing reasonable doubt, an acquittal is the only possible verdict.

Third, devastatingly, the state failed to stand behind its own witnesses. De la Rionda used a PowerPoint presentation, in which he sometimes just put up a slide, scrolled through, and expected the jury to read and absorb it without comment from him, as though he'd gotten tired of doing a closing argument at all. One of his slides read, "SAO doesn't choose Witnesses. Don't go to central casting and order one up." Using jargon or unknown abbreviations is another poor communication technique. What do you suppose *SAO* is? It took me a few minutes to figure out that acronym stood for *state attorneys' office*. Were the jurors expected to know that?

More significantly, what was to be gained by slamming one's own witnesses in closing arguments? Final arguments should be focused on convicting the defendant, not saving face for the lawyers. Prosecutors should have championed Rachel Jeantel, for example, reminding the jury not only that she was impressively good with dates and times, but also that the essence of her story never changed: that Trayvon feared the creepy man following him, tried to get away from him, and when confronted, said, "Why are you following me?" whereupon Zimmerman said, "What are you doing around here?" and then assaulted Trayvon—the reasonable inference to be drawn from Jeantel's testimony that Trayvon's headset was "bumped" and then she heard sounds of "wet grass." Jeantel had familiarity with and a clear understanding of the sounds of Trayvon's headset—she'd been on the phone with him all day, off and on. Trayvon's final words were *defensive*, "Get off, get off."

Credibility is the issue for every witness, the state should have explained. Credibility has nothing to do with skin color, gender, or size. It has nothing to do with a speech impediment or one's hesitancy to be hurled into a courtroom on live TV, in the center of an extraordinarily high-profile case. If anything, Jeantel's reluctance to be a part of this case *bolsters* her credibility, as she wasn't rushing in to create a story or become famous. Believability should be measured by a witness's truthfulness and integrity. Yes, Jeantel had fibbed about herself before trial (name and age to protect her privacy, and the white lie she gave to avoid going to Trayvon's funeral), but she never wavered about what she heard on that phone call, and that's why she is credible. She knew that some of the conversation she relayed would not be well received (*creepy-ass cracka, nigga*), but she put it out there honestly, warts and all. Plus, her testimony matches up with the cell phone records and even Zimmerman's story—that Trayvon was running from him. She calls Zimmerman "a hard-breathing man,"[79] and indeed, on his recorded police call, he is breathing heavily. Her story checks out, over and over again, because it is the truth.

Instead of doing that, the state considered Jeantel a throwaway witness by the end, offering several negative comments about her, and making only the weakest efforts to support her testimony.

Fourth, one of the state's biggest failures was in not putting together all the evidence to show that Trayvon could not have seen and reached for the gun at the most critical moment in the altercation. As we've seen, a mannequin was available for use by the attorneys, but the prosecution's use of it in closing was brief and clumsy. The state's attorney straddled it for a few seconds, yelling, "How does he get the gun out?" Again, the question invited speculation rather than certainty. But we know that Zimmerman somehow *did* get the gun out, so the question went nowhere. The subject wasn't how Zimmerman, trained in the use of his own gun, and in the adrenaline of the situation, got it out. The issue—missed by the state at this most critical phase of the trial—was that Trayvon could not have seen it through the bulk of Zimmerman's body, inside the back of his pants, behind him in the rainy darkness— and without that, Zimmerman's self-defense claim failed.

The prosecutor suggested that the jury get down on the floor in the jury room and reenact the altercation themselves (to see whether Zimmerman could get the gun out). Asking the jury to experiment was foolhardy. The jury might not do it, for any number of reasons, including the awkwardness of women who were strangers to one another a month earlier physically straddling one another. (In fact, they didn't do it.) They might attempt it, but in an incorrect position, with no one there to correct them, which would throw the whole demonstration off. This is why it was essential that the prosecution, in closing, *demonstrate every detail of it for them,* with the gun in the concealed holster, the shirt and jacket, and even a patch of grass, reminding the jury of the darkness and the rain. And again, the issue was not whether Zimmerman got the gun out, because we all know he did. Instead, prosecutors had to prove that he did not have a legitimate *reason* to pull his gun. If Trayvon did not know that Zimmerman had a gun, and was not threatening his life, Zimmerman could not claim self-defense.

Instead, the prosecutors spent a great deal of their precious closing argument time on tangents and nonissues. The prosecutors seemed to feel that being loud—for instance, yelling the self-evident "THE TRUTH DOES NOT LIE!" and repeating melodramatic uncontested facts like, "Two men were there that night; one is dead"—would suffice. Focusing primarily on Phase 1 of the story, the prosecutors repeated over and over again that Trayvon was unarmed, walking home from the store. I imagined the jurors thinking, *Yes, we know that. No one has claimed otherwise. Please tell us why the shooting was murder. Because that's what we have to decide.*

The state insulted the jurors' intelligence with red herrings like, "Buying Skittles is not a crime!" (Did anyone say it was?) "Trayvon Martin didn't do anything wrong at the 7-Eleven. He bought that candy!" (Did anyone say he didn't? *Please tell me how that proves murder.*) In his rebuttal closing, prosecutor John Guy called Trayvon a "child" dozens of times—this was jarring, as it was the first time in the trial anyone had done that. Technically, legally speaking, yes, Trayvon was a child. But most of us don't think of a five-foot-eleven seventeen-year-old, especially one who clearly punched Zimmerman squarely in the face, as a child. Floridians don't—they send kids younger than that to prison for life without parole sentences in record numbers. Either way, the issue was a distraction, a desperate new last-ditch effort to gain sympathy for "the victim," whom the state had entirely failed to humanize during the presentation of evidence. And as Maddy recalled so vividly, the jurors were then instructed not to decide the case based on their hearts.

The theme of the state's closing was that Zimmerman had told a "web of lies." Going piecemeal through the evidence (rather than synthesizing it), they asked the jury to consider why Zimmerman had apparently lied about details of his story, such as his claim to police that he didn't know what street he was on (the community only has three streets) or that he couldn't see the nearest house number in the dark. But most people in a stressful situation will forget commonly known information, and minor inconsistencies in retelling the same story are understandable. The bigger problem was that Zimmerman was not on trial for lying, he was on trial for murder. So the prosecution needed to connect Zimmerman's "web of lies" with the murder charges, and they never did so.

"This case is not about Standing Your Ground," Guy said. "It's about *staying in your car*."[80] A nice rhetorical flourish—the state had a few of those—but Zimmerman was not on trial for getting out of his car, even though the police told him not to, nor for walking around the neighborhood looking for Trayvon. Nor could he be, as none of these acts are illegal, which everyone conceded by the end of the trial. He was on trial for murder, and the prosecution throughout seemed unwilling to confront that charge. Pointing out Zimmerman's falsehoods and ugly words was a step in the right direction, and relevant to the element of intent, but was not sufficient to get a conviction.

Sure, some of Zimmerman's lies were big. His head could not have been banged on concrete at the time of the shooting, as his body was a substantial distance from concrete. In addition, no blood was seen on the sidewalk when crime scene investigators looked that night. And Zimmerman had blood dripping off both the front and back of his head when photographed immediately after the shooting (from the punch to his nose, and from two tiny cuts on the back of his head), so one would expect to see blood on the concrete if his head had been slammed into it. The state should have argued not only that Zimmerman lied, but that his lies *meant his version must be rejected entirely as not credible*, and then invited the jury to come along with the state's theory of the case, supported by the evidence and reasonable inferences from that evidence. But the prosecution offered no alternate scenario.

And that was the state's biggest blunder in summation: its failure to offer its own theory of the case. For the most part, as they had throughout the trial, prosecutors went along with the defense's version of what happened that night, arguing only the details around the edges. For example, the state attorney wondered how Trayvon could have put his hand over Zimmerman's mouth, as Zimmerman had maintained, and simultaneously pounded his head on the cement. Since he could have done one then the other in rapid succession, this weak argument went nowhere, and as we've seen, *wondering* equals reasonable doubt. The visual the jury was left with was that Trayvon punched Zimmerman, he went down, Trayvon banged Zimmerman's head on the concrete, saw and reached for the gun, and then Zimmerman drew his gun and killed him—the defense story.

The jury sorely needed an alternative, one that the state could have easily put together for them by pulling out the key testimony from its own witnesses. Such as:

> Members of the jury, we know what really happened that night. When the defendant got out of the car to confront Trayvon, he was convinced that Trayvon was an armed criminal, and he wanted to keep him there until the police arrived, so that he didn't get away like all the other "fucking punks." We know that from Zimmerman's own recorded words. So what did he do, alone, on that dark night, when he went after him? What's the reasonable inference? He drew his gun. Trayvon saw the gun all right, but

not in the way Zimmerman told it. We know from two defense witnesses, Adam Pollack and Dennis Root, that Zimmerman had no physical fighting skills whatsoever. He was a one on a scale of one to ten in his martial arts class. He was overweight and not athletic. And he knew it.

Which is precisely the reason he carried a gun, to compensate for that deficit. Many of us keep guns in our homes for self-defense, but few of us walk around with concealed weapons when we're going to Target.

But unfortunately for Trayvon Martin, George Zimmerman was a man who regularly lived in unreasonable fear. We know from his prior police calls about other black men in the neighborhood that he didn't want to go near them. He didn't want to approach "suspects." Zimmerman feared African-American men in his neighborhood. All of his police calls about suspicious persons in the prior six months were about black men, even though the community is 20 percent African American. Never mind that, they're all suspicious! And here was another one, walking down the street. Trayvon Martin, a "real suspicious guy." Zimmerman's ill will toward Trayvon was instantaneous, his decision that he must be a criminal so conclusive that he didn't want to give the police dispatcher his address for fear Trayvon would hear it and come after him. And we know that Zimmerman did not want him to escape—"These assholes, they always get away." This one, this time, was not going to get away.

He told the police Trayvon was reaching into his waistband (the inference being that Trayvon had his own weapon—another reason Zimmerman was scared). Like so much of what

Zimmerman said that night, this is an exaggeration or an outright lie. Because Trayvon had no weapon.

Listen to what Rachel Jeantel told you about the moment when Zimmerman and Trayvon met. She heard the exchange, and she's the only one who did. Trayvon asked a reasonable question, "Why are you following me?" A respectful answer would have been, "Hey, I'm Neighborhood Watch, so just wondering if you live here or you're visiting someone?" "I'm staying over at Brandy Green's, that house on the end," Trayvon would have said. And that would have been the end of it.

Instead, Zimmerman, hopped up on the ill will he harbored toward a lot of black males walking down the street in his community, responds with the hostile, "What are you doing around here?" Zimmerman then grabs or shoves him, because Rachel Jeantel hears a thump on the headset clipped to Trayvon's hoodie. That thump means Zimmerman touched him, without Trayvon's consent—an assault. At that point, Trayvon, surely frightened, has every right to defend himself and stand his ground, so he lands one good punch to Zimmerman's face. A tussle ensued, where it's not particularly significant who was on top and who was on the bottom at any given point. We know that Zimmerman's "Trayvon saw the gun through my body" story is preposterous. We know that Zimmerman had to draw his gun while standing or while he was on top, because it's physically impossible while he's down. Zimmerman drew his gun early in the incident because he was afraid, because he didn't want Trayvon to get away, because he wanted control over the situation. The most reasonable inference to draw from the evidence is that he drew it when he approached Trayvon initially. With the gun pointed at Trayvon, Zimmerman likely continued the profane insulting rant he started on his police call, for a horrible forty seconds, as Trayvon screamed for help, hoping this armed madman would not do the unthinkable.

[Play the Lauer 911 call, with the high-pitched screams.] Remember, Rachel Jeantel told you that Trayvon had a "baby" voice. Listen to these screams, of the terrified teenager with the baby voice. No one has ever said Zimmerman had a high-pitched voice—and you've heard his voice yourself multiple times. And why would he need to scream for help? He's the one with the gun.

But Trayvon had fought back, and now Zimmerman was in a panic. The same panic that caused him to say his head was being banged on the concrete dozens of times, though his lawyer now admits that's not true. He's also even angrier now, angry that this kid, this punk, had the nerve to stand up to him. In anger and in panic, Zimmerman fired his gun at Trayvon. And at that precise moment, Trayvon's screaming stopped. [Play the portion of the Lauer 911 call again, where the screaming stops suddenly with the gunshot.]

Killing in panic is not self-defense. Killing in anger is not self-defense. Killing because a kid you followed responded by punching you in the face is not self-defense. In each of these situations, Zimmerman is guilty of either manslaughter or murder.

What is manslaughter? [Put up slide of jury instruction on manslaughter.] The intentional taking of a human life without justification. Intentional? Easy. Zimmerman admitted he shot intentionally. He did exactly what he meant to do. So we can check intent right off. And Trayvon was a human being, though Zimmerman saw him not as an individual, but as a member of a group, black males, and therefore criminal. Human life, check. Justification? That's another word for self-defense. And since we've proved to you with the physical evidence that Zimmerman's story of self-defense is a lie, not possible, that's out. That's why manslaughter very easily fits the facts of this case. Guilty. At a minimum, guilty of manslaughter.

But we have charged Zimmerman with a top charge of second-degree murder, and that's been proved, too, with the evidence and the reasonable inferences you should draw from the evidence. Second-degree murder is simply manslaughter (intentional killing) with just one additional element: hatred, malice, or ill will. It can be hard to get inside a human mind and see what lurks there, but in this case it's easy because we have Zimmerman's own words, recorded, that tell us all the dark, hateful thoughts he had about Trayvon right before he shot him. Upon seeing Trayvon for the first time, Zimmerman thought, criminal, asshole. Upon meeting up with him, Zimmerman delivered the belligerent, "What are you doing around here?" Now, do you think Zimmerman got warmer and fuzzier toward Trayvon after he grabbed or shoved Trayvon, and Trayvon responded by punching Zimmerman in the face? Of course not. Zimmerman surely got even angrier at that point. He's now furious, enraged. This "fucking punk" punched him! *BAM*. That, members of the jury, is an intentional killing with hatred, malice, or ill will. And after he shot him, more ill will—Zimmerman turned this dying boy facedown to the dirt and spread his arms, his final insult and humiliation to Trayvon, who had done nothing wrong. At the police station later, Zimmerman still insults him by calling him a suspect. This is the same ill will he'd harbored since the moment he laid eyes on Trayvon. And if all of that is not enough, and you still have any doubt about the ill will Zimmerman had in his heart toward this innocent teenager, consider this: five months later, after he'd lawyered up and had time to calm down and reflect on the case and choose his words carefully, he sits beside his lawyer, with a friendly interviewer, Sean Hannity, and says he has no regrets and that his shooting of Trayvon was "God's plan." Did God want Trayvon to die that night?

The defense has never had an explanation for that chilling, malicious statement.

Every word he's uttered about the teenager has been insulting and false. Every action he took toward him was predatory. That's how we know to a certainty that before, during, and after the shooting, Zimmerman harbored ill will toward Trayvon. Certainly at the moment when he pulled that trigger, he did. And he probably still does today.

Zimmerman, as we know from his college professor, had been taught the law of self-defense, and he was one of the best students, getting an A in the class. So after he shot Trayvon, he knew what he had to do: claim self-defense. That would be his only hope, since the police arrived and there he was, the proverbial smoking gun still on him. Trayvon was unarmed, though, and had never touched the gun, so his fingerprints wouldn't be on it. What was left for this star criminal justice student? He had to quickly come up with a story, that he was not just hit once, because that wouldn't justify a deadly shooting, but that he was getting beaten to a pulp, and then Trayvon went for the gun, threatening him. Yes, that's it—he reached for the gun! That was Zimmerman's story, and he almost got away with it.

But now we know the truth. We know that Zimmerman killed Trayvon intentionally, with ill will toward this boy he'd never met, and that his self-defense story doesn't match up with his own concealed gun and holster. We all have sympathy toward Trayvon, and his family, but this case is not about the emotion, it's about the proof, the proof that Zimmerman's story is impossible and therefore fabricated to cover his crime. All the evidence in this case points to Zimmerman as the predator, who followed an innocent unarmed minor, confronted him, started the fight, then needlessly shot to kill him. He almost fooled the police. But you know better. You now know conclusively that his self-defense story is a lie. Once that's out, conviction is the only remaining option. And he should be convicted, because he was a menace that night, to his community, and to a kid who just wanted to get away from him, so he could keep joking with Rachel Jeantel and watch the basketball game. And because Zimmerman chose to take the law into his own hands instead of following the police instructions, Trayvon didn't make it home that night. And he never will.

For that reason, you must return the only verdict that is consistent with the evidence: guilty.

The state was not legally required to come up with its own version of what happened that night, but without one, they were doomed to fail. I have never seen prosecutors win without their own theory of the case. The jury simply will not do the job for them. Here they were required to explain how the proof fulfilled the elements of the crime they'd charged Zimmerman with, and they never did it. Left with only questions from the prosecutors and the defense's version of the story, it's surprising the jury took as long as they did, sixteen hours, to acquit Zimmerman. Inside the jury room, the voices for conviction were desperate for the facts and law to support their side. But as the hours went by, they couldn't locate them because the state had not given them anything close to the roadmap they needed.

# EIGHT

## *It's Not Over*

WHY DID THE prosecution make so many blunders? Was it negligence or intentional?

I can't say they meant to throw the case. A few, like defense attorney Mark Geragos, made that allegation based on the prosecution's poor performance. But I have no real evidence of that. Special prosecutor Angela Corey, who did not personally try the case but who oversaw it, did appear delighted in her press conference right after the verdict, as if she was pleased with the "not guilty" verdict, but perhaps that was just a politician's "never let 'em see you sweat" smile for the cameras. In contrast, her two courtroom prosecutors, de la Rionda and Guy, seemed genuinely deflated. They appeared to work hard, and they looked like they wanted to win as much as any courtroom lawyer. That the police who initially failed to arrest Zimmerman, believing his self-defense story, were vindicated by the acquittal is insufficient to make such a serious allegation.

Was it inexperience—simple incompetence? More likely, but still, implausible. Lead prosecutor de la Rionda had obtained convictions in eighty prior murder cases, he said after the trial, losing only one other. He knew how to bring cases home to juries. So why did it not happen here?

The most likely explanation is that, like the police who did not want to arrest Zimmerman, they just did not believe in their case. As we've seen, they did not choose this case. It landed on their laps, and they could not plea bargain or dismiss it. They were stuck with it. Sure, they tried the case. But they only went through the motions.

Angela Corey made a very telling public statement immediately after the verdict:

> What we promised fifteen months ago was to get all the facts before a jury. That's what we've done. The focus needs to be on how the system worked, and how now everyone in this country can say they know the facts and can make up their own minds about the guilt of George Zimmerman.[81]

What a peculiar view of the role of a criminal trial, coming from the special prosecutor. Her team's job was simply to put forward all the evidence, so that everyone could make up his own mind about guilt? Prosecutors are not documentary filmmakers or journalists. One does not need lawyers to expose facts. Prosecutors are there to advocate, to make the case against the defendant in the courtroom, not just throw out all the facts and see what sticks. In that role, they failed miserably.

Did the state attorneys truly believe that Trayvon was the innocent victim and Zimmerman the aggressor? Probably not. Certainly they did not behave in the courtroom as though they had the evidence to convict. As a result, they did not appear to have looked hard enough at the evidence. Assigned what Corey believed was a difficult case—she called it "difficult" or "tough" five times in her post-verdict press conference—Corey made it even more challenging for her team by choosing to charge Zimmerman with second-degree murder rather than simply manslaughter. Had the jury been given only that lower charge, and the prosecutors explained and focused on manslaughter, the prosecutors would have had a lower bar. If it's a difficult case to begin with, why make it more difficult for your courtroom team?

As advocates, the state attorneys did just a perfunctory job. Their trial strategy was not to argue for conviction but to toss all the evidence and witnesses before the jury and let them sort it out, if they could. They appeared to think that the passion was the best part of the case, so that's what they argued, sympathy for Trayvon (while surely knowing, as seasoned prosecutors, that that would not be enough—it's not a memorial service, it's a murder trial). They stayed away from Phase 2 because they didn't think they could win it. They didn't bring in additional experts because they didn't believe the science *could* prove another theory of the case. They were all over the place in handling the race issue because like most Americans, they felt uncomfortable talking about race and probably themselves believed in the logical fallacy that if African Americans had robbed one home in the neighborhood it was reasonable to be suspicious about all others walking the streets. And it seems that they didn't put together a clear theory of the case to give the jury because in their heart of hearts, they believed Zimmerman's.

Of the four prosecutors who took to the microphones after the not-guilty verdict, only one, Bernie de la Rionda, said he was disappointed with the verdict. His boss, Angela Corey, concluded the press conference[82] by insisting, "The focus needs to be on how the system worked." It worked? So Zimmerman's acquittal was the right verdict? Is there some other interpretation of these words?

And thus, in a series of missteps, this very winnable case was lost. Though Zimmerman's story of the shooting was belied by the physical evidence, though he expressed overt hostility toward Trayvon from the moment he laid eyes on the minor, though he admitted to no remorse afterward and gloated months after the shooting that the killing was "God's plan," the defense won the trial by painting Trayvon just as Zimmerman had, as "a real suspicious guy," a "match" to burglars.

At Pastor Durham's Greater Friendship Baptist Church in Daytona Beach the Sunday morning after the verdict, men openly wept in the pews, "men in their fifties, sixties, seventies." For that congregation, Pastor Durham said, Trayvon's family "was the embodiment of mainstream America. Even when you look mainstream and live in a nice community, somehow America is not fully liberated because we hold these biases against individuals based on skin color."[83]

Justice was not blind, and it especially was not colorblind.

After the verdict, Americans demonstrated in one hundred cities[84] across the country in "Justice For Trayvon" rallies. On July 20, 2013—a hot summer day, when anger over injustice is most likely to turn violent—the most divisive trial in the country led to millions loudly but almost entirely peacefully marching to voice their opposition to the verdict. In Miami, a little black boy carried a handwritten sign that read, "I AM NOT A SUSPECT!!" In Atlanta, another African-American child's sign read, "BLACK LIFE MATTERS,"[85] reminiscent of the Memphis sanitation marchers' signs[86] from 1968, searing in their simplicity, "I AM A MAN."

*She's a human being.*

*He's not an animal.*

How little we had progressed in fifty years.

Ugly social media posts abounded:

I want to thank god . . . for that bullet that killed trayvon martin.

Congrats to my boy Zimmerman for getting off the hook killing that dumb nigger.

The stupid nigger shoulda never went to by Skittles, stupid fucker had the munchies.

Hostile words were not limited to anonymous Internet nobodies. "Hallelujah!"[87] bestselling conservative author Ann Coulter said of the verdict, claiming that Zimmerman was "mugged" by Trayvon (conveniently garnering attention for her just-released book of the same name, though even Zimmerman had never claimed such a thing). Musician and gun activist Ted Nugent announced that racism had been over since the 1960s and joined the blame-the-victim chorus with his patronizing, "Nothing of consequence existed to deter or compromise a black American's dream if they got an alarm clock, if they set it, and if they took good care of themselves."[88]

Fox News anchor Bill O'Reilly accused the NAACP and those speaking out against the verdict as being motivated by money. "The grievance industry," he said, "there's a lot of money in it, there's a lot of power in it."[89] O'Reilly should know. He airs his own grievances nightly on his popular Fox News program, reportedly earning $20 million per year. (O'Reilly's comment would be laughable if it weren't so insulting to a heartbroken community. Singer Stevie Wonder, on the other hand, announced he would no longer perform in Stand Your Ground states like Florida. He gave up income derived from touring in more than twenty-seven states.)

The former head of South Carolina's GOP, Todd Kincannon, tweeted, "Trayvon Martin was a dangerous thug who needed to be put down like a rabid dog."

(Months earlier, Kincannon had amused himself during the Super Bowl by tweeting what he thought were funny zingers about the dead boy, like, "This Super Bowl sucks more dick than adult Trayvon Martin would have for drug money.")[90]

A Volusia County, Florida, police officer posted online[91] a cartoon of Trayvon Martin with the caption, "THOSE SKITTLES WERE TO DIE FOR," and another of Rachel Jeantel on the witness stand, uglified as Shrek. "Another thug gone," read one of the police officer's messages. "Pull up your pants and act respectful. Bye bye thug r.i.p."

The trial was over, but the fight against dehumanization was not.

A MONTH AFTER the verdict, Zimmerman went to the manufacturer of the gun he'd used to kill Trayvon, KelTec. He was treated like a celebrity, was given a tour of the factory by the owner's son, and smiled for a picture[92] with an employee.

Less than two months after the verdict, another 911 call was made, another accusation that Zimmerman was threatening someone with his gun. Zimmerman's estranged wife Shellie Zimmerman, who had filed for divorce after the trial claiming Zimmerman now thought he was "invincible,"[93] called the emergency number to report that Zimmerman had punched her father in the face, threatened her with his gun, and smashed her iPad that she was using to video record the entire incident. Zimmerman claimed he only acted in self-defense after both Shellie and her father assaulted him.

Shellie declined to press charges, claiming in an interview that the police said they'd put her in jail if she pursued the matter. She was on probation for perjury at the time, as she'd lied under oath at Zimmerman's bail hearing the year before.

Two months later, Zimmerman's new live-in girlfriend, Samantha Scheibe, made strikingly similar allegations against him, claiming, like Shellie Zimmerman, that when she'd asked him to leave her home he became belligerent, threatening her with his gun. Zimmerman denied her allegations, claiming she was the one who'd "gone crazy" on him. Scheibe later recanted her story, saying the police had exerted undue pressure on her.

Zimmerman may be the Teflon defendant, with accusations of criminal violence periodically made against him with few legal consequences. I spoke with Florida attorney David Chico, who was the prosecutor assigned to yet another Zimmerman case in 2005 (and who also, coincidentally, represents Maddy pro bono). In that case, Chico said, Zimmerman was at a bar with a friend who was arrested for underage drinking by a uniformed police officer. Zimmerman tried to speak with the arresting officer, and when refused, Zimmerman became angry and pushed the officer. Aggression toward a uniformed police officer is a serious offense, and Zimmerman was arrested and charged with two felonies, "resisting an officer with violence" and "battery of a law enforcement officer."[94] "For some mysterious reason," Chico said, "the charging prosecutor decided to reduce it to a misdemeanor. I don't know why." After three years, the records were destroyed. Chico recalls that Zimmerman was ordered into a twelve-hour anger management class, mandated fifty hours of community service, and required to pay a fine. "George Zimmerman is so lucky," Chico said.

A month after he was accused of shoving the police officer, in August 2005, Zimmerman's then-fiancée alleged domestic violence and sought a restraining order against him. He responded by seeking a restraining order against her as well, and both were granted.[95]

Neither of Zimmerman's prior incidents of alleged violence came in to his murder trial, where he sat throughout, preternaturally calm.

ACCORDING TO HIS brother,[96] Zimmerman now wears a bulletproof vest and a disguise whenever he goes out, and he never leaves home without carrying a concealed gun on his person and at least one other firearm in his car. "There's even more reason now, isn't there?" said his lawyer, pointing out that Zimmerman is eyed warily by people who recognize him wherever he goes.

Ironically, it is now Zimmerman who is viewed as the real suspicious guy.

IS FURTHER LEGAL recourse against Zimmerman possible? Trayvon's family could bring a civil case against Zimmerman, similar to the action the estate of Nicole Brown Simpson successfully brought against O. J. Simpson in 1997 after he'd been acquitted of murder in his criminal trial. But civil lawsuits result in money damages only, and Zimmerman has few resources. The U.S. Department of Justice is reportedly investigating whether Zimmerman could be charged with federal civil rights violations, as happened in the Rodney King case in 1992 after four police officers were acquitted in state court despite the fact that their beating of King, an African-American unarmed motorist, was captured on videotape. As time ticks on, and those charges are not forthcoming, the possibility seems increasingly remote.

The Florida criminal justice system offers no recourse for the prosecution's shortcomings in this trial. "Ineffective assistance of counsel" is a legal theory that defendants sometimes use to get trial convictions reversed, when their lawyers are incompetent. It does not apply to prosecutors. There is no legal remedy for crime victims who believe the state failed them in bringing a killer to justice.

The Double Jeopardy clause to the U.S. Constitution means that Zimmerman can never be retried for the crime of murder or manslaughter for killing Trayvon, even if new evidence emerged, even if he confessed, even if new prosecutors wanted to take a fresh look at the case. The state cannot appeal his acquittal.

THE TRIAL IS over, and despite Corey's blithe proclamation, the system did not work. And as long as the root causes of the shooting of Trayvon Martin and the acquittal of George Zimmerman remain unexamined, the injustice lingers. That's why for many, particularly in the African-American community, it's not over, not even close. Since the Trayvon Martin shooting, more unarmed young black Americans have been shot and killed by whites who instantly and unreasonably feared they were criminals, as we shall see. The shootings continue. Justice remains elusive.

Maddy wants to move forward now and is willing to speak out about her experience in the hope it will be used to change the law so that in future cases, jurors like her who know in their hearts that a murder was committed will have the law on their side. Though this case could have been won based on existing law, in the bigger picture, she's right. Laws are created by us, in an effort to achieve fairness and accountability, and those laws should be reformed by us when they aren't working. And Stand Your Ground and gun laws are ripe for review.

But truly confronting this disturbing trial and verdict requires more than legal reform. Because getting convictions after racially profiled young people are killed is not the real solution. Saving those lives before they're gone is. And to prevent future tragedies, we need a new, unflinching look at the uncomfortable issue of race, staring down the buried biases of a nation that so often determine whom we deem suspicious and why.

# PART TWO

## FEAR AND LAWLESSNESS IN
## SUSPICION NATION

*"Please use my story, please use my tragedy, please use my broken heart to say to yourself, 'We cannot let this happen to anybody else's child.'"*

—SYBRINA FULTON, MOTHER OF TRAYVON MARTIN

TRAYVON MARTIN'S DEATH was not a tragic *accident*, unforeseeable, unstoppable, as though an asteroid had smashed into the earth without warning, taking a life. Human-made stereotypes and laws created all the conditions that led to the death of Sybrina Fulton's son and that made George Zimmerman's acquittal by far the most likely outcome. Those biases and legal rules remain in effect, polluting our behavior as we interact with our neighbors, impeding just results when those interactions turn violent. At the root of all of it is fear—overblown fear of crime, inordinate fear of strangers, deep-seated fear of difference, and in particular, lingering, unspoken fear that African Americans are criminals. So many of us are suspicious. We eye each other cautiously. And in twenty-first-century America, that fear is often armed, locked and loaded. And so, the body count continues to rise in an atmosphere of increasing lawlessness.

Three months after the shooting of Trayvon Martin, John Spooner, an elderly white resident of Milwaukee, Wisconsin, was convinced that his thirteen-year-old African-American neighbor Darius Simmons was a burglar who had stolen his cache of shotguns a few days earlier. As Darius and his mother collected their family's garbage cans from the curb, Spooner confronted the boy, gun in hand. Darius put his hands up, and his mother asked Spooner "why he had that gun on my baby."

Security footage shows that the boy quickly moved back, and then Spooner shot him once in the chest. As Darius turned and ran, Spooner fired a second shot at his back. He tried to fire a third shot, but his gun jammed. Darius ran a little further, then collapsed and died in the street in his mother's arms. Darius's home was searched immediately after the shooting. No guns were found. At his trial, Spooner showed no remorse and said that he also had wanted to kill Darius's older brother, who had run into the street to help Darius after the shooting. Spooner testified that his shooting of Darius was "justice," and that "I wanted those shotguns back. They were a big part of my life." (Spooner was convicted of first-degree intentional homicide, largely due to the videotape from his own security cameras, which depicted him going after the child without any pretense of self-defense.)

Nine months after the shooting of Trayvon Martin, four black teenaged boys were in a car stopped at a gas station in Jacksonville, Florida. Michael Dunn, forty-six, complained about the loud music emanating from the boys' SUV, and a verbal exchange followed. Dunn, who is white, says he thought the boys had a gun, and so he opened fire into their vehicle, killing Jordan Davis, seventeen. Jordan and his three friends, it turned out, were unarmed. After the shooting, Dunn went to a hotel, ate pizza, and went to sleep. He was arrested the next morning, two hours away from the crime scene. In a letter written from jail as he awaited trial for first-degree murder and three counts of attempted murder, Dunn called his shooting victim a "thug."

Eighteen months after the shooting of Trayvon Martin, Jonathan Ferrell, twenty-four, was driving home at 2 AM in Charlotte, North Carolina, when he crashed his car, causing him to climb out the rear window to escape. He went to a nearby house and banged on the door to summon help. The white woman inside, afraid, called 911. Police arrived and Ferrell ran toward them. A white police officer fired twelve shots at him, hitting him ten times. Ferrell's fiancée said, "I feel like if somebody had just taken a step back and really figured out what was going wrong with him, they would have known he didn't cause a threat to anybody."

Ferrell, an African-American football player for Florida A&M University, died instantly that night, September 14, 2013. He was unarmed, had no drugs in his system, and had only a small amount of alcohol in his blood, less than the legal limit permitted for driving. The officer was charged with voluntary manslaughter.

Twenty months after the shooting of Trayvon Martin, another tragedy occurred in a suburb of Detroit, eerily similar to the Jonathan Ferrell shooting that preceded it. In Dearborn Heights, Michigan, nineteen-year-old Renisha McBride's car had broken down and her cell phone had died. After knocking on a door for help at 4 AM, McBride, who was African-American, was fatally shot in the face by a fifty-four-year-old white homeowner who feared she was a burglar. Prosecutors say the homeowner, Theodore Wafer, opened his front door and fired through his locked screen door. "I can't imagine in my wildest dreams what that man feared from her to shoot her in the face," her mother, Monica McBride, said. "I would like to know why. She brought him no danger." For nearly two weeks, no arrest was made, though the shooter was known immediately and McBride, while inebriated, had no weapon. After community outcry and national media attention, Wafer was charged with second-degree murder, manslaughter, and felony firearm possession.

Stories like these—showcasing overblown suspicion of unarmed African Americans; fear of crime; children or young adults gunned down, often with a lack of accountability or outrage—persist. Racial profiling by police officers continues too, and is sometimes defended, though many police departments have made efforts to diversify and train officers to look beyond race. But how do we address shootings by ordinary citizens? What reordering of our culture and laws is necessary to protect and preserve basic human life?

American media performs well when covering breaking news and dramatic events that capture the public's attention, like a high-stakes murder trial. It has far less interest in digging deep into the root causes of these horrendous stories, and it often perpetuates the very stereotypes that lead to the tragedies it covers. And so the stories recur, and we remain *shocked, stunned, saddened*—cable TV attention-grabbing words—each time. But once we understand that we as a nation created the underlying conditions that enable these crimes, we can see why they happen with alarming regularity, and we can then enact reforms.

As I was interviewed about the Zimmerman case, I was often asked, "With all the shootings in America, why *this* case? Why has it garnered so much attention?"—as if an incident that occurs frequently is not newsworthy. To the contrary: if we have a persistent problem, we should talk about it more, not less. And what's the implication of that question, that we are wasting time focusing on the killing of an ordinary citizen? Why *not* talk about this case?

The real answer: because we can only take them one by one. Pulling back and looking at the big picture, looking hard at all the people gunned down in America—especially young people of color—can lead to despair.

*At least we are talking about one*, I thought. We're talking about it because Trayvon's life was precious, just as every life is precious. We're talking about it because it was not only tragic, it was preventable. And unlike most American homicide cases that don't involve sexy white women or celebrities, Trayvon's case was able to get some media attention. Tomorrow, let's talk about another one. And another one after that.

Let's talk about all of them.

And then let's stop talking about them one by one, and let's have an unflinching examination into why our society allows so many Trayvon Martins—gun homicide victims and racially profiled youth—to happen. And let's start understanding where we've gone wrong, and then focus on known solutions that can help us save lives and become a less violent and more inclusive people.

# NINE

## *"Everyone's a Little Bit Racist"*

*"There is no immaculate perception."*

—FRIEDRICH NIETZSCHE

AFTER THE ZIMMERMAN verdict, some people, including Maddy the juror, expressed that our laws needed to be changed to prevent injustices like this one from happening in the future. And as we'll see later in this book, some legal reforms would save lives and provide better accountability. But the first root problem is one so many deny exists at all: the persistence of racial bias in America. While we'd like to believe otherwise, we have not yet arrived at our goal of racial equality. But by understanding the way racial bias operates today—so different than a generation ago—and building on a solid body of social science research, we can propel ourselves much closer to that goal.

IN 1930, STANFORD sociology professor Richard LaPiere[97] set off for a two-year road trip driving across the United States with his friends, a young Chinese couple. At that time, anti-Chinese sentiment was at an all-time high, with white Americans overwhelmingly in agreement with the California Supreme Court's[98] assessment that "They are a race of people whom nature has marked as inferior." "Yellow peril" fears that the American way of life was at risk from Chinese immigrants bent on its destruction raged. Hundreds of Chinese had suffered lynchings in the preceding decades. Anti-Chinese riots erupted in Denver, Los Angeles, and other cities. Chinese Americans were run out of towns, forced to live in ghettos, and excluded from most jobs. The Chinese Exclusion Act, the only U.S. law ever to ban immigration based on race, prohibited immigration from China. The phrase "Chinaman's chance," meaning no chance at all, caught on after the conviction of a white man for murdering a Chinese railroad worker was overturned because all the eyewitnesses were Chinese.[99]

As a result of this hostile climate, LaPiere worried about being turned away from hotels and restaurants as he traveled with his foreign companions. He was pleasantly surprised, then, when they were politely received at virtually all of the sixty-six hotels and campsites and 184 restaurants they chose randomly along the route of their epic journey. In only one, "a rather inferior auto camp," did the proprietor take one look at LaPiere's friends and say, with the bigot's typical imprecision, "We don't take Japs!" (Happily, they promptly secured alternate lodgings that night at "a more pretentious establishment, and with an extra flourish of hospitality.")[100]

But other than that one bad experience, LaPiere and the Chinese couple received overwhelmingly hospitable, friendly service across America. Sure, people were curious, especially outside the big cities, as many Americans at that time had never laid eyes on a Chinese national.

LaPiere reported that their curiosity generally turned into solicitousness, and he was delighted with the experience overall. His cheerful conclusion revealed how steeped even he was in the dehumanizing attitudes of his time:

> A Chinese companion is to be recommended to the white traveling in his native land. Strange features when combined with "human" [*why is this in quotation marks?*] speech and actions seems, at times, to heighten sympathetic response, perhaps on the same principle that makes us uncommonly sympathetic towards the dog that has a "human" expression on his face.

Ah yes, the Chinese, like dogs, can seem *almost human*. This from a man who spent a great deal of his professional life analyzing and opposing his countrymen's own unexamined biases.

For LaPiere was not just a traveler. His journey wasn't simply a prolonged holiday; it was a social experiment, one with profound implications that launched a still-burgeoning field of social psychology.

Allowing six months to pass so that memories of his visits could fade, LaPiere then sent out questionnaires to each of the establishments he and his friends had visited, asking, "Would you accept members of the Chinese race as guests in your establishment?" Possible answers: "Yes," "No," or "Uncertain; Depend upon on circumstances." With persistence, he obtained answers from 128 of the hotels and restaurants, about half of those they'd visited.

Remarkably, in the questionnaire answers, LaPiere received the opposite results from what he'd personally experienced. Ninety-two percent of the restaurant owners answered "No," flatly denying that they would accept Chinese patrons. Ninety-one percent of the hotel owners also answered "No." The remainder checked "Uncertain." Only one out of the whole bunch answered yes, that Chinese travelers would be welcome, a female owner of a small campground who included a "chatty letter describing the nice visit she had had with a Chinese gentleman and his sweet wife during the previous summer."

In answering LaPiere's questionnaire, the Depression-era business owners overwhelmingly wanted to be seen as conforming to the accepted, overt racism of the day, reporting that *no, of course not,* they would *not* offer a room or a meal to Chinese customers. When presented with the very same situation months earlier, though, they had actually done so, with notable kindness, either because they decided to be decent and hospitable to their fellow humans (or "humans"), or because they wanted to earn a buck when they could. (Most of the time, upon arriving at a new establishment, LaPiere sent the couple in ahead of him, so that he could determine whether they'd be welcomed even without the presence of a white man as their companion.) As Albert Einstein said, "Few people are capable of expressing with equanimity opinions which differ from the prejudices of their social environment." Einstein himself had been driven out of his native Germany around that time, his cottage turned into an Aryan youth camp, his books burned by the Nazis, his university position eliminated because he was Jewish.

LaPiere published his results in 1934. Don't believe what people say in response to questionnaires, he concluded. If social scientists want to measure attitudes, relying on self-reporting is an ineffective way to go about it. The only way to know for sure how someone will behave in a given situation is to measure their *actual behavior* in that situation. We now know for sure, based on LaPiere's classic work and the chain of research it spawned that continues to the present day, that our responses to questions may be wildly inaccurate and instead tend to parrot back the socially acceptable answer of our time. What we say and what we do are two different things. Sometimes this is because we know what we do, but we can't admit it (we lie to others), and sometimes it's because we are not consciously aware of our own behaviors (we lie to ourselves).

Either way, asking people about their racial biases is as unreliable today as it was eighty years ago. The politically correct answer has changed, but our actions still speak louder than our words.

TODAY, ALMOST NO one will admit to racial animus of any kind. We profess to be egalitarian, to judge others, as Martin Luther King, Jr. admonished, not on the color of their skin but on the content of their character. Outside the world of extremists (Aryan Nation, skinheads, Neo Nazis), almost no one will call him- or herself racist. The word itself is a vile insult.

And yet evidence of racial bias is all around us, though a yawning perception gap divides whites and blacks on our understanding of it. About three times as many[101] blacks as whites say that blacks are treated less fairly than whites at work, in stores or restaurants, in public schools, and by the health care system. And even when looking at the criminal justice system, where injustices against African Americans have been long known and well documented, mainly it is blacks who see racial discrimination and whites who do not. According to a Pew Research Center poll,[102] twice as many blacks as whites say that African Americans are treated less fairly by the police. More than twice as many blacks as whites say that blacks are treated less fairly by the courts.

In fact, astonishingly, a 2011 study[103] by researchers at Tufts University and Harvard Business School found that "Whites believe that they have replaced blacks as the primary victims of racial discrimination in contemporary America."

Some accuse African Americans of "playing the race card," of seeing bias where none exists. So how can we get to the truth as to the extent of racial bias that still remains in America? To measure it today, researchers can't bring in a bunch of subjects and straightforwardly ask them whether they are bigots, because everyone will simply deny it. So like Richard LaPiere before them, social scientists have gotten creative. For example, in a 2012 poll that was ostensibly about the presidential election, after a long list of political questions, the Associated Press snuck in some questions about the characteristics of people of color. When asked to associate adjectives with different racial groups, the majority called African Americans violent, lazy, and irresponsible[104]—the worst stereotypes about blacks that have lingered since the days of slavery, when the system required degradation and dehumanization to justify enslavement. Yet surely these very same people, if contacted individually and not anonymously, would strongly deny harboring any racial biases.

This disturbing poll result is consistent with the results of clever, cheat-proof tests of our subconscious attitudes developed and refined by social scientists over the last fifteen years and administered internationally. For instance, when contemporary Germans are asked, "Do you like Turks?" they invariably respond, "yes," because they consider themselves modern, unprejudiced citizens. They are then asked to rapidly click computer keys next to positive words such as "love" or "laughter" when German faces flash onscreen, and then they're instructed to try again with Turkish faces. Another round has them quickly click on negative words next to German and then Turkish faces as they appear on the monitor. Surprise! They can much more easily and speedily connect happy terms with people who look like themselves. When the Turkish faces appear before them, they must pause and then *push themselves* to click on words like "joy" or "wonderful." They can much more quickly connect negative words like "terrible," "horrible," or "nasty" with the foreign, darker faces. The very same Germans who report no ethnic bias against Turkish people have automatic negative associations with them, biases that they are either unable or unwilling to reveal.

And so it is with domestic attitudes about African Americans in the twenty-first century. Presented with this "Implicit Bias Test" developed by Harvard University researchers, three-quarters of white Americans show significant racial bias against blacks. The majority of Asian Americans do too.[105] And 50 percent of African Americans display racial bias against their own group. That is, the majority of both white and Asian Americans more readily connect "evil" with black faces and "glorious" with white faces, and so do half of African Americans.[106]

In a sense, the Implicit Bias Test is a grown-up version of the famous doll study. In 1950, psychologists Kenneth and Mamie Clark interviewed sixteen black children from South Carolina, ages six to nine. Each child was shown two baby dolls that were identical in every way, except that one had a darker complexion. They asked the children questions like, "Which is the nice doll?" and "Which is the pretty doll?" Over and over again, the children associated the positive attributes with the white doll and negative attributes with the black doll. Most heartbreaking was the response to the final question, "Which doll looks most like you?" as each child pointed to the doll they had consistently identified as being ugly and bad. In less than ten years on earth, these youngsters absorbed the message that their skin color marked them as unattractive, undesirable, even evil.

The Clark doll study was cited in the landmark 1954 Supreme Court case *Brown v. Board of Education* as proof that segregated schools conveyed the message that African-American children were second-class citizens, branding them with the stigma of inferiority. Relying on the doll study and other evidence, the high court ruled that legalized separation of the races was unconstitutional, ordering schools to integrate "with all deliberate speed." Desegregation had a slow start, but it picked up in the late 1960s through the 1980s as school districts used various means, including forced bussing, to achieve racial diversity in their student bodies. Then a series of court cases dismantling enforcement of *Brown v. Board* led to resegregation nationwide, resulting in nearly all of the early gains being erased. Today most students do not attend racially diverse schools. Black and Hispanic kids attend the most segregated schools of all.[107]

Although the battle to desegregate schools was mostly lost, American society has changed in many ways since 1950. One would expect the Clark doll study, if administered to twenty-first-century children, to show better results, right? A few years ago, a Harlem, New York, day care center set out to answer that question and repeated the study[108] with twenty-one children. Fifteen of the African-American youngsters responded like this:

ADULT FEMALE QUESTIONER: "Can you show me the doll that looks bad?"

A preschool-aged black girl quickly picks up and shows the black doll.

"And why does that doll look bad?"

"Because she's black," the little girl answers emphatically.

"And why is this the nice doll?"

"Because she's white."

The outcome was the same, unchanged since 1950. Most black pre-schoolers linked negative attributes to the doll that looked more like them. Sixty years had passed, but little African-American kids still struggled under the stigma of inferiority.

Why are the results the same? Because children pick up the cultural cues all around them, and those messages remain overwhelmingly negative about African Americans. In the area of physical beauty, for example, magazines at supermarket checkout counters, eye level for kids, feature gleaming, alluring celebrity faces—white faces, almost always. Blacks continue to be routinely shut out of "beauty" positions, such as modeling in New York City fashion shows.[109] Many in the fashion industry believe discrimination against dark-skinned models is getting worse, not better, and their numbers have declined in the last few decades. African-American models are often told, "We already have our black girl." Their representation is only about 6 percent, less than half their numbers in the population at large, and for some fashion lines, it's zero.

Popular culture's message: if you want to be desired, be white. *People* magazine's annual honor should be called Sexiest White Man Alive, since twenty-seven of the last twenty-eight stars to grace its "Sexiest Man" cover have been white. (We'll always have Denzel, back in 1996.) Reality shows popular with young people have few dark-skinned cast members who aren't the walking embodiment of a demeaning racial stereotype, like the Ghetto Ho or the Angry Black Woman. The attractive, eligible star of every episode of ABC's hugely popular shows *The Bachelor* and *The Bachelorette* have been white, every season (seventeen for the former, nine for the latter), every time. A few token minority contestants appear on those shows initially, to be voted off and disposed of early.

And in that sense, the reality shows reflect reality. Because while most single people insist that they are open to dating people of different races, in online dating sites, blacks are often overlooked and whites are preferred. A report[110] from the popular online dating site OKCupid.com found that African-American women received fewer responses than any other group, even though they sent the most messages[111] seeking dates on the site. The study points out that its website users are younger and more progressive than the rest of the population, and that nearly everyone in the study said that interracial marriage was a fine idea. But when it came to responding to messages, white, Asian, and Hispanic women all preferred white men. And everyone shunned black women. The study concluded: "Men don't write black women back. Or rather, they write them back far less often than they should. Black women reply the most, yet get by far the fewest replies. Essentially every race—*including other blacks*—singles them out for the cold shoulder."[112]

Each decision maker who chooses the white model for his fashion show, the white "Sexiest Man" winner for her magazine cover, the white cast member for his reality show, or the white woman on a dating site would surely say that she is not racist—*oh, absolutely not, I have black friends!*—and that it "just happened" that the white person was chosen this time, and last time, and the time before that, and, well, all the other times too. As defense attorney O'Mara said of Zimmerman's racial profiling, "It's just happenstance." But each of these choices reinforces all the others, snowballing to produce a powerful cultural message that white is "wonderful" (Implicit Bias Test results) and black is "bad" (doll studies)—a message so prevalent and powerful that preschoolers can be counted upon to repeat it back, to the point of self-humiliation.

Implicit bias against those with darker skin goes beyond children's assessments of good and bad and adult decisions on physical allure and dating. More perniciously, we are quicker to see aggressiveness and violence in African Americans even when whites engage in identical behavior. For example, in one study,[113] 75 percent of whites observing a black person shoving a white person called the behavior violent, but only 17 percent characterized the identical act performed by a white person (shoving a black person) as violent. Many called the latter simply "playing around." Both black and white subjects are more likely to rate computer-generated African-American faces as hostile compared to identical (except for skin color) white faces.[114]

The stereotype that blacks are criminals—dangerous, violent—runs deep. We are so quick to assume that African-American men are suspicious that many of us see weapons in their hands when there are none, for example. In another study,[115] participants were shown a face, then an object. They were more likely to misidentify a nonthreatening object as threatening when a black face preceded it, and they were more likely to mistake a dangerous item as safe when a white face preceded it. "He's got his hand in his waistband," Zimmerman said to the police dispatcher of Trayvon Martin. "And he's a black male." A moment later he added, "He's got something in his hands." What Zimmerman saw as suspicious was probably a cell phone. Many Americans, including police officers, make the same mistake Zimmerman did, magically "seeing" a weapon in the hands of an unarmed black male.

Social psychologists at the University of Colorado asked subjects to watch a video and then make a split-second decision to shoot when they perceived that the character who flashed on screen threatened them. In experiment after experiment—subjects were undergraduates, DMV customers, mall food-court patrons, and police officers—mistakes followed a pattern: they shot more unarmed blacks than unarmed whites, and they failed to shoot more whites than blacks who were holding weapons. Recounting the results of four separate studies, researchers wrote, "In the case of African-American targets, participants simply set a lower threshold for the decision to shoot." That trend held true even when the participants themselves were African-American.[116]

The association of dark skin with violence includes assumptions made about darker and lighter-skinned African Americans. Decision makers become increasingly harsh when the accused has a darker complexion and is "more stereotypically black"; they are more lenient when the accused is lighter-skinned and has more "white" features. Thus judges and jurors impose more punitive sentences on more "Afrocentric" defendants.[117]

All of these subconscious conclusions that African Americans are violent, or armed, or worthy of more severe treatment have profound implications for a criminal justice system in which deciding who was aggressive in a high-pressure confrontation is a monumental determination. So many decisions of police and prosecutors, judges and juries turn on gut assessments of who provoked a street fight, who pulled a weapon first, who verbally threatened the other, whether a victim appeared to be reaching in his waistband for a gun—or was it just Skittles? And all those players in the criminal justice system have the same unacknowledged racial biases as the rest of twenty-first-century Americans, affecting their perceptions; while at the same time most would strongly reject the idea that prejudice had any role at all in their judgments.

Most of us think that one is either racist or one is not, and certainly that *we are not*. An accusation of racism is a serious charge and is often hotly denied. And yet the field of testing for implicit biases opens up a third option: that while we would like to think of ourselves as open-minded and egalitarian, most of us have subliminally absorbed long-standing and widespread cultural messages that affect our decision-making processes when it comes to sizing up African Americans.

And so racial bias festers, perniciously, under the smooth surface where no one admits to prejudice at all. Three-quarters[118] of blacks say they have personally experienced race discrimination.[119] And evidence of extensive differential treatment confirms that our unacknowledged stereotypes continue to mar the lives of African Americans.

Some voice the frustration that in discussions about race, America's gains are ignored. And certainly some advances are real and worth celebrating. Slavery and the explicit, legally enforced racism of the Jim Crow era are over. (Though surely the brutality of those years was an exceedingly low bar to surpass.) Under federal, state, and local laws, overt racial discrimination in jobs and housing is illegal everywhere in the United States. Explicit racists, like Keith Bardwell, the Louisiana Justice of the Peace who recently refused to marry interracial couples[120] on the grounds he was concerned for their future children, are widely reviled. (Bardwell was forced to resign shortly after the story became public.)

Some extraordinary African Americans have achieved greatness that would have been unthinkable fifty years ago. Bardwell need only have looked to our highest office to see how off the mark he was about the limited futures of children of biracial marriages. President Obama, elected and then re-elected by majorities of Americans of every race, winner of the Nobel Peace Prize, is also a bestselling author whose first book is largely about his struggles with and pride in his racial identity. His presence in the Oval Office carries enormous symbolism for the gains America has made toward racial equality. No European nation has ever elected a member of a racial minority as head of state. In the prior administration of George W. Bush, Colin Powell and Condoleezza Rice were appointed to the President's cabinet as back-to-back Secretaries of State. Actors like Will Smith or Jamie Foxx and musicians like Michael Jackson, Jay-Z, Beyoncé, and Rihanna are beloved as crossover performers. Oprah Winfrey ranked number one on *Forbes*'s list of most powerful people, known and admired worldwide. Prominent black CEOs include Ursula Burns, who runs Xerox, a $22 billion company, and Kenneth Chenault, chief executive of American Express, with annual revenues of $33 billion.

Young people today study African-American history in school, read literature written by great black authors, and annually commemorate a holiday honoring one of the bravest and most brilliant leaders in our nation's history, Dr. Martin Luther King, Jr. (None of this happened when I was in school in the 1970s.) Thurgood Marshall was one of the primary dismantlers of school segregation, and since his ascension to the U.S. Supreme Court, it's now understood that the Court will forever-more include at least one African-American justice.

And so on. Search nearly any field, and prominent African Americans will emerge. It's far more difficult to be the first black something in America today than it was a generation ago.

Many stories of individual achievement are out there, inspiring, magnificent, well worth telling. A few African Americans have risen to stratospheric levels of achievement. But as they've cracked the glass ceiling, by nearly any measure, as a group the vast majority of blacks remain trapped on the "sticky floor" of subpar schools, housing, jobs, and income. Disappointingly, many of these indicators have barely budged in a half century. At the same time, the illusion of modern-day racial equality allows these vestiges of racial inequality to fester, mostly unchallenged.

In 1962 and 1963, at the height of Jim Crow–era racial segregation, a majority of whites believed that blacks and whites had equal opportunities in employment and education. This was before the existence of legal protections against race discrimination in America, as African Americans were barred in much of the country from all but the worst schools, jobs, living conditions, and most anything that would have been a step toward a middle-class life, as African Americans in the Deep South were being fire-hosed and set upon by police dogs and imprisoned and killed for sitting at lunch counters, participating in peaceful demonstrations, or attempting to vote. *Most whites at that time said that there was equal treatment for blacks.* As far as they were concerned, everything was just fine, and the civil rights agitators were just stirring up trouble. (As Dr. Martin Luther King, Jr.'s daughter, Dr. Bernice King, reminds us, her father was the most hated man in America at the time of his death.[121])

Just about the same number of white Americans today, 54 percent, say they believe there is equal treatment for minority groups under the law. We are still walking around in mass denial.

A BIG PART of the problem is continued social segregation, as most of us live in communities dominated by our own race. George Zimmerman, for example, was on the lookout for people he didn't know, which sounds like a reasonable approach for a neighborhood watch volunteer. But it appeared from the trial testimony of his friends and family that the people he knew were overwhelmingly white, increasing the odds that an innocent African American in his neighborhood would be considered suspicious. Brandy Green, Zimmerman's African-American neighbor and Tracy and Trayvon Martin's host, for example, was unknown to him. One of the most awkward moments in the trial was deep into the defense case when an older black woman, Eloise Dilligard, home ill, testified literally from her sickbed via Skype. The only African-American witness called by the defense, Dilligard was asked several times whether she considered Zimmerman a friend, and each time she pointedly refused to take the bait, firmly correcting defense attorney Mark O'Mara as to her relationship with his client: "a friendly neighbor."

In this aspect, Zimmerman is little different from the rest of us. Most white Americans have few or no real black friends. Families, too, typically are monoracial. While interracial marriages have risen in the last generation, still only 2 percent of marriages[122] are between black and white spouses.

The races aren't just segregated. Separate but equal remains inherently unequal. Black Americans today continue to live in much poorer neighborhoods than white Americans, just as they did fifty or a hundred years ago. In fact, according to a 2011 Brown University study,[123] the average *affluent* black household lives in a poorer neighborhood than the average lower-income white resident. Blacks are the most segregated racial group in America, the study concludes, living in areas with significantly worse public schools, safety, environmental quality, and public health. As Malcolm X said in 1964, "America preaches integration and practices segregation." Still true.

Today, black unemployment is significantly higher[124] than it was in 1954, when the Supreme Court ordered schools to be desegregated in *Brown v. Board of Education.* This is in part because when whites fled from city neighborhoods to avoid sending their kids to integrated schools, the good jobs followed.

Black income relative to white income has barely moved in the last fifty years, from 55 percent to 59 percent. That is, the average black person earns just over half of what the average white person takes home. And in the last thirty years, the median net worth for African Americans[125] has gone *down*, and remains a tiny percentage of white median net worth. The average white family has a whopping twenty times[126] the wealth of the average black family. African Americans carry significantly more debt relative to their income than whites. Socioeconomically, many blacks remain where their grandparents were fifty years ago, "smothering in an airtight cage of poverty in the midst of an affluent society," as Dr. King described it in his Letter from a Birmingham Jail.[127]

Some readers may object to attributing any of these disparities to racial bias, on the grounds that individual responsibility may explain these numbers. Arguments may be made in the employment sector, for example, that individual African Americans bear some responsibility for their educational attainment, choice of career, job performance, and other factors that bear upon their personal income and ability to accumulate wealth.

And all things being equal, individual responsibility would play the largest role in net worth outcomes. The most qualified candidate would get the job, the highest achieving employee would be rewarded the promotion and the raise. But as we shall see when we drill down in two important areas, all things are not equal, not even close. As a result, high barriers to good jobs and middle class income remain insurmountable for many African Americans.

When we're assessing results, a hard look at *beginnings* is imperative. Unequal educational opportunities in the early years of students' lives produce more dropouts and poorly qualified job applicants. Disproportionate policing in inner-city neighborhoods, where many young people have their first encounters with the criminal justice system, and the consequences that flow from arrests and criminal records create lifetime challenges for many African Americans, who can be barred from jobs, schools, housing, and other basics of life for crimes as trivial as marijuana possession.

That's why racial disparities in public schools and the criminal justice system matter profoundly, because in each case racial inequality in the early stages produces grossly unfair outcomes for Americans of color— outcomes that are then used against them in justifying further disparities, creating vicious cycles. And each of these systems is funded entirely by tax dollars and is controlled by public policies we as a nation make. An understanding of implicit racial biases at play in these two institutions— schools and the justice system—is critical to understanding the very different positions of American blacks and whites in the twenty-first century.

## Pushed Out and Locked Out

LET'S START WITH education. For the most part, forget individual responsibility here. A child cannot be blamed for an underfunded or poor-performing school, for barriers that only the most extraordinary children can surmount. Most kids of all races go to their nearest public school, and our shameful choice as a nation to let inner-city kids languish in understaffed, overcrowded classrooms with shorter school years and fewer class and extracurricular offerings limit their opportunities for success.

Nationwide we've slashed and burned school budgets. Majority-African-American schools, already suffering, have been hit the hardest. For example, in the summer of 2013, Philadelphia's school district, whose students are 85 percent black, laid off a jaw-dropping 3,783 school employees, including assistant principals, guidance counselors, administrative support staff, and nurses. Lacking teachers, Philadelphia schools can no longer afford the luxury of separate first-, second-, and third-grade classes, so students of different ages and abilities are combined[128] in mixed-grade classrooms. Twenty-four schools were closed entirely, their students packed into the remaining schools. Art, music,[129] and athletic programs were eliminated, as if these were frilly extras children in one of the world's richest nations should simply live without.

Shortly thereafter, in October 2013, asthmatic sixth grader Laporshia Massey[130] died after feeling sick in a Philadelphia public school. No school nurse was on duty. No one called 911. One in five children in the school district suffers from asthma, a common inner-city ailment. The City of Brotherly Love, the birthplace of the Declaration of Independence, the Constitution, and the abolitionist movement, had decided that the health of its schoolchildren was no longer worth funding, though school nurses, facing budget cuts months earlier, had warned that deaths of children would likely occur.

While Philadelphia's majority black schools may have suffered the most recent round of deep cuts, they are in line with the cuts and underfunding associated with most black schools around the country. Majority black schools are significantly poorer, are less likely to offer[131] academically challenging classes like calculus or algebra, and are less likely to have gifted-and-talented programs, arts, or even physical education classes. Teachers in those schools are more likely to be inexperienced and working for lower pay than teachers in majority white schools.

Shouldn't we spend *more* per pupil in economically disadvantaged neighborhoods to help poor kids with the tougher challenges they face? When we know that inner-city children are less likely to have had the advantages of preschool, or even decent nutrition, wouldn't we want to give them more educational support? Yet confoundingly, by any measure, as a nation we spend significantly less on students of color, who are clustered in poor neighborhoods, than we do on white students in mostly suburban neighborhoods. The disparity[132] is most pronounced in the comparison between students in schools that are more than 90 percent white versus students in schools that are more than 90 percent black. (Remember, most of our children are once again attending segregated schools.) Disgracefully, we bestow an average of $733 more per year of public money on each white child's education in those schools than on the black students.[133] For the average predominately African-American school, this is a loss of about a half million dollars a year, money that could hire a dozen new teachers or nine experienced ones (and thus smaller classes and more personal attention); school counselors to help troubled kids and encourage college enrollment; tutors; or equipment like computers, or even books. Many low-income school districts lack supplies as basic as textbooks. "We mostly don't get homework in my math class because we don't have books," said Silas Moultrie,[134] an eighth grader in San Francisco. In poor areas of New York City, some schools have next to no textbooks[135] at all, and many teachers lead classes in fields in which they are not certified or proficient.

These disparities take a direct hit on students of color. We know, for example, that African-American males are far less likely to graduate high school[136] (only a bare majority, 52 percent, finish) or attend college than boys in other racial groups. A big part of the problem is what one educational reform group, the Schott Foundation, calls a "pushout" and "lockout"[137] crisis. That is, black boys, often struggling in those bare-bones, underfunded schools, are frequently disciplined for even minor misbehavior with suspensions, which cut down on their learning time and "push" them out of educational opportunities. (When I talk about suspensions in this book, I'm talking about out-of-school suspensions, where kids are banned from school premises. Some schools use the less-punitive form, in-school suspensions, where students remain on campus, supervised by a teacher in another classroom.) The students who remain behind in school are "locked out" of better educational opportunities available to white kids in school systems that provide smaller classes, adequate materials and facilities, highly-trained teachers, and other resources that are critical to their success. Predominately white schools arc also more likely to use corrective measures in response to children's misbehavior, such as counseling, calling in parents for conferences, and coming up with a step-by-step remedial plan the student signs to teach the student better conduct, all while the child remains in school, attending classes.

To see how African-American boys are so often pushed out of school, we need look no further than Trayvon Martin. In the public discussion of the case, some raised Trayvon's three school suspensions in the months prior to his altercation with Zimmerman in an attempt to show that he was the violent, aggressive type who would instigate a fight with a stranger, as Zimmerman described. It's likely that this is what the juror who believed Trayvon was a "bad kid" was referring to, as the media had extensively reported on his suspensions, though no evidence on this subject came into the trial.

And indeed Trayvon had been suspended three times in his junior year of high school in the months prior to his death. The reason his father said that he removed Trayvon from his home, friends, and neighborhood in Miami and took him to Sanford, four hours north, was to help Trayvon focus on "priorities" during that third suspension. Because Trayvon was not going to school in Miami on Monday morning he found himself in Sanford on the night of Sunday, February 26, 2012.

Three suspensions? Those unfamiliar with modern school rules may conclude that Trayvon was delinquent, or at least a troublemaker. But today being kept out of school doesn't necessarily mean that at all. Because with little fanfare, public schools have ratcheted up suspensions as disciplinary tools for nonviolent offenses, and African-American boys like Trayvon too often bear the brunt of this punishment.

Once disfavored based on the radical notion that we actually want children to be in school, suspensions have skyrocketed in the last few decades for infractions major and minor. After fighting, the second biggest category warranting suspension is truancy, tardiness, or cutting a class. This has all the logic of punishing a kid for drinking a beer by insisting he guzzle a fifth of bourbon. Other categories warranting suspension in some schools are bringing a cell phone to school or publicly displaying affection, which are both considered subsets of "willful defiance." Students have been forced to sit home for days on end after criticizing teachers on Facebook.[138] A six-year-old was suspended for

forty-five days for bringing a camping tool to school that contained a
fork, spoon, and knife.[139] The situation is absurdly out of hand.

Since the early 1970s, the percentage of students suspended from
school has doubled. Nationwide, the trend is toward more mandatory
suspensions from school, for longer periods of time. This began in 1994
when the federal government began its zero tolerance policy against
kids bringing guns to school—a laudable concept, but which spawned
a host of other "zero tolerance" laws, getting kids kicked out of school
for minor infractions. For example, in New York City in 1998, only
seven offenses warranted zero tolerance mandatory suspensions. That
number quadrupled to twenty-eight categories of mandatory suspensions by 2009.

This punitive treatment is a policy cousin to our country's choice
to imprison five times more Americans today than a generation ago,
spawning a culture of mass incarceration that we can no longer afford.
Similarly, in our schools, with little fanfare or public discussion, we've
instituted punitive policies resulting in mass suspensions, particularly
for minority kids. And just as authority figures' implicit racial biases
disadvantage blacks in the criminal justice system, African Americans,
especially boys, find themselves disproportionately subject to school suspensions for perceived suspicious behavior.

Two million middle and high school students are forced to stay home
each year, missing out on classroom instruction. Given that the purpose
of schools is to educate, banning children from schools should be a last
resort, reserved for those students who pose a threat to the safety of
others. Instead, forcing troubled or angry kids to stay away has caused
a host of problems for children and has not improved overall school discipline or performance. (Notably, some cities like Baltimore have gone

in the other direction, working to keep at-risk kids engaged in school, with some success.)

And while suspensions have increased for all racial groups, African-American suspensions have skyrocketed at *eleven times* the rate of other groups. Black male students were the most likely to be suspended (and disabled black males the most likely of all). A Children's Defense Fund study of almost three thousand schools from the 1970s showed that black students back then were also more likely to be suspended, but the disproportionality has climbed sharply since. Today African-American students are suspended more than three times as often as their white classmates, twice as often as their Latino classmates, and more than ten times as often as their Asian classmates in middle and high schools nationwide.

Why has the rate at which black students are suspended shot up so dramatically in a generation? A big part of the problem is that notwithstanding all the talk of "zero tolerance," most suspensions are discretionary, varying widely from school to school, even within the same school district. The same suspicions and fears that lead to racial profiling on the streets are in play in the schools as well. Civil rights leaders find the statistics "appalling." Gloria Sweet-Love,[140] who served on a Tennessee school board for two decades and is now the state's leader for the National Association for the Advancement of Colored People (NAACP), explains that white teachers are more likely to deem a black student "threatening" instead of simply disobedient, and therefore more likely to "make an example" of him or her.

We can see this by analyzing the racial disparity in suspensions in Trayvon's state, county, and even his school, and by comparing his particular offenses with the punishments he was given. Was Trayvon's race a factor in his suspensions?

Florida, Trayvon Martin's home state, has seen a rash of lawsuits brought by the NAACP and the Southern Poverty Law Center over its racial bias in the doling out of suspensions and other harsh disciplinary actions. In Okaloosa County, for example, 50 percent of school arrests involved African-American students, even though they make up just 12 percent of the school population. African-American students were six times more likely to be arrested at school than white students. In Flagler County, African-American students account for 70 percent of expulsions, even though they represent only 16 percent of the student population. In Miami-Dade County Public Schools, where Trayvon was enrolled, half of all students who received multiple out-of-school suspensions in 2009 were black. At Dr. Michael M. Krop High School, Trayvon's school, again nearly half of the 105 suspensions in 2009 were given to black students, who made up only 24 percent of the school's enrollment. Any numbers revealing this level of significant racial disparity should be unsettling, but these are especially so given that we are talking about schoolchildren, and forcing them out of their classrooms.

With this context, let's examine Trayvon's suspensions. Were they justified? Was he appropriately "pushed out"? The three suspensions he'd been given that school year were for tardiness, writing the letters "WTF" on a locker, and possessing a plastic bag with marijuana residue. Each time the decision was made by high school administrators to push Trayvon out of school, though he was planning on taking the SAT and going to college like his older brother Jahvaris. (Trayvon had hoped to pursue a career in aviation.)

As with any student, each of these suspensions increased his odds of failure, disconnecting him from his teachers, disrupting his classroom attendance and participation. Even a single suspension can double a student's odds of dropping out, and multiple suspensions make the possibility of graduation even more remote.[141] Put another way, if we wanted to increase the number of high school dropouts in America, we'd suspend more kids for petty offenses, causing them to fall behind in their classes and disconnect from school until they just decide to give up on it entirely.

Ironically, Trayvon's own high school student handbook[142] preaches this concept, stating that "Miami-Dade County Public Schools believes attendance in school is critical to a student's success." Is there anyone who would argue with that? Yet its "You're on your own, kid" policy toward suspended students is consistent with that of most schools, which burden children with the obligation of making an extra effort to keep up once they've been barred from school and fallen behind. Trayvon's high school student handbook reads:

> Suspensions. The responsibility for securing written assignments missed during the suspension period will be the responsibility of the student. Under no circumstances are teachers required to make special provisions to comply with this procedure.

The message to kids: Ordered to miss school? Teachers aren't going to make any particular effort to help you catch up. You figure it out.

A close look at Trayvon's offenses[143] and his school's own policies about the consequences that should flow from them raise serious questions about whether he was treated fairly for his infractions. Trayvon's school set forth a detailed five-tiered disciplinary policy in an effort to make clear what punishments would be warranted for various types of misbehavior, ranging from petty "Level I" offenses like inappropriate public displays of affection or unauthorized use of electronic devices to hardcore "Level V" offenses like armed robbery or homicide. Trayvon's first offense, tardiness/truancy, is not listed anywhere at any level. The closest violation, the more serious "cutting classes," is listed as a Level I offense. According to the school policy, this would not warrant a suspension but instead lesser corrections such as calling parents, a reprimand, a student conference, peer mediation, or revocation of privileges to engage in student social activities. Which makes more sense—let's take kids who've made small mistakes and pull them back into school by helping them modify their behavior, not push them out for it.

So why was the heavy penalty of suspension imposed upon Trayvon when it wasn't called for under the school's own written policy? Was his race a factor in the school's decision to push him out, as appears to happen frequently in his school, county, and state?

His second suspension, for writing on a locker, would have fallen under the school's Level II category for disruptive behavior. One incident of graffiti would have warranted, according to Krop High's own plan, calling Trayvon's parents or instituting a "school-based program that focuses on modifying the student's inappropriate behavior or promotes positive behavior." Suspension would have been appropriate only for Level II "serious or habitual infractions." Yet Trayvon's offense consisted only of writing three letters on a locker one time. Even taking into account his prior "offense" for tardiness, this action could not rise to the level of "serious" or "habitual."

So why was he suspended a second time? Why did the school not use the opportunity as a teaching moment, helping him learn the lessons of respect for school property, appropriate language in appropriate contexts, and free speech and its limits, as their own policy required?

Trayvon's third offense, possessing an empty baggie with marijuana residue, would have arguably been a Level III offense, possession of a controlled substance. (Is residue a substance?) Under the Krop High rules, the principal should have called Trayvon's parents for this one, then handed down a one- to ten-day suspension. Trayvon got the maximum penalty, a ten-day suspension.[144] And thus his father took him to Sanford.

Why did he get the maximum? Other factors may have been at play in the decisions to punish Trayvon with three suspensions his junior year, but based on publicly available information, he appears to have been trapped in precisely the type of overly punitive "pushout" cycle that leads to a disproportionately high number of students of color being kept from attending school. Writing on lockers, being late for class, or possessing marijuana are behaviors that require adult intervention, but they are also extremely common teenaged offenses that should lead to *more* engagement with the misbehaving kid, not relegating him to the streets or a home where adult supervision may not be present. No one could have predicted the horrific outcome that befell Trayvon in Sanford, Florida, and his school administrators are in no way responsible for Zimmerman's shooting of Trayvon. But officials should be accountable for decisions that erect more barriers to success for African-American kids when better options are available.

Of course all schools need options to deal with unruly kids. Many teachers would prefer to send children to talk over their problems with the school guidance counselor. But in this era of budget cuts, school counselors have been eliminated in many districts. Similarly, fewer teachers are available for after-school detention, to coach teams, or to lead music or drama classes, which motivate students' good behavior so that they can stay on the team, in the band, or in a school play. Suspended students often wind up alone, walking the streets, bored, or spending time with other kids who are dropouts or who have also been suspended—a recipe for failure. In 2013, the American Pediatrics Association called for pediatricians across the United States to take stronger steps to discourage out-of-school suspensions and expulsions because they are so harmful to children's chances of success, and with no benefit to the schools. The APA concluded that "research has demonstrated . . . that schools with higher rates of out-of-school suspension and expulsion are not safer for students or faculty." So concerned was the APA about the impact of mass suspensions on children's lives that it called upon its member pediatricians to inquire during checkups about whether children are being suspended and to advocate for preventative programs and those that administer consequences for rule-breakers within the schools.

Suspending schoolchildren, who are then ten times as likely to drop out, has profound short- and long-term consequences for them. High school dropouts are all but unemployable in today's tough job market, where 60 percent of new jobs now require a college education. They're last hired, first fired, and will earn[145] $200,000 less over their lifetimes than their peers who finish high school, and one million dollars less than college graduates. The United States high school graduation rate is already miserably low, ranking twenty-second out of twenty-seven developed countries. Almost no high school dropout will ever earn more than $40,000 per year,[146] making supporting a family extremely difficult. Those who don't finish high school are more likely to be illiterate, to become teenaged parents, to abuse alcohol and drugs, to wind up in prison, even to commit suicide. So helping kids complete school, rather than pushing them out, ought to be our priority.

When we choose to spend significantly less of our education dollars on predominately black schools, we can expect the kids in those overcrowded schools with crumbling plaster, nonfunctioning toilets, poor lighting, inadequate ventilation, and inoperative heating and cooling systems to perform poorly on tests, and they do.[147] When we cut art and music and drama and sports and all the "extras" that made school fun for many of us, we can expect children attending boring, bare-bones schools to rebel and have more disciplinary problems, and they do. And when we push out and lock out large numbers of African-American boys, in particular, for minor infractions that many successful adults committed when we were kids (cutting class, writing on a locker, smoking marijuana), we should expect hostility toward school in general, falling behind in classes, and ultimately giving up on the enterprise altogether, as so often happens.

Certainly rules that are not helping out kids to begin with, and which are administered in a racially disparate manner, causing so many African-American kids to be pushed out of their own schools, spiking their drop-out rates, must be reformed. When we disadvantage this group of kids at the beginning of their lives, we ensure that their lives will be poorer, sicker, rife with unemployment and struggle. We ensure that those job, income, and wealth numbers for African Americans don't budge, as they haven't in the last half century. It's no secret that education is the key to success in adulthood. Yet we allow rampant inequality in underfunding of inner-city and majority-black schools, together with grossly differential treatment of students of color, and then expect them to compete with kids who had all the advantages of personal attention from experienced teachers, extracurricular activities, tutors, and counselors, and who, at a minimum, were kept in classrooms learning whenever possible.

A country that allows all this to continue right under our noses, despite report after report about how inner-city schools are little more than dropout factories or prison pipelines, cannot seriously contend that it is an egalitarian nation. A country that shrugs at its segregated schools, knowing that racially ghettoized schools teach little black kids that they are inferior, has lost its right to claim that everyone in America has equality of opportunity. A country that pays substantially more per pupil for white suburban kids than for black inner-city students cannot pretend when it comes to high school graduation, college admissions, and the job market that everyone begins at the same starting line and has an equal shot at success. And if urban kids weren't failing fast enough, now we're actively pushing them out of classrooms in record numbers via the new insanity of mass suspensions.

Racial bias need not be explicit to be shattering and self-perpetuating. No one has to say, "Let's discriminate against African-American kids today." No one has to be a Racist with a capital R, donning a white hood, spewing racial epithets or committing hate crimes. The common implicit racial bias that African Americans are less good and less worthy can lead to results that are just as insidious, namely a culture that turns a blind eye to policies that harm children of color and allow them to struggle in inferior schools, subject to harsher discipline, throwing up obstacles to their achievement and success, ensuring that the cycle of poverty continues for the next generation.

African-American children as young as six get the message loud and clear that they matter less to us. Who among us can tell them that they are wrong?

## *"Et Tu, America?"*

*"In our courts, when it's a white man's word against a black man's,*
*the white man always wins. They're ugly, but those are the facts*
*of life . . . The one place where a man ought to get a square deal*
*is a courtroom, be he any color of the rainbow, but people have*
*a way of carrying their resentments right into a jury box."*

—HARPER LEE, *TO KILL A MOCKINGBIRD*

THE SECOND MAJOR public sphere in which racial bias runs rampant
is the American criminal justice system. Shine a light in any corner of
it, from initial arrest to sentencing and parole, and you'll discover that
blacks bear the brunt of our most highly punitive laws, experiencing
our criminal justice system markedly differently than whites. African
Americans are far more likely to be watched, stopped, charged with
petty crimes, convicted, and sentenced to longer terms than members of
other races. As crime victims like Trayvon Martin, African Americans
are more likely to be seen as aggressors, dangerous, violent, even when
they are unarmed or have no criminal record, with only the defendant's
word to support that narrative.

In polls, overwhelming majorities of blacks[148] believe that African
Americans are treated differently by police and the courts. Only half as
many whites agree. Unfortunately, the complaints of African Americans
are borne out by the research, which reveals that disparity at every turn.

Consider juries, which should be drawn randomly from the community, and which we'd hope would reflect the diversity of the local
population. In reality, that's rarely the case. In most places in the United
States, African Americans in court are highly unlikely to have a jury
of their peers. Of the six women who served on the Zimmerman jury,

for example, five were white. The sixth, Maddy, identifies as Hispanic. When the jury was empaneled, many commentators felt that the lack of African Americans on the panel in this racially-charged case was unfortunate, but that it "just happened," the luck of the draw.

But as it turns out, it's the norm for minorities, especially African-American men, to be underrepresented on American juries, as a direct result of laws barring them from jury service. Most states prohibit felons from jury duty and even voting—usually for life. Those with a criminal record, even veterans, even those who did their time years ago and have been contributing, taxpaying citizens ever since, cannot serve on juries. More than two million African Americans cannot vote or be jurors because of felon disenfranchisement laws—four times higher than the rest of the population. (We'll see why so many blacks have criminal records in a moment.)

According to one Georgia study,[149] for example, in some counties more than half of African-American men are excluded from jury service because of prior criminal convictions. Nationwide, according to another study,[150] almost one-third of black men are barred from jury duty. In Seminole County, Florida, where the Zimmerman trial took place, jurors are automatically disqualified if they have ever been convicted of a felony, or if they are currently facing prosecution—rules that apply in most of the United States. (Some states have provisions where ex-cons can petition for reinstatement of their jury rights, but who spends time and money for the inconvenience of serving on a jury?)

The disqualification of these large numbers of black men from juries is particularly disturbing given that so many black men are caught up in the criminal justice system and face trials themselves—yet they are the least likely to get a jury of their peers. In the Zimmerman case, the defense's theory of self-defense meant that in a very real sense, Trayvon Martin was on trial, accused of being a hair-trigger homicidal assailant. As we've seen, while both whites and blacks harbor implicit racial biases, whites are far more likely to judge a young African-American male as aggressive in nonthreatening situations. Thus the absence of African-American jurors in the case, as in many cases, could very well determine the outcome.

And yet because of our little-known and rarely discussed jury exclusion laws, it was unlikely that Trayvon Martin would get a panel of his peers. And in fact, he did not. (This is a particular problem in Florida, where nearly all cases seat just six jurors. In states with twelve jurors, the odds of at least one or two nonwhite jurors increase.)

Authority figures in the courtroom too are also less likely to be black. Prosecutors, as we've seen, are the most powerful players in the system, yet few are African-American. Nationwide only about 5 percent[151] of state attorneys are black, and many counties in America have no black prosecutors at all. This lack of diversity means that determinations as to who was the aggressor, who was the victim, who gets charged and for what crime is missing the voices and experiences of African Americans, who are more likely to see members of their own race as individuals and are less likely to see dark skin as inherently criminal. (While many blacks harbor implicit racial biases, they do so in significantly lower numbers than whites, as we've seen, and blacks are far more cognizant of racial biases at play in the criminal justice system.) None of the Zimmerman trial courtroom prosecutors were African-American, for example, and they readily accepted most of the defense version of the altercation, especially the allegation that Trayvon was on top and assaulting Zimmerman. In addition, they seemed entirely unable to communicate with their star witness, Rachel Jeantel, who spoke in an urban dialect. These types of problems are not unusual when many of those swept into the system as defendants, victims, or witnesses are African-American but few of the attorneys are.

African Americans are underrepresented as judges too, and studies[152] show that especially in cases where race is an issue, black judges rule differently. An African-American judge may have had a different perspective in the Zimmerman trial as to whether lawyers would be permitted to use the words "racial profiling" and whether evidence of the Bertalan burglary was relevant to Trayvon's inherent suspiciousness. Even the image of a strong, authoritative African-American judge in the case may have undermined some of the blacks-are-criminals messaging at play in the case.

While those administering justice—judges, lawyers, and jurors—are disproportionately white, those being judged are disproportionately black. This is in part because of where we send police to look for crime—overwhelmingly, it's inner-city, majority-black neighborhoods—and in part due to the more punitive treatment African Americans receive once they're swept up into the system.

From start to finish, it's a major advantage to show up with white skin in the American criminal justice system. We know that in judgment calls where a suspect may be held or let go, African Americans are more likely to be detained[153] than whites accused of the same crimes. If arrested, whites are more likely to be permitted to plead down to a lesser crime. When discretion may be exercised, such as by prosecutors offering plea bargains, African Americans are offered deals with higher charges and stiffer sentencing. When they are tried and convicted, whites get lighter sentences than blacks for the same crimes. In one study, judges[154] were found to impose as much as eight additional months on black defendants than on whites committing identical offenses.

The War on Drugs has swept up such vast numbers of African Americans into prisons and second-class citizenship thereafter that it's been aptly called The New Jim Crow by prominent Ohio State law professor Michelle Alexander. In at least fifteen states, blacks are admitted to prison on drug charges twenty to fifty-seven times more than whites, though blacks and whites use at the same rates, and whites are more likely to sell drugs.[155] To achieve that astonishing disparity, racial biases are at play among thousands of policy makers (who determine that it's acceptable for policing to be focused intensely in inner-city neighborhoods), police officers (like those found to engage in racial profiling), prosecutors (who routinely exercise their discretion in favor of leniency for white but not black defendants), judges (who impose different sentences on whites and blacks for similar crimes), and juries (who are more likely to see blacks as aggressors and whites as victims).

Most of these are people with good intentions who would be deeply offended at being called racist. Some have black friends or family members. Some are people of color themselves. All that is interesting but not particularly relevant. Because the system's outcomes demonstrate irrefutably the widespread acceptance and practice of racial discrimination in the administration of justice. While many in America take it as a given that blacks are more likely to be criminals, the horrific level of criminalization and mass incarceration of African Americans has in fact occurred only recently. African Americans are now incarcerated at more than twenty-six times the level they were in 1983, and Latinos are imprisoned twenty-two times more. (Whites are incarcerated at "only" eight times the level they were in the early '80s.)

The racial discrepancy is stark and especially outrageous for juveniles. For first-time child offenders, African Americans are six times as likely as whites to be sentenced to prison *for identical crimes*. African-American youth are significantly more likely to be arrested, more likely to be tried in adult court, and more likely to be sent to adult state prison, where they meet other criminals; rarely receive counseling, educational, or vocational training; and then enter the pipeline, primed for a lifetime of nearly impossible burdens once they're released. Nowhere is this more unjust than in the area of drug prosecutions, as we've seen, with its appallingly unequal enforcement against African Americans. It's even worse for black youth, who are ten times as likely to be prosecuted for drug possession, though they are *less* likely to use and abuse drugs than white youth, according to a 2011 large-scale Duke University study.[156]

There is no justification for these numbers. There is no way to sugarcoat what's happening here: blatant race discrimination against African-American children—in an outfit that has "justice" in its title and stone-engraved words about liberty and equality over many of its entryways, statues of a blindfolded lady justice gracing its hallways.

Take a close look at any stage of our criminal justice system, and the research documenting racial bias jumps out. Even defense attorneys, who one presumes represent many black defendants, can be ignorant to the extent of the injustice. Right after the verdict in the Trayvon Martin case, Zimmerman defense attorney Mark O'Mara threw out a whopper of a reverse-racism claim. He said[157] that his client "never would have been charged with a crime" if he were black.

In what country is O'Mara living? Certainly not the United States, where clear and persistent discrimination against African Americans in our criminal justice system is ubiquitous and well documented.

Racial bias extends from jury selection all the way to the end of the line, to life and death decisions in capital cases. It's long been known that the race of the victim is the most important factor in determining whether or not a convicted American murderer gets the death penalty, a sentence we reserve for a small percentage of killers—the "worst of the worst." Consistent with our undervaluing of black lives, one who takes the life of a white victim is at least four times more likely[158] to receive a death sentence than one who takes the life of an African-American victim. In a study[159] from the state of Georgia that was used for the basis of a race discrimination claim that went all the way to the U.S. Supreme Court, a defendant who had killed a white victim there was *sixteen times* more likely to get the death penalty.

From beginning to end, African Americans fare worse in our criminal justice system, as implicit racial biases subject them to more scrutiny, more charges, more incarceration. It's a Catch-22: caught up in more sweeps, sentenced to longer terms, black behavior is more likely to be criminalized, and then blacks are more likely to be seen as criminals. More police are then sent to inner-city neighborhoods, more blacks are arrested, and the vicious cycle continues.

## *"Whites Commit Crimes but Blacks Are Criminals"*

UNDERLYING MUCH OF that subconscious racial bias is the most enduring, corrosive racial stereotype in America: the black-as-criminal mindset. Historian David Levering Lewis summarizes it: *"Whites commit crimes but blacks are criminals."*[160] While whites can and do commit a great deal of minor and major crimes, the race as a whole is never tainted by those acts. But when blacks violate the law, all members of the race are considered suspect. I used to anchor a show on Court TV, and when we heard about a new arrest for some horrific crime, my African-American co-host would whisper, "Please don't let him be black." It would never enter my mind to wish that a bad guy not be white, because no matter how sick the crime, other members of the white race are not impugned.

Remember Zimmerman's false syllogism? A few blacks committed burglary, Trayvon was black, therefore Trayvon was a criminal. Similar logic is used daily in the assumptions police and citizens make about African Americans, especially young males.

The black-man-as-criminal stereotype runs deep. The archetype is so prevalent that the majority of whites *and African Americans* agreed with the statement "blacks are aggressive or violent" in a national survey.[161] In support of these findings, other research indicates that the public generally associates violent street crime with African Americans. Other nationwide research has shown that the public perceives that blacks are involved in a greater percentage of violent crime than official statistics indicate they actually are.[162]

Notice how the reasoning about race runs right to insulting conclusions (blacks are criminals), but never to positives, which would be equally (il)logical. No one thinks:

1. Barack Obama is our president, and he's African-American.

2. That kid walking down the street is African-American.

3. He's probably a future president!

The standard assumption that criminals are black and blacks are criminals is so prevalent that in one study, 60 percent of viewers who viewed a crime story with no picture of the perpetrator falsely recalled seeing one, and of those, 70 percent believed he was African-American.[163] When we think about crime, we "see black," even when it's not present at all.

Where did this insulting stereotype come from? The black-as-criminal image has been with us at least since the nineteenth century, when explicit racism portrayed African-American slaves' essential nature as ignorant and savage, in need of the "civilizing" influence of the white man. At that time, little black crime actually occurred, as slaves' lives were rigorously controlled, and they could be and often were swiftly put to death for perceived offenses against the slave owners, who acted as judge, jury, and executioner. As Chief Justice Roger B. Taney said in the famous 1857 *Dred Scott v. Sandford*[164] decision about the Founding Fathers' mindset in drafting the Constitution:

> Blacks had no rights which the white man was bound to respect; and that the negro might justly and lawfully be reduced to slavery for his benefit. He was bought and sold and treated as an ordinary article of merchandise and traffic, whenever profit could be made by it.

In contrast, white slavers, who should have been the real criminals, imprisoned African Americans on their plantations, forcing them to live short, harsh lives in extreme poverty, working without any compensation, constantly subjecting them to beatings and threats of violence. Female slaves were often raped by white male slave owners. Well into the twentieth century, lynchings of blacks in the southern United States were not only common but were social events where white families would bring the children and a picnic lunch and would take pictures of the hanging to be made into commemorative postcards. On average, an African-American man, woman, or child was hanged, generally by a white mob, once a week, every week, between 1882 and 1930, as police actively participated or stood by and condoned the murders. Lynchings continued until the 1950s, as thousands of black Americans were hanged for offenses like "disputing with a white man." (A much smaller number of whites were lynched[165] as well, often for taking the side of a black person.)

Though the United States was founded as a slave nation, with the subjugation of African Americans written into our Constitution, and though our history brims with centuries of repulsive acts of viciousness perpetrated by whites against millions of African Americans, no white-as-criminal trope ever took hold. This can only be attributed to the triumph of propaganda over reality. From the Reconstruction Era onward, academics churned out pseudoscientific papers linking blackness with criminality, "studies" which were then championed by journalists and even reformers as the basis for the view that blacks were innately inferior. Decreased funding to African-American schools and neighborhoods was justified on this ground, as were many forms of discrimination.[166]

What about more recently? Most of us see our history of slavery, Jim Crow, and lynchings as shameful and repellent, yet we still believe the black-as-criminal attitude is justified based on current crime fears. Is it?

It depends on what we choose to fear. How about serial killers? What criminal is more terrifying than a madman killing again and again, escaping the law? America's most notorious serial killers, striking fear as their body counts mount, have almost always turned out to be white, and gruesome beyond imagining. Albert DeSalvo, the Boston Strangler, terrorized his city in the 1960s, sexually assaulting and murdering thirteen women. David Berkowitz, New York City's "Son of Sam," killed six and wounded seven in the late 1970s, terrifying the city until his apprehension. Ted Bundy, who called himself "the most coldhearted son of a bitch you'll ever meet," confessed to thirty murders in the 1970s. He was on the loose, killing women in Washington, Idaho, Utah, and Colorado for years before he was apprehended. Chicago serial killer John Wayne Gacy, who dressed as a clown and performed at children's hospitals, murdered thirty-three teenaged boys and young men in the 1970s, burying twenty-seven in the crawl space under his house. He described his sexual release in committing murder as "the ultimate thrill." Gary Ridgway, Washington State's Green River Killer, was convicted of killing forty-eight girls and young women but admitted to ninety murders during the 1980s and 1990s. He returned to the corpses he left along the river to have sexual intercourse with them. Ted Kaczynski, the Unabomber, killed three and terrorized many others, sending mail bombs with his antitechnology screeds to universities and airports for seventeen years, until 1995. Jeffrey Dahmer, the Milwaukee Cannibal, raped, murdered, and dismembered seventeen men and boys over thirteen years, until 1991. Dennis Rader, known as BTK for his signature "bind, torture, and kill" modus operandi, killed ten in Wichita, Kansas, and was on the loose for decades until his 2005 apprehension.

Though each of these men was white, striking again and again in towns and cities across the United States, garnering intense media coverage of their crimes and captures, no fear of white men emerged. Their murders were considered individual acts for which they alone were responsible.

Prominent American organized crime families have long been run by white men like John Gotti, widely reputed to be responsible for at least thirty murders, including executions he ordered of members of his own crime family whom he suspected of being informants. James "Whitey"

Bulger killed at least eleven of his organized crime associates and did not face justice until he was eighty-four years old. He was sentenced to life in prison in late 2013. The judge sentencing him pronounced, "The scope, callousness, and depravity of [his] crimes are almost unfathomable." Yet none of us looks at white men with concern that they are mob bosses.

Rampage killers are often in the news. Nearly everyone who has murdered a large number of people in one criminal event has been white. American bomber Timothy McVeigh took 168 lives at the federal building in Oklahoma City in 1995, many of them preschoolers at day care, in the worst incident of domestic terrorism until 9/11. Dylan Klebold and Eric Harris, the Columbine High School killers, shot thirteen of their fellow high school students, then took their own lives in 1999. Adam Lanza killed his mother, then a classroom full of six- and seven-year-olds and six school personnel before killing himself at Newtown Elementary School in Connecticut in 2012. Earlier that year, James Holmes shot twelve moviegoers in Aurora, Colorado. All these men are white, as is the case for virtually all shooters on the long and growing list of mass killings in America. (The major exception is not an African American but Korean student Seung-Hui Cho, who committed the worst mass shooting in our history, killing thirty-three people at Virginia Tech University before turning his gun on himself in 2007.) Yet even though these shocking events generate round-the-clock media attention for days or weeks afterward, that level of attention does not scare anyone away from white men.

Shocking cases of white women killing their own children occur regularly. In 1995, Susan Smith murdered her two sons, then told police an African-American man did it. (So prevalent is the black-as-criminal stereotype that racial hoaxes are common and often effective in distracting attention.) Andrea Yates drowned all five of her young children in 2001.

In one of the highest profile cases of the last few years, Casey Anthony was tried (and acquitted) for the murder of her daughter Caylee. No one concludes white women are baby killers.

Every American presidential assassin—the killers of Presidents Abraham Lincoln, James Garfield, William McKinley, and John F. Kennedy—has been white, as was the killer of JFK's assassin, and the murderers of Martin Luther King, Jr. and Robert F. Kennedy. Ronald Reagan's attempted assassin was white, and so were all those who made attempts on the lives of Presidents Theodore Roosevelt, Franklin D. Roosevelt, and Gerald Ford (Ford's two attempted killers diverged not on racial but on gender lines, as both were white women).

In our nation's history, so many of the sickest, most appalling crimes have been committed by whites. Yet no matter how sadistic the crime, no matter how young the victims, no matter how much fear is engendered in a community, no matter how much media attention and public discussion the crimes of whites engender, the race itself is never sullied. One does not look at a white man or woman and feel concern that pale skin enhances the likelihood that he or she is an assassin, a bomber, a murderer.

It is the black-as-criminal stereotype that endures, sometimes buried, sometimes expressed in private to trusted confidants, and other times stated openly by those who do not fear being called racist. President Obama, in his remarks the week after the Zimmerman verdict, noted that African-American men are disproportionately involved in the criminal justice system, acknowledging the concerns about black criminals. He'd previously discussed his white grandmother, Madelyn Dunham, who had sacrificed for him and helped to raise him, but who had confessed her anxieties about black men who passed her on the street. During the

Zimmerman case, *Washington Post* columnist Richard Cohen[167] spoke for many when he openly wrote of his fear of African-American men. Even civil rights leader Jesse Jackson admits, "There is nothing more painful to me . . . than to walk down the street and hear footsteps and start thinking about robbery, then look around and see somebody white and feel relieved."[168]

Most everyone in the debate about the black-as-criminal stereotype accepts as fact that African-American males commit a grossly disproportionate amount of crime. On the right, this is generally used as evidence justifying anxiety about African Americans on the streets, in stores, or near white homes. On the left, root causes of crime are examined (failing schools, poverty, joblessness) in an effort to explain and reduce the numbers. But few scrutinize the numbers themselves to see who really is committing serious crimes in America, to determine based on reason and logic whether suspicions of African Americans actually make sense.

Let's look at run-of-the-mill crimes today. Who's committing them? Who should be feared? Again, it depends on what categories of offenses we choose to fear. Whites are disproportionately arrested for some crimes, such as arson, driving under the influence,[169] and vandalism.[170] That is, even with the focus of police resources on black communities, whites are convicted of these offenses at numbers greater than their percentage of the population. Drunk driving is a real menace, killing over 10,000 Americans per year, according to the National Highway Traffic Safety Administration data. Yet no one eyes a white driver next to him on the road and says, "Aha, light-skinned guy, he's probably drunk, I'm calling the police." The statistics don't matter. Our perceptions do.

How much crime overall is committed by African Americans? You'd be surprised at how difficult it is to strip away anxieties and emotions and arrive at the factual answer to this question. Most go quickly to FBI arrest or incarceration statistics, to see who has been convicted and sentenced for various offenses, broken down by race. But this data doesn't include every state or even consistent reporting from one police department to the next. Nevertheless, this FBI data shows that African Americans, who comprise 13 percent of our population, represent 38 percent of inmates in state and federal prisons. That is, blacks are locked up at nearly three times their rate in population, a shockingly high number. This statistic is often used in support of the black-as-criminal conclusion.

But these numbers are almost entirely useless, because they are both over- and under-inclusive. They include a small number of people who may be innocent as well as a very large number of inmates incarcerated for nonviolent offenses, especially marijuana possession, which does not strike fear in the hearts of most people. Worse, these numbers are flawed because they do not reflect who's *committing* the crime, merely who has been *apprehended and locked up*. They leave out all the burglars and rapists and killers who are still on the loose.

And the statistics don't take into account unequal policing. Many people are unaware of the huge disparity of law enforcement resources applied to majority-black urban neighborhoods in comparison to the relatively lax policing of white suburbs. Police departments send legions of officers to patrol inner-city neighborhoods with high concentrations of blacks, stopping, questioning, and frisking African Americans (and Hispanics), and where law enforcement has more eyes on a community, it finds more offenses. Once in the "sticky" criminal justice system, young men of color are likely to find themselves under correctional control, monitored, and watched for many years, even after release from incarceration. To make room for the skyrocketing number of Americans (disproportionately men of color) incarcerated in the last few decades, we've slashed and generally eliminated prison counseling, drug-treatment programs, education, and vocational programs. Once released, ex-cons are legally discriminated against by employers and are denied food stamps, access to public housing, school loans, professional licenses, and many other basic services. As a result, the United States has a high recidivism rate, as drug dealing and other criminal enterprises are the rare occupations that offer jobs to released former inmates. In inner-city neighborhoods, it's easy to fall under correctional control, and once in, it's tough to get out.

The chief problem with arrest and incarceration statistics, compiled so diligently by law enforcement annually and relied upon heavily by most legal analysts, is that they are only as good as the humans making decisions as to where to focus police, what crimes to charge, what plea bargains to offer, what sentences to impose. As we've seen, nearly everyone harbors implicit racial fears and assumptions, and the humans staffing our criminal justice system are no better nor worse than the rest of us. We know that at every turn, similarly situated African Americans are treated more punitively than whites in the criminal justice system.

Thus the decisions made at the entry point to the criminal justice system—community policing decisions as to who gets watched, who gets stopped, who gets questioned, who gets patted down for contraband—powerfully determine not who *is* a criminal, but who gets *labeled* as criminal. All things being equal, inmate numbers would easily tell us who has broken the law. But again, almost nothing is equal in our justice system.

For example, arrests. We know that overall, blacks and whites use marijuana at about the same rate[171] (whites are more likely to sell).

Among young people aged eighteen to twenty-five, the most common age to be caught up in the criminal justice system, whites are more likely to have smoked marijuana. This is contrary to the widely held association of drug use with African Americans. When we include other narcotics, whites constitute the vast majority of drug users. Yet in one survey, when subjects were asked, "Would you close your eyes for a second, envision a drug user, and describe that person to me?" *Ninety-five percent* of respondents pictured a black drug user.[172]

Nationwide, four times[173] as many African Americans as whites are arrested for marijuana possession. In Iowa and the District of Columbia, the number jumps to *eight times* as many. How does this happen? Because police departments, partly driven by a desire to increase their drug arrest statistics, concentrate on minority or poorer neighborhoods. Focusing on low-level offenses is easier and cheaper than investigating serious crimes and drives those arrest numbers high, triggering increased funding. And so hundreds of thousands[174] of inner-city residents are arrested, convicted, and incarcerated for having a joint, a brownie, or a baggie of marijuana in their pocket, even though the majority of Americans favor legalization.

When was the last time you saw a drug sweep in the suburbs?

If one reasoned only from arrest records, one would conclude that blacks are four times as likely as whites to smoke marijuana. And we know that would be wrong. Reasoning backward from arrest or imprisonment statistics to conclude that minority groups are violent criminals is equally flawed.

We know that police disproportionately target neighborhoods of color, so that's where the vast majority of *arrests* occur. That does not necessarily mean that's where most of the criminals are. To drill down on this, let's take a look at a timely case study of focused policing, where due to a federal judge's intervention, the police themselves compiled massive data as they patrolled, stopped, questioned, and frisked millions of citizens over many years in America's largest city.

## Watched, Followed, Stopped, Frisked

WHEN ZIMMERMAN LOOKED out his car window and labeled Trayvon "suspicious," he was using the very language law enforcement is constitutionally required to consider before stopping citizens on the street. (Not a coincidence. He was familiar with legal language from his neighborhood watch training and his criminal justice class.) In *Terry v. Ohio* (1968), the United States Supreme Court required police officers to have a "reasonable"—there's that requirement again—"reasonable articulable suspicion"[175] that someone is engaged in criminal activity and is dangerous before stopping, questioning, and frisking her. (This was a step down from the requirement up to that time that the police have probable cause or a warrant before stopping a citizen. The court reasoned that police needed this lower standard to protect themselves and others on the streets.) In the decades since the Terry case, police stops have become commonplace, at least in urban communities of color, based on law enforcement's purportedly "reasonable suspicions" of criminality. But since police officers, like the rest of us, walk around with unexamined implicit racial biases, how truly reasonable have those stops been? Given that suspicion is subjective, how often have the educated hunches of trained police officers been borne out by a finding of a criminal offense?

Consider New York City, one of the most liberal and ethnically diverse cities in America, with a similarly racially mixed police force, the NYPD.

In the summer of 2013, New York was harshly criticized by a federal judge for its ongoing racial profiling and harassment of *millions* of its boys and men of color. After reviewing mountains of the police's own data describing many years of police stops throughout the city, and after presiding over several full-blown trials on various aspects of New York's "stop and frisk" policy, U.S. District Court Judge Shira Sheindlin[176] ordered the New York police to stop the practice on the grounds that it violated the constitutional rights of the men and boys of color so often stopped and frisked. Concluding that blacks and Hispanics were stopped and frisked excessively (blacks and Hispanics, 52 percent of New York City's population, constituted 83 percent of police stops), and treated differently than whites once stops were made, Judge Scheindlin ordered a variety of remedial measures to fix the problem, including the appointment of an independent monitor to oversee police practices. Though whites were more likely to be found with weapons or contraband (generally drugs), for instance, minorities were more likely to be subjected to force.

Pause for a moment and contemplate that *whites were more likely to be found with weapons or contraband*. In fact, when stopped by the NYPD, white New Yorkers were almost twice as likely to be carrying a weapon than African Americans. According to a study[177] by then Public Advocate (now New York City mayor) Bill de Blasio, police found a weapon in one out of every forty-nine stops of white New Yorkers, but in only one of every seventy-one stops of Latinos and ninety-three stops of black New Yorkers. De Blasio's study also revealed that whites were more often found with contraband than blacks. Thus racial profiling does not make sense even if we cared nothing about the dignity of black and Hispanic Americans, and we concerned ourselves only with crime prevention.

In addition, racial profiling is extremely inefficient. Unlike civilians like Zimmerman, police are trained in how to spot suspicious persons. Race alone, they know (or should know), is insufficient. New York City police did not randomly stop people, such as every tenth person walking down the street. Instead, they stopped those who were doing something in particular that caught police attention and raised concerns of criminality. For example, a bulge in a pocket that might be a gun; looking around anxiously or appearing to case a property; running. But even of this group of people deemed "articulably suspicious" in the eyes of skilled police officers, how many of them were actually criminals? How often were the cops right in their assessments?

Almost never.

Nearly nine in ten young men of color stopped in New York under its "stop and frisk" policy were *entirely innocent of any crime*. Of those found with contraband, the offenses were most often minor—an open bottle of alcohol, marijuana possession. Only 1 percent of these "suspicious" young men of color who'd been stopped by trained police officers were found with weapons (carrying concealed firearms is generally illegal in New York City because the permit is difficult to obtain, unlike Sanford, Florida, where Zimmerman's concealed firearm permit was easily approved and entirely legal).

Overwhelmingly, then, just about all of the "suspicious" young men of color were simply ordinary citizens going about their day-to-day lives. Though police are more trained than the rest of us to observe and identify questionable behavior, in ninety-nine out of one hundred incidents, the men weren't doing much of anything wrong. "It is better that ten guilty persons escape than that one innocent suffer," the English jurist William Blackstone said, a principle that underlies our system's respect for civil liberties and its requirement of the presumption of innocence and proof beyond a reasonable doubt. NYPD had flipped the concept on its head, hassling ninety-nine innocents for every one wrongdoer.

Under the Fourth Amendment to the U.S. Constitution, as we've seen, reasonable suspicion is required before police officers may stop and frisk civilians. But New York City police, the judge found, cast a wide net that often seemed to include nearly all young men of color in some neighborhoods, with only the fuzziest of justifications for those law enforcement interruptions of their lives. Many of the over four million stops conducted by New York City police and analyzed in the *Floyd* case were justified by police, for example, as based on a suspect's claimed "Furtive Movements" or an allegedly "Suspicious Bulge"— actual boxes police officers checked on after-the-fact forms to explain the stop and frisk.

This is reminiscent of George Zimmerman explaining on a recorded police call that he became suspicious of Trayvon because he was, ostensibly, walking slowly in the rain, and Zimmerman reported his concern that Trayvon put his hand in his waistband, implying he had a weapon. After Trayvon was shot and killed, it became clear that he was not carrying any contraband, but merely a soft drink and candy. Similarly, in analyzing the NYPD, Judge Scheindlin recounts story after story of black boys and men who were simply walking home, minding their own business, when they were suddenly accosted by police officers cursing at them, shoving them up against fences or police cars, handcuffing them without justification. Police often said the young men appeared to move in suspicious ways or had something unusual in their pockets, which often turned out to be a wallet or phone. That nearly everyone now carries a cell phone, the judge points out, does not give the police carte blanche to suspect every pocket bulge is a weapon and harass community members.

When may race be taken into account in determining who is suspicious? In the Zimmerman trial, the defense argued that the fact of a recent neighborhood burglary conducted by two African-American men justified Zimmerman's heightened suspicion of Trayvon, because Trayvon, due to his race and youth, was a "match." And in the NYPD case, the city said that crime statistics justified their stops and frisks of black and Hispanic men and boys. Judge Scheindlin sensibly held that race may be taken into account as one of many factors when looking for a particular suspect, but *"it is impermissible to subject all members of a racially defined group to heightened police enforcement because some members of that group are criminals. The Equal Protection Clause does not permit race-based suspicion."* (My emphasis.)

In the NYPD case, Judge Scheindlin found the city to be "deliberately indifferent" to overwhelming racial bias in its police stops of citizens—that is, though officials had often been warned of its unconstitutional nature, they closed their eyes to the racial profiling inherent in their policing. That same blindness lies at the core of the widespread inferior treatment of African Americans throughout the criminal justice system, once those racially profiled young men (mostly) are arrested, charged, pleaded out (usually), and incarcerated.

And that indifference allows the humiliation of racial profiling to continue. Because too often the stops are not only inconvenient, they're downright insulting.

We can get a sense of the indignity of racial profiling from the testimony of some of the participants in the NYPD case. Leroy Downs is a black resident of Staten Island, a borough of New York City. One evening after work, he was standing in front of his home, talking on his cell phone. Two plainclothes police officers accused him in an aggressive tone of smoking marijuana, told him to "get the fuck against the fence," and shoved his back against his fence. Downs explained that he was a drug counselor and had merely been holding the microphone on the cord to his cell phone up to his mouth. Without asking permission, the police officers patted him down and removed the contents of his pockets: a wallet, keys, and a bag of cookies. They also searched his wallet. Walking back to their car, the officers told Downs that he was lucky they didn't lock him up. This is but one example of many times Downs has been stopped by New York police based on false suspicions that he'd engaged in criminal behavior.

David Ourlicht, a college student of mixed black and white heritage, was walking to a deli near his dormitory in Queens, New York, when police officers pulled up and asked him what he was doing in the area and where he was going. After providing his ID, Ourlicht asked the officer if he could take down his name as well. At that point, a patrol car arrived and the officer said, "Okay, now you're going to get the full treatment, up against the wall." Ourlicht faced the wall, hands above his head, while the police frisked him. They found only his cell phone, a five-subject notebook, pens, keys, wallet, passport, and iPod. He was then ordered to sit on the ground while they wrote him a ticket for disorderly conduct.

Clive Lino, a thirty-two-year-old African-American social worker in the Bronx, New York, has been stopped and frisked by the NYPD multiple times. One evening he was standing on a subway platform carrying a plastic bag containing some food he was bringing home from a visit with his mother. Police officers surrounded him, and one put his hand into Lino's pocket. Lino was told to wait, causing him to miss his train. He asked why he was being detained and was told to "shut the fuck up."

After he was told to put his "fucking bag down," he was frisked and further detained until the officers ran his ID and released him.

A thirteen-year-old African-American boy,[178] the son of a former cop, was handcuffed and then detained for six hours because he allegedly reached into his pants' waistband. Other police officers punched and then pepper-sprayed a thirty-eight-year-old veteran who was discussing Memorial Day plans with friends on a street corner.

Each time a citizen is stopped on the street, on a bus or train or on a highway, he's reminded that he's seen by authorities as different, "other." He's reminded that he must be wary of the police, who consistently view him as suspicious, dangerous, worthy of being watched. Any ordinary activity—going to school, coming home from mom's house, going out for some food—may be marred by intrusive police questioning or pat-downs.

And that's just for those who are simply hassled, not arrested and charged with crimes. For those swept into criminal justice system processing, on top of the humiliation that flows from being the object of racial profiling, once released after serving time, few opportunities exist for a second chance to regain a footing in American life. The job market blacklists African-American ex-offenders once they're released, singling them out for especially negative treatment. A few years ago, Princeton sociology professors sent black and white men with identical resumes to a wide variety of businesses looking to hire, from couriers to cashiers, deli clerks to telemarketers, undergoing 3,500 job interviews across New York City. The study's[179] authors minimized the applicants' nonracial differences to the greatest extent possible—their personalities, communication skills, and level of education (they all reported they were high school grads). Some of the job seekers told prospective employers they had felony drug convictions and had served eighteen months in prison.

Others reported clean records. The result? When both had a prison record, the white ex-offender got the job three times as often as the black ex-offender. When neither had been in trouble with the law, black men were half as likely to get the job as the white male applicants. White men with felony records were as or more likely than black men with no criminal histories to get the job. (This mirrors common workplace discrimination regardless of any felony record. A white-sounding name on a resume is 50 percent more likely to get a job interview than a black-sounding name. Emily and Greg are more employable than Lakisha and Jamal.[180])

This is why fixing racial bias at the *beginning* is so important. Failing schools produce uneducated, unskilled, unemployable young people, as we've seen. And most of those swept into correctional control are young people too, many under the age of eighteen, most under twenty-five. A young African-American man with a simple drug conviction will not get the job, and without employment, his life will falter. (And surely each of those employers who offers his white counterpart the job would say she is not racist, she just liked the other candidate better, and it "just happened.")

The pain experienced by victims of racial profiling runs the gamut from anger at police, alienation from the community, loss of job opportunities, and of course the worst outcome, the grief at the loss of a loved one, as experienced by the families of Trayvon Martin and other young people whose lives were extinguished based on incorrect assumptions that they were violent, aggressive, or armed. That horror is then magnified by the perpetrator escaping accountability in our justice system, where we have the right to demand absolute fairness. It's one level of pain when a beloved family member is lost because an *individual* commits a hotheaded, violent act; quite another when calm, rational players in our *system of justice* review the matter and nevertheless back someone like Zimmerman. Trayvon's brother, Jahvaris Fulton, summed up that pain in three searing words on the day that George Zimmerman was acquitted: "Et tu, America?"[181]

Echoing the last words of Shakespeare's Julius Caesar when he discovered that his close friend Brutus had conspired with his enemies to kill him, Fulton's words cried out against his own country's betrayal of his American family. Georgetown University Professor Maurice Jackson echoed the sentiment: "Like Trayvon Martin's father, my heart is broken. I am sad to say that I expected this verdict," he said. "There is much to love about our country, but there are also things that happen to black people every day that make you want to put your head down and cry."[182]

All the data compiled by the NYPD about their own stops simply confirms what social psychology studies have told us about racial bias: that we are more wary of our African-American neighbors, that we see ordinary matters like pocket bulges, hanging out on street corners, or walking to the deli as suspicious, and that overwhelmingly, our suspicions are wrong. The statistics also establish that police focus their attention on our citizens of color, stopping large numbers of them, looking for crimes. Although the African Americans stopped were less likely to be carrying drugs or contraband, when greater numbers of them are frisked, a greater number of apprehended black criminals will result. And thus the perception of the black criminal is self-perpetuating and is a self-fulfilling prophecy.

Does police data get us any closer to answering the question as to whether African Americans commit more crimes than whites? Not really. What it does underscore is that race-based policing is the norm— that darker-skinned people are more likely to be seen as suspicious by police, and those suspicions are nearly always wrong. When one group is disproportionately watched and stopped, more of that group will be fed into the criminal justice system. Because the inputs are distorted, we can't rely on arrest and incarceration numbers to determine who the criminals are. Garbage in, garbage out.

The best we can do with current data is to look at self-reports, where people acknowledge what behavior they've engaged in. As we've seen, self-reports have limited value, at least when it comes to discussing racial bias. And even on an anonymous survey, we can't expect subjects to own up to major crimes like burglary or murder. But a surprising number of people will cop to using illegal narcotics, owning prohibited guns, or street fighting. And there's no reason to believe that one race would tend to lie on self-reports any more than another, so we can use this data in comparing white and black criminality.

When asked about drug use, whites and blacks report consuming illegal narcotics at roughly the same rates, though as we've seen, blacks are arrested for marijuana possession at four times the rate of whites. In the area of weapon possession, whites report carrying illegal guns more frequently than blacks, according to the Centers for Disease Control and Prevention's annual Youth Risk Behavior Survey. This is consistent with what NYPD cops found in their stops and frisks: more white New Yorkers carried unlawful firearms. Yet African-American youth are arrested for weapons offenses at a rate more than twice that of whites (69 per 100,000, versus 30 per 100,000).

What about violent crime? African-American youth report[183] being in a physical fight at a similar rate to white youth, though blacks are arrested for aggravated assault, a major felony, at a rate nearly three times that of whites (137 per 100,000, versus 48 per 100,000).

Self-reporting reveals no particular association between criminality and African Americans at a level greater than whites. Those numbers, the only ones available that remove police racial profiling and disproportionate inner-city policing from the equation, do not provide any support for the black-as-criminal stereotype.

We also know that offenders tend to prey on people like themselves. That is, most crimes are crimes of opportunity, committed in one's own neighborhood. Because our country remains residentially segregated, most of the time, criminals target people of their own race. We hear a fair amount about black-on-black crime, as we should, because its victims cry out for justice. Overwhelmingly, black criminals rape, rob, and kill black victims. Yet we hear little about its mirror image, equally prevalent white-on-white crime. White offenders commonly prey on other whites. In a thirty-year study, 86 percent[184] of white murder victims were killed by other whites. Ninety-four percent[185] of African-American murder victims lost their lives at the hands of other African Americans.

Is fear of black criminality reasonable? If you play the odds and are white, no. Whites are far more likely to be victimized by other whites. And overall, whites are the majority of criminals and convicts.[186] This remains true even as the number of white Americans relative to the rest of the population decreases.

Cross-racial crimes are relatively rare. In 2011, for example, in our country of 314 million people,[187] whites were killed by blacks 448 times,[188] according to FBI statistics (recognizing the limitations of these statistics discussed above). Whites were killed by whites 2,630 times. Seventy-eight percent of the population is white (including white Hispanics), for a total of 244,920,000 white Americans. In other words, a white person has a one in 547,000 chance of being killed by an African American. The odds are nearly *six times higher* that a white American will be killed by a white person.

Put another way, Zimmerman was about as likely to be hit by lightning when he got out of his car that winter evening as he was to be killed by Trayvon. (Zimmerman's odds of being hit by lightning in Florida were one in 614,549—odds that rose as he exited his car into that rainy February night.)[189]

On the other hand, if you are African-American and live in a low-income, segregated neighborhood, fear of black crime is reasonable, but I doubt you need me to tell you that. As has always been the case, violent crimes occur more often in poor neighborhoods, and so many black Americans, as we've seen, remain locked in a cycle of poverty, in inner cities where crime is high relative to wealthier residential areas. Economically disadvantaged people have fewer options and more desperation, and they commit more street crime, nearly always against their poor neighbors. This is an issue of socioeconomic class, not race. In a study[190] of over 9000 American neighborhoods in sixty-four metropolitan areas, Ohio State researchers found that poverty, not race, breeds violent crime. Whites in economically disadvantaged neighborhoods committed crime at the same rates as African Americans in similar poor communities. (The researchers called their book *Divergent Social Worlds*, lamenting how difficult it could be to find statistically significant numbers of wealthy majority-black neighborhoods or economically disadvantaged white areas so that they could compare apples to apples. "The divergence is still tremendous," they said.)

FINALLY, A WORD about fear. To answer the question, "Should we fear black criminality?" let's take a moment to focus less on the race question and more on the fear factor. Our anxieties about crime in general are grossly distorted. Despite all the scary local news stories ("If it bleeds, it leads"), crime has dropped significantly in the last generation. The number of violent offenses has fallen by 32 percent[191] since 1990 across America as a whole. In our major cities, it has plummeted a whopping 64 percent. A debate rages as to why: from the legalization of abortion, to less lead in paint, to more sobriety among young people, to more cops on the streets. For whatever reasons, crime is now down[192] to 1960s levels, and in many places, it's still falling. As George Zimmerman and many others like him were preoccupied with crime, it continued to drop nationwide, most notably in the South,[193] where Zimmerman lived.

Our anxiety about crime is much like our other irrational fears, based more on emotion than reason. If what we fear most is death, murder isn't even in the top ten causes of death for Americans. According to the CDC,[194] in order of lethality, Americans died from these top killers in 2010, the most recent year, as of this writing, for which full data was available:

1. Heart disease: 597,689

2. Cancer: 574,743

3. Chronic lower respiratory diseases: 138,080

4. Stroke (cerebrovascular diseases): 129,476

5. Accidents (unintentional injuries): 120,859

6. Alzheimer's disease: 83,494

7. Diabetes: 69,071

8. Nephritis, nephrotic syndrome, and nephrosis: 50,476

9. Influenza and Pneumonia: 50,097

10. Intentional self-harm (suicide): 38,364

Since heart disease tops the list, if you want to fear the most prolific killer among us, fear cheeseburgers. Consider number 5. Most accidents occur at home. You're better off checking for uneven and slippery surfaces inside your home than worrying about threats on the outside. And consider number 10 on the list. You are more likely to die at your own hand than be killed by an assailant of any race. Or number 9: getting a flu shot is a better use of your time than worrying about your neighbors.

Our biggest worries bear little relationship to actual danger. In our prosperous, democratic country, bordered by oceans on the east and west and friendly neighbors to the north and south, we are a nation dominated by fear. Anxiety disorders[195] are America's number one mental health problem, and we consume more psychiatric medications for our uneasiness than any other nation on earth. A series of books from Seth Mnookin's *The Panic Virus* to Michael Specter's *Denialism* and Chris Mooney's *Unscientific America* decries America's irrational terrors. Parents worry that a stranger will abduct and murder their child, for example, an extraordinarily rare event, while accidents, cancer, and genetic conditions are the top causes of death[196] for children aged one to fourteen. (As author Lenore Skenazy points out, if you actually wanted your child to be kidnapped, you'd have to leave her outside unattended for about 750,000 years.[197]) Many of us are frightened by flying, yet we jump in and out of our cars all day, worry free, where we are twenty times more likely to be injured or killed. We feel so irrationally safe behind the wheel of these dangerous vehicles that huge numbers of us cavalierly text while driving, or drive impaired or tired.

Just as most of us are more comfortable in cars because we live with them daily, most of us are more relaxed with our own race because we live in families and neighborhoods that are dominated by members of them. We want to feel safe and secure and so we don't like to look at the hard facts that those same people are the most likely to commit crimes against us. A child, for example, is nine times more likely to be molested by a family member than a stranger. A burglary is most likely to be committed by someone who lives in the same neighborhood, and who shares the same skin color, as his or her victim. But fear of the Other, especially fear of the black man as criminal, has such a deep, ingrained history in America that it lives on, irrational as it is for most of us.

Does the black-as-criminal stereotype reflect reality? The real answer is that with so much racial bias permeating our system, operating cumulatively to produce a bloated population of black inmates that is not representative of the African-American population's contribution to crime, we can't know for sure what percent of, say, burglars, are black. (Only 10 percent of burglars are caught.) When black youth are rounded up for drug crimes while whites use marijuana, cocaine, methamphetamines, and other popular narcotics with relative impunity; when young people of color are watched, stopped, and frisked as a matter of course while whites are not; when black offenders are treated more harshly than whites for the same crimes; when black ex-cons are released into impoverished communities and barred from the necessities of life; we will continue to bear the disgrace of pushing out African Americans not only from schools but from our communities, locking them out of our neighborhoods and into prisons.

Having said all that, if for some reason you choose to fear crime, though statistically you should fear accidents or diabetes far more, *and you are black*, then yes, fear black criminals. Similarly, if you elect to walk around with anxiety over being assaulted, though rationally speaking you'd do better concerning yourself with preventing strokes or Alzheimer's, and you are white, fear your white neighbors. Because we know that most crime is *intra*racial.

What makes little sense is for whites to fear blacks. Those anxieties should be relegated to the dustbins of our ignominious history of slavery and overt racism, understood as lingering vestiges of those days. The black-as-criminal stereotype should be seen today not only for its illogic but also for the pain it causes racially profiled young people of color, for the barrage of indignities we heap upon them in response to our irrational fears, for the alienation we are causing to millions of Americans as we eye them with suspicion, set our police upon them, round them up and incarcerate them for minor offenses like marijuana possession that the majority of Americans of all races have committed at some point in our lives. It's time to call out this deep-seated stereotype for what it is: a toxic lie that stands in the way of our becoming the egalitarian, racially inclusive nation we aspire to be.

## And Now for the Good News

*"The challenge has been to tell what I view as the truth about racism without causing disabling despair."*

—HARVARD LAW PROFESSOR DERRICK BELL

THE MOUNTAIN OF evidence establishing the persistence of racial bias in America can lead to despondency, but let's not allow that, for there is also encouraging news giving us reason for hope. The overwhelming majority[198] of whites (75 percent) and blacks (90 percent) believe that the criminal justice system *should* operate in a race-neutral fashion and favor federal government intervention to ensure that whites and people of color receive equal treatment at the hands of police and the courts.

The people want fairness.

It's not 1930. Our explicit values no longer support racism, but instead favor equality, hands down. The solution is simply to bring our actions, conscious and unconscious, into alignment with our explicit values of nondiscrimination. The happy news is that this is eminently doable.

Implicit racial biases are in operation everywhere, not just the criminal justice system. In one study,[199] hundreds of doctors in Atlanta and Boston were given vignettes featuring black and white patients with the same medical history of coronary artery disease. The physicians reported no explicit preferences for black or white patients (like everyone in these studies, they profess that they are not racist), but their interpretations of the patients presented to them and their recommendations proved otherwise. White patients were more likely to be taken seriously and sent for treatment, and black patients were viewed as less cooperative, even though the doctors were presented with identical behaviors and symptoms. This only replicates many medical studies[200] finding that doctors spend more time with white patients, pay more attention to their symptoms, and refer them to specialists and treatment more often.

But doctors, like most of the rest of us, *want* to live up to their expressed egalitarian values. And it turns out that when they are made aware of unconscious biases, they are able to change their behavior. Once they learn the disappointing news that they are giving short shrift to their African-American patients, they learn to pause, consider, then override their implicit biases, treating black and white patients fairly.[201] With motivated professionals, education leads to better practices in relatively short order.

Similar work has been done with police officers. Police departments occasionally investigate Racists with a capital R in their ranks, eliminating them when found as the rare bad apples (see, e.g., the odious Mark Fuhrman in the O.J. Simpson murder case, who was caught on tape calling African Americans "niggers" forty-one times and admitting to targeting for arrest black males driving in cars with white women). While that's a good start, it's still stuck in the old "you're either racist or you're not" mindset. Newer thinking approaches the matter in an entirely different way, essentially conveying this message: "We all want to be fair to everyone regardless of skin color. But most of us would be surprised to learn that we carry around with us hidden racial stereotypes that affect some of our judgments and decisions about people we come into contact with on a daily basis. Even many African Americans harbor some racial biases against their own group. Many well-meaning people do. You're not a bad person if you, like most Americans, have these implicit racial biases. We want to make you aware of them and then help you do your job in a way that's fair to people of every color."

Police officers can then be trained to intentionally override their implicit biases. The Chicago Police Department, for example, has new recruits respond to mock calls from computer simulations. Most of the rookies initially react to the situations presented to them based on racial and gender stereotypes, focusing more on young men of color, for instance. (Implicit biases about gender, sexual orientation, and age are also present in most of us, according to legions of studies.) They are then surprised to see how unproductive reliance on those biases was, as the trainer reveals that they missed a woman with a gun and a male sex-crime victim, but they stopped a law-abiding young man of color.[202] The message: Well-meaning people—even you!—have implicit biases, and acting on them produces unjust and ineffective results. Awareness is the first step. Multiple follow-up training sessions then teach recruits how to override prejudices and conform their conduct to their values. The result: better policing.

Diversity in the workforce also minimizes implicit biases, for police officers and the rest of us. Not only do employers with multiracial staff get the benefit of a mix of people from different cultural backgrounds, but when people get to know one another as individuals rather than group members, stereotypes diminish. (This was one of the primary reasons courts used to order schools to desegregate.)

Jurors, too, can learn about racial biases and be instructed to override them, in a nonthreatening manner. Most jurors in American courtrooms are read overly broad instructions to the effect that they are not to decide cases based on emotions or prejudice. The Zimmerman jury was so instructed. But that is meaningless to most of us who consider ourselves nonracist, fair-minded people. Few think they *are* deciding a case based on stereotypes to begin with. Thus few panelists even consider that this instruction has anything to do with the racial issues in the case before them.

U.S. District Court Judge Mark Bennett[203] has improved upon this bland language, building on implicit bias research. He educates jurors about implicit racial biases before the trial even begins, during jury selection, and again at the end, just before they go to deliberate. Note how he brings up the subject in such a nonthreatening manner, even including himself in it:

Do not decide the case based on "implicit biases." As we discussed in jury selection, everyone, including me, has feelings, assumptions, perceptions, fears, and stereotypes, that is, "implicit biases," that we may not be aware of. These hidden thoughts can impact what we see and hear, how we remember what we see and hear, and how we make important decisions. Because you are making very important decisions in this case, I strongly encourage you to evaluate the evidence carefully and to resist jumping to conclusions based on personal likes or dislikes, generalizations, gut feelings, prejudices, sympathies, stereotypes, or biases. The law demands that you return a just verdict, based solely on the evidence, your individual evaluation of that evidence, your reason and common sense, and these instructions. Our system of justice is counting on you to render a fair decision based on the evidence, not on biases.

That too is an excellent start, but it fails to explicitly talk about race. If, as in the Zimmerman case, the two primary parties in the case are of different races, race must be discussed explicitly, fearlessly, and inclusively, and the judge is just the person to do it in jury instructions. Building upon Judge Bennett's instruction, the jury should be told:

Almost everyone, including me, has feelings, assumptions, perceptions, fears, and stereotypes, that is, "implicit biases," that we may not be aware of. Often these are racial biases, where we assume that one race is more likely to be aggressive, violent, or criminal, for example. These judgments, though common, are often inaccurate and have no place in my courtroom. Though we don't think we're prejudiced, many well-meaning people turn out to harbor stereotypical thinking about those of other races. In this case, please consider whether you, like most of us, have those hidden stereotypes, and if so, put them aside here. In this courtroom you are forbidden from making assumptions based upon the skin color of anyone in this case. You must decide this case only upon the evidence before you and ignore the fact that the two men in this case are of different racial backgrounds because skin color tells you nothing about their behavior that night. When in doubt, consider switching the races of the two men in your mind to see whether you're operating based on sub-conscious racial judgments.

Above all else, please insist that this case be decided based on the evidence and not on racial stereotypes.

Not talking about race has not worked for us, not in doctor's offices, police stations, nor in courtrooms. Not talking about race allows the fallacy to continue, that there are only two options, perfect colorblindness or overt racism. Yet we know that implicit bias works covertly, affecting our interpretation of ambiguous evidence (Who was threatening whom? Who was the initial aggressor? Whose fears were reasonable?) and that *not* talking about it allows it to continue to operate, unchecked. "Playing the race card" has acquired such a negative connotation that many good-faith conversations about race are swept up in the charge. But there's another path, which begins not with finger-pointing ("You're a racist!") but with the shared knowledge that we all still have room to evolve.

In the course of writing this book, I took the Implicit Bias Test[204] for myself. I grew up with friends of all races; I've demonstrated for racial equality in America and against apartheid in South Africa and in favor of women's and LGBT rights. As the daughter of an outspoken civil rights lawyer, I became a civil rights lawyer myself, representing many victims of invidious discrimination since 1986. I have spent a lifetime speaking, writing, and advocating against all forms of prejudice. My children are biracial. (Shall I go on with my antiracism credentials? Do you already know where this is going?) I was thus quite confident that I would not be one to harbor any kind of racial bias.

I cringe writing this, but the result of my test, out of the options "slight," "moderate," or "strong," was moderate racial bias. Certain this was a mistake—surely I was tired? Computer error? Something?—I immediately repeated the test, with the same result.

Profoundly disturbed, I considered the implications. That we all are truly steeped in a culture with so many negative, stereotypical images of people of color that we cannot avoid harboring racial biases. That this includes me, though I passionately believe that we are all children of God and deserving of fair, egalitarian treatment. That our nation's loathsome history of enslavement and segregation and violence toward African Americans in particular could only have been justified by a dehumanizing mindset so potent that it still lingers in our collective DNA. Including mine.

Still disturbed by my findings, I had several friends and family members take the test, and they too mostly tested "moderate" racial bias, including those who were nonwhite. This made me feel worse. It seemed none of us were immune to implicit racial bias. I remembered the fact that many African Americans test positive for implicit racial bias against their own race, something I had now experienced firsthand, the most heartbreaking outcome of all.

How does anyone contend with implicit racial bias? As the Twelve Steppers say, the first step is admitting you have a problem. Okay, it's there, in me too, I had to concede. I had to acknowledge the bias existed, as it does in so many of us, in order to confront it honestly. In an effort to override my subconscious prejudices, I brought to the forefront the great love and admiration I have for my dearest girlfriends of color; the kindness of one, the work ethic of another, her humor, her impressive intelligence. On the next retest, the result: no racial bias. (Remember, this is a test that cannot be tricked or cheated, as it measures response times in rapidly associating positive words with each race, then negative.)

I leave it to the psychologists to explain exactly how this mental process works. But I believe that seeing individuals rather than group members is a substantial part of it. As is simple awareness and a decision not to accept the presence of implicit biases.

The encouraging news is that reversing implicit biases can be done. And in the case of the criminal justice system—and our society broadly—it must be done. Becoming aware of the prejudices we don't want to admit even to ourselves is the painful, humbling part of the process, but after that, consciously overriding them is achievable. (And is probably a lifelong endeavor.)

The fix is thinking and talking about race in settings where racial bias affects outcomes. The research is clear that bringing implicit racial biases to the surface in nonaccusatory, sensitive, constructive conversations can cure them. Because most of us want to be fair—we want that deeply, passionately. We loathe these lingering stereotypes festering in us. White mock jurors, when notified about racial issues in a case, for example, are able to work with and overcome those issues and deliver fairer outcomes.

As the song "Everyone's a Little Bit Racist" from the Broadway musical *Avenue Q* satirized:

If we all could just admit
That we are racist a little bit,
Even though we all know
That it's wrong,
Maybe it would help us
Get along.

Sweeping problems under the rug has never worked. Pretending that race isn't a factor, as at the Zimmerman trial, when it plainly is, only exacerbates the injustice. Any discomfort we experience discovering our own implicit biases and talking about race is nothing compared to the pain of our fellow citizens being harassed, alienated, incarcerated, or even killed based on false assumptions. From our schools to our prisons, in our encounters with strangers on the street, coworkers, and friends, we are long overdue to complete the struggle toward equality and remove the constraints of racial bias once and for all.

# TEN

## *One Nation, Overgunned*

Y EMEN IS A tiny country on the Arabian Peninsula that is one
of the poorest, least developed places in the world. The average
Yemeni brings home roughly $100 in monthly wages. Corruption has
run rampant in its government and security forces for as long as anyone can remember. Tribal conflicts and outright civil war have marked
Yemen's modern history. Slavery was not abolished there until 1962.
The country ranks dead last on a list of 135 countries in the Global
Gender Gap report, as discrimination and violence against women are
common there, as are child brides forced into marriage as young as nine
years old. Genital mutilation is practiced on girls. Many Yemenis, especially women, are illiterate.[205]

In contrast, the United Kingdom is a flourishing, peaceful, egalitarian democracy. We share a common language and culture with the UK
(and obsess over their royalty). Most of our law derives from British
common law, and millions of Americans (including me) are of British
descent. As our closest ally, the British could count on our soldiers to
fight alongside them in World War I and World War II, and we relied on
their support in our recent wars in Afghanistan and Iraq.

It's therefore improbable that we would have more in common with
Yemen than we do with England in any sphere of public policy, but in one
important area, we do: gun ownership. The United States has more guns per
capita than any other country in the world. The only country that comes
close—and not all that close—is Yemen, with its frequent strife, separatist
insurgencies, and active branch of Al Qaeda. Americans count nearly one
firearm for every man, woman, and child (ninety per one hundred residents). Yemen is number two, at fifty-five guns per one hundred people.

Some Americans have substantially more than one weapon, maintain-
ing stockpiles that would generate alarm in any other developed country.
Four months after his acquittal, police searched George Zimmerman's
home after his second accusation of domestic violence in two months.
They discovered his entirely legal arsenal: a 12-gauge high-capacity shotgun (the weapon he was accused of pointing at his live-in girlfriend's
face), an AR-15 assault rifle, and three handguns—a Glock 19, an
Interarms .380-caliber, and a Taurus 9mm, according to a police warrant.[206] He also possessed one hundred rounds of ammunition. Since up
to that point, November 2013, none of the three domestic violence accusations made against him in eight years nor his murder trial had resulted
in a conviction, Zimmerman was free to arm himself to the teeth, and he
did. An Ohio gun advocacy group even sent him a $12,150.37 check[207]
after his murder trial acquittal to buy more firearms.

When Zimmerman's stockpile of weapons and ammunition was
revealed, his friend Frank Taaffe appeared on television to defend him. He
shrugged off the allegations, as well as any concerns about Zimmerman's
continued gun ownership. "Boys will have their toys," he said.

Surely law-abiding gun owners cringed alongside gun control advocates at such a flippant comment. Prior to Zimmerman's murder trial,

some in the gun rights community rallied around George Zimmerman, proclaiming him the poster boy for the right to own, conceal, and carry a gun, and to use it in self-defense. "If he hadn't, he'd be dead from that thug Trayvon Martin," one of them told me on Twitter. But after the trial, as he was twice accused of threatening the women closest to him with his firearms, the voices supporting Zimmerman's gun rights faded. Why? Because gun rights are one thing; firearms in the hands of an allegedly irresponsible hothead are quite another. While guns remain a contentious issue in America, surely we can all agree that gun owners must behave reasonably with their weapons.

Our current gun laws are a crazy patchwork of regulations, varying by state, county, and even by town. After the Zimmerman verdict, for example, the city of Sanford banned neighborhood watch volunteers from carrying guns. Everyone else, though, may still wear a concealed weapon, and in Florida, many do. More than 900,000 people are currently licensed to carry a secret gun in the state, and the process to obtain one is "pretty freakin' easy," according to a gun store staffer[208] there. A gun safety course can consist entirely of an applicant's walking to the back of the store, shooting a Glock at two targets, then filling out some paperwork. Florida's "shall issue"[209] concealed carry laws, like those in many states, widely authorize untrained citizens to walk around with guns hidden in their clothing. "Shall issue" means that local officials have no discretion. A citizen who wants a concealed weapon permit and who meets the minimal requirements (age, no criminal record) *shall* be granted one.

Our country is filled with Zimmermans—citizens with multiple legal firearms. It's also filled with those who have pointed their gun at another, pulled the trigger, and taken a life. We're not just number one in possessing guns, we're at the top of the list for using them for their intended purpose: to kill. If the argument that more guns reduce gun violence were correct, we'd have the fewest firearm homicides on the planet. Instead, America is first in firearm-related deaths in the developed world, according to the United Nations. Our gun murder rate is twenty times the average for all other developed countries. Imagine. Americans are not two or three times more likely—that would be disconcerting enough—but *twenty times* as likely to die from a bullet than citizens of other Organization for Economic Co-operation and Development (OECD) countries such as Australia or Canada, with whom we share many common values. (The countries with the fewest gun homicides, with numbers so tiny they chart at zero per 100,000, are Japan, South Korea, and Iceland, all of which have strict gun laws.)

If a foreign power came to the United States and killed eighty-five Americans, we'd declare war on them. But as eighty-five Americans die daily from preventable firearm murders, suicides, and accidents, we collectively shrug at our nation's own self-inflicted injuries.

In the UK, where guns must be licensed and are difficult to obtain legally, firearms are used rarely, even in murders: just one of thirteen homicides there is gun related. In the United States, guns are easily available nearly everywhere and are the most popular murder weapon, used in two out of three homicides. As a result, though the UK has triple the crime rate of the United States, it has fewer homicides. The British suffer from their crime rate but don't die from it. Why? Because guns are by far the quickest, most effective way to kill, and criminals in the UK can't get their hands on them.

Consider everyone's favorite rock-and-roll band, the Beatles. Singer-songwriter John Lennon was attacked by a crazed fan in gun-loving America in 1980. His assailant shot him in front of his Manhattan home with five hollow-point bullets, and Lennon died immediately. Lennon's former bandmate George Harrison was attacked by a crazed fan in gun-controlled England in 1999. His assailant broke into Harrison's home, where he stabbed him in the chest with a large knife. Harrison fought him off and survived. This is the life-or-death difference in outcome ordinary Brits and Americans experience daily, as Brits are far more likely to live through even vicious criminal assaults and continue on with their lives. In the United States, human life so often terminates from a moment of anger, from a stray bullet, from a hothead's or madman's quick decision to pull a trigger, with irreversible consequences.

The numbers in America are so high and impersonal they're difficult to fathom. Though our frequent, appalling mass shootings (do they even still shock us, really?) garner all the media attention, every day in America forty people die from the criminal use of guns, their stories not mentioned in the press at all. Hundreds of our children perish from gun accidents annually, most often at the hands of young boys who could not resist the magnetic temptation to touch, hold, point, and shoot the family firearm, which their parents did not lock away.[210]

One of those forty we do know, if only by his name, is Trayvon Martin. Yet notwithstanding all the public discussion of the case, and the widely broadcast and analyzed trial, he is better known as a shooting victim than a flesh-and-blood young man. In the courtroom, the state attorneys failed to humanize him, as we've seen, calling him "the victim." Who was he? Inspired by his uncle Ronald Fulton, a former Navy aviation mechanic who is quadriplegic, Trayvon was fascinated by airplanes and aspired to a future in aviation.[211] Trayvon was part of a close-knit family, so close that he fed and cared for his uncle after his car accident and held his playing cards for him at card parties. Trayvon chose to express his connection to family members past and present on his clothing and even on his skin. At the time he was shot, on his hoodie was a pinned-on button bearing a picture of his cousin, Cory Johnson, who died in 2008 at age thirty-six. Travyon had tattoos of his mother's name, Sybrina, as well as his grandmother's and great-grandmother's names. The rest is known only to his family and friends, as they struggle to hold on to memories of this high school junior who would never go to a senior prom, graduate from high school, go to college, marry, be a father, have a career, or attend family events. As it is for Trayvon, so it is for the forty Americans killed yesterday, today, and tomorrow by preventable firearm homicides. They recede into our history, too often unacknowledged, the details of their lives blurring with the passage of time, remembered by the criminal justice system, if at all, simply as another shooting victim. We can't possibly take in the hopes and dreams of the lives lost daily, hourly, the grief of their families, the lives that could have been, if only we'd decided to rein in our guns.

Homicides are one facet of America's sad gun deaths; the other is gun suicides. The states with the highest rates of gun ownership are also the states with the most suicides, as having a gun in one's home substantially increases the risk that someone will take his own life in that home. Though other means may be used for suicide, guns are by far the most lethal method. Suicidal acts with guns are fatal 85 percent of the time. Suicide attempts with pills kill in just 2 percent of cases.[212] Many people who unsuccessfully attempt suicide go on to lead productive lives.

And that's only the deaths. For every person dead from a bullet, four more are injured, most commonly from gunfire to the eyes, face, or abdomen. Nonfatal gunshot wounds often cause severe, lifelong injuries such as major disfigurement and permanent disability.

After horrific mass shootings in their countries, most other developed nations passed strict gun control, registration or tracking legislation, which for the most part solved the problem of gun violence. Occasionally one hears of a mass shooting in, say, Norway or France, but overall their citizens are at far lower risk of being slaughtered in gunfire than Americans. American children die from shooting incidents eleven times as often as children in other high-income countries. Our rural children are shot as often as our urban children—country kids most often by firearm accidents, city kids from gun homicides. Firearms are one of the leading causes of accidental death for American children and teenagers. Virtually every other developed country has discovered that these deaths are preventable and has passed gun laws to protect their children. We have not.

The cost, mostly to taxpayers, of medical treatment, criminal justice proceedings, security precautions, and reductions in quality of life due to sky-high American gun violence has been estimated at $100 billion annually.[213]

Is there hope for tightening America's gun laws? After twenty first graders and six female staffers were executed at Sandy Hook Elementary School in December 2012 by a mentally ill young man armed with a semi-automatic weapon, the popular AR-15 Bushmaster rifle, a public outcry pushed for more gun regulation. President Obama advocated expanded background checks for gun buyers, reinstating the assault weapons ban that had expired in 2004, bans on high-capacity magazines, and funding for research into gun violence. Congress briefly considered and then rejected all of these reforms. To many who view America's gun violence problem as out of control, this was cause for despair.

With three hundred million guns in America, and sales surging, it's unrealistic to expect America to ban guns outright, like Japan, which has only about ten gun homicides per year to our 12,000. Neither President Obama nor any other serious advocate has proposed a ban. But there remain positive signs that sensible gun reforms restricting ownership to law-abiding adults of sound mind, and tightening up the safety, handling, and licensing requirements, can save lives and prevent injury. To get there, let's dispel some commonly held myths about America and guns.

## GUN MYTH #1: THE SECOND AMENDMENT PROHIBITS ANY RESTRICTIONS ON GUN RIGHTS.

WHAT ABOUT THE Second Amendment to the U.S. Constitution? Does it prevent the state or federal government from enacting gun laws? Don't Americans have the right to "bear arms"?

Short answer: Don't fall for the hype about the Second Amendment. The landmark 2008 U.S. Supreme Court decision, *Heller v. District of Columbia*, did uphold the Second Amendment right of Americans to own guns in our homes but the Supreme Court also took pains to carve out many exceptions allowing for reasonable restrictions on that right. This is true of our constitutional rights generally—they are not absolute. We must all be *reasonable*. Just as we have the First Amendment right of free speech, one may not yell fire in a crowded theater, nor threaten anyone, nor disturb the peace, nor protest in a prohibited area, nor violate a copyright, nor defame nor sexually harass a coworker—many restrictions on speech are legally recognized. Similarly, in the over eight hundred Second Amendment cases challenging gun laws in the United States since the *Heller* case was decided, 96 percent of the firearm regulations were left standing. Laws that have been upheld include prohibiting felons and those committing domestic violence misdemeanors from owning guns—for life; restrictions on machine guns and assault weapons; laws requiring gun registration; laws forbidding guns in national parks and publicly owned places; and laws banning firearm possession by parents delinquent in child support payments.[214]

To be clear: it's not the courts, nor the Second Amendment, that keep us from reforming the law to minimize gun violence. "We made it clear in *Heller* that our holding did not cast doubt" on many forms of gun control, the Supreme Court said in a follow-up 2010 gun case. "We repeat those assurances here."[215] A generation ago, conservative Supreme Court Chief Justice Warren Burger put it more strongly: "The Second Amendment has been the subject of one of the greatest pieces of fraud, repeat the word 'fraud,' on the American public by special interest groups that I have ever seen in my lifetime."

## GUN MYTH #2: THE GUN LOBBY IS ALL POWERFUL.

SECOND, WHILE MANY view the nation's leading gun lobby, the National Rifle Association, as invincible, this is far from the truth. The NRA has had many successes, but the perception of its strength is overblown. A Sunlight Foundation report reveals that the NRA had the worst return on investment of all major political contributors in the 2012 election. Its clout is nowhere near the public perception of it as an all-powerful force in American politics. Thousands of gun regulations have been passed in cities, states, and the nation over the objections of the gun lobby, and they continue to be passed. And all those court challenges to firearms restrictions since *Heller*? They were overwhelmingly lost by the gun rights side of the cases, many of which were funded by the gun lobby.

## GUN MYTH #3: AMERICANS OPPOSE ANY GUN REGULATIONS.

IT IS TRUE that the United States is not going to eliminate firearms, like Japan or England, but it is equally true that the public supports laws requiring gun owners to be responsible with their weapons, and this is fertile ground for tightening up our gun laws. A large well of support exists for the idea that law-abiding people can own handguns and rifles, but subject to licensing, registration, and periodic safety training. For example, nine out of ten Americans say yes to universal background checks, including three of four NRA members. Currently only those buying from licensed dealers—60 percent—undergo the check, leaving a huge loophole for criminals to buy guns. Gang members, who are major weapons users in the United States, go to unregulated gun shows, buy a bunch of guns, and hand them out to their members. Requiring background checks across the board would make this more difficult. Other reasonable measures that would save lives is a loophole-free assault weapon ban and prohibition on large ammunition clips that would prevent troubled young men like the Sandy Hook Elementary School shooter from taking twenty-six lives so swiftly. Tucson, Arizona, shooter Jared Loughner, who injured Congresswoman Gabby Giffords and killed six others, was stopped by a sixty-one-year-old woman who pounced on him and grabbed the magazine of his Glock as he paused to reload. This ended the carnage. Bullets built to shatter in the body for maximum damage should be prohibited. And requiring a real waiting period before gun purchases would reduce spur-of-the-moment, hot-tempered killings and suicides because studies show that when people have to wait at least a week, many change their minds and commit no acts of violence.

At a minimum, gun owners should be required to demonstrate proficient safety skills on a recurring basis in order to continue to own these dangerous, lethal devices. We must undergo training and testing, updated every few years, to gain a license to drive a car. Operate a vehicle irresponsibly, and that license is revoked because we want to reduce vehicular homicides. The same should be true for gun ownership. And unlike firearms, cars have a benevolent primary use: transportation. Use a car as intended and you get to work smoothly. Use a gun as intended and you take a life.

Gun rights advocates such as NRA Executive Vice President Wayne LaPierre point to countries like Switzerland and Israel as models for the proposition that high levels of gun ownership can coexist with low homicide rates. First, those countries have a lot of guns compared only to other first-world countries, not compared to the United States. Israel has one-thirteenth the gun possession rate of America, a tiny fraction. Even fewer Israelis would own guns were it not for the hundreds of thousands possessing firearms as part of their mandatory military service. Forty percent of gun applicants are rejected in Israel, the highest rejection rate in the Western world. Though Israel is marked by frequent acts of terrorism against it, for the most part Israelis leave defense to the security professionals.

But Switzerland and Israel do allow more gun ownership than other Western nations (outside the United States), and they have little gun violence. How do they do it? They require licensing, training, and permits for those who want to keep firearms, and annual (or even more frequent) permit renewals to be sure that the reasons for gun ownership remain valid. Safety training, permits, and licensing will not reduce gun deaths to zero, but they do make a difference.

No single measure will stop all the heartbreaking gun deaths in America. But with our high number of gunfire victims and lax gun laws, we can save many lives by requiring gun owners to behave like grown-ups with their deadly weapons. If we reduced American gun violence by just one homicide per day, we'd save the equivalent number of lives as were lost in the Sandy Hook Elementary School slaughter every month.

A generation ago, antismoking activists were told they could never prevail against Big Tobacco, one of the wealthiest industries in the world, which had used its power to beat back many proposals to limit cigarette smoking in public places. But Americans sick of cancer deaths persevered and now have largely prevailed in that fight, passing nationwide antismoking ordinances, levying hefty taxes on cigarettes, and forcing the industry to pay for antismoking educational campaigns. Cigarettes remain legal but carefully regulated, and as a result, millions of lives have been saved and improved. Just as decreasing smoking decreases cancer deaths, reducing guns reduces gun violence. Sure, cancer from other sources remains, and some killers will find other ways to kill. But cutting down on the use of the most efficient death delivery systems necessarily means fewer devastated crime-victim families, fewer people caged in our overcrowded prisons, and reduced costs to taxpayers for police, the criminal justice system, hospital emergency rooms, and medical care.

While some states and municipalities regulate guns, nationwide our gun laws are more accurately a state of lawlessness. After many horrific school shootings—twenty-six more in the year after Sandy Hook—we learned that the shooters obtained their firearms legally. Our inaction, our failure to fill the legal void by restricting even high-powered automatic weapons, enables the next madman to arm himself and prevents law enforcement from stopping him until after he has killed.

Our gun laws have veered back and forth over our nation's short history. Concealed carry, for example, was reviled in the nineteenth century. As Adam Winkler points out in his book *Gunfight*,[216] an Alabama court once called the secret carrying of weapons an "evil practice," and a Louisiana court wrote that concealed carry created a "tendency to secret advantages and unmanly associations." By 1907, nearly all states had laws prohibiting the carrying of concealed weapons. In the first decade of the twenty-first century, concealed carry is permitted in all fifty states.

Our gun laws can be rewritten as often as we like until we get it right. Where there is lawlessness, order can be imposed. Sybrina Fulton implored us to use her family's tragedy to take action to prevent others from becoming grieving mothers, as do many mothers of American children dead from gun violence. We don't have to guess or even debate whether gun restrictions would save lives: the records in dozens of other advanced countries spanning decades proves they do. Our tears and condolences in response to the daily gunfire and the periodic incidents of mass carnage in schools, malls, and workplaces are not enough when we know what needs to be done and fail to comport ourselves like other civilized nations.

# ELEVEN

## *Bring It On, Make My Day, Stand Your Ground*

W HEN EXACTLY DID we stop prioritizing saving human lives?
I'm pegging it to 2005.

Before that year, the number of guns and gun deaths in America was
high, to be sure. But penalties for gun violence were also high, placing
an elevated level of personal responsibility on firearms owners. It was
almost a setup: guns were easily available, but one misstep—a negligent
shooting, even simply brandishing a gun or firing a warning shot in the
air—could have dire consequences. In most states a crime committed
with a firearm warranted a "gun enhancement," meaning the perpetrator got extra years tacked onto his sentence for introducing a gun in
the course of a crime. California's "10-20-life" law, for example, adds
ten years to the underlying felony sentence when a gun is used in the
crime; twenty years if the gun was fired; and twenty-five years to life
if a gun user kills or seriously injures his or her victim with that gun.
These sentences are on top of the sentence required for the underlying
crime, such as robbery. "Use a Gun and You're Done,"[217] as the law is
nicknamed, is intended to deter criminals from bringing deadly weapons
to their encounters in the first place. The idea behind gun enhancements
is to allow law-abiding Americans to own guns while at the same time

dealing harshly with those who commit crimes with them. Because carrying guns into volatile situations increases the likelihood of carnage, we hope (though evidence for it is scant) that catchy phrases and long prison sentences will motivate criminals to leave their firearms at home. Why? *Because we want to save the lives of our citizens. Because human life is paramount.*

Prior to 2005, a standard element of self-defense law also was intended to save lives: the requirement of retreat. I learned this as a skill in Krav Maga, a no-nonsense, practical martial arts class, years ago. The first rule of self-defense, the hulking, testosterone-charged Israeli commando taught us, was the "Nike defense." If an attacker came at us, our first move, drilled into us in training exercises, was to quickly scan the area for an escape route. If one was available, we were to run like hell. Only if confined, or restrained, or locked in a room, were we to fight back. We learned the effective, even brutal fighting techniques that could neutralize or kill an assailant, but the most important lesson was restraint, the learned reflex to look for a way out first before doing any harm. Training fighters to run away from a threat may be unsatisfying to macho impulses, but more people wake up breathing the next day. Also, conveniently, this lesson dovetailed with the law at the time, which permitted the use of force in self-defense only where withdrawal from the altercation was not possible. In short, the law, and sensible self-defense training, required *de-escalation*. Flight, not fight.

To be honest, over the years Americans have never been entirely comfortable with the requirement of retreat, nor was it mandatory in every situation even prior to 2005. The Castle Doctrine, in effect in most states nationwide since the beginning of our republic, allows inhabitants of a residence to shoot to kill intruders in their home when a threat is perceived, even if withdrawal is possible. When the sanctity of our home is violated, we are not required to run out the back door, hop a fence, and scurry off, even if that would save more human lives. A line was drawn around the perimeter of our property. "A man's home is his castle," (as is a woman's) and Judge Benjamin N. Cardozo[218] said of it a century ago:

> If assailed there, he may stand his ground, and resist the attack. He is under no duty to take to the fields and the highways, a fugitive from his own home . . . Flight is for sanctuary and shelter, and shelter if not sanctuary, is in the home.

A home is where one runs *to*, not *from*. Being a *fugitive, taking to the fields and highways*, tail between one's trembling legs—the image is unseemly, undignified. Most of us would probably embrace the Castle Doctrine because the idea of forcing a homeowner to run away, or stand by and not defend her own home, just feels alien and wrong.

That is, until you consider the real-life consequences of allowing citizens the unrestricted right to shoot someone on their property.

Yoshihiro Hattori[219] was a sixteen-year-old Japanese exchange student staying with a family in Baton Rouge, Louisiana, in 1992. He loved American culture, jazz, and dancing. One night in October he was off to a Halloween party with his homestay teenaged "brother," Webb Haymaker. Yoshi, as his family called him, was dressed for the Halloween party in a white tuxedo and gaudy jewelry as the John Travolta character from the movie *Saturday Night Fever*. Webb confused the address, and they wound up at the wrong house, though it had Halloween decorations and lights on inside. The boys rang the doorbell and announced that they were there for the party. When there was no answer, they headed back to their car. Inside the home, meanwhile, Bonnie Peairs had looked through the window, seen the boys, and screamed for her husband to get his gun. Rodney Peairs quickly emerged from his home with his .44-caliber Magnum revolver and yelled "freeze."

Hailing from a country with strict gun control laws, Yoshi had no familiarity with firearms whatsoever. "Freeze" was a word that Yoshi, with very limited English skills, probably did not understand. He may have thought the gun was a Halloween prop. When he continued to move and wave his arms, perhaps mimicking Travolta's famous disco dancing moves, Rodney Peairs pulled the trigger, killing him.

The jury deliberated just three hours. Peairs was acquitted under Louisiana's version of the Castle Doctrine, called the "shoot the burglar" law there. The defense depicted Peairs as a down-home, regular guy who enjoyed "sugar on his grits," just as they did. His fears were their fears. "In your house, if you want to do it, you have the legal right to answer everybody that comes to your door with a gun," the defense attorney had argued in closing argument, a correct statement of the law. "A man's home is his castle," one dismissed potential juror had said, questioning why the case had even gone to trial.[220]

Yoshi was not a burglar. He never entered the Peairs home. He had no criminal intent whatsoever. There was nothing reasonable about the Peairs' fear. Nevertheless, the Castle Doctrine protected Rodney Peairs, to the great shock of Yoshi's family, which has spent the last two decades fighting unsuccessfully for stricter American gun control laws. In Yoshi's name, they've established a peace park and a foundation[221] that brings American students abroad to experience virtually gun-free Japan.

While the concept of protecting one's own home seems sensible, the death of young Yoshi is a reminder that answering the door with a loaded firearm increases the chance of accidental shootings based on mistaken identity, misunderstandings, or wrongheaded suspicions. And even inside one's home, tragic mistakes can occur from gunfire at intruders. In Florida, a ten-year-old and a fourteen-year-old boy trespassed onto a property with several trailer homes, attracted by piles of junk and old parade floats as their father worked at a nearby warehouse. Discovering some piles of wood, they knocked on the doors of the trailers to ask permission to take the wood to build a fort in a nearby forest. Finding the door to one home slightly ajar, they entered. Within seconds, the elderly homeowner, seated inside, picked up his gun and shot and killed fourteen-year-old Eric Brooks. A Florida appellate court said that the resident's fear that the boys were burglars was enough for him to shoot to kill in his own home, and reversed his conviction.[222] Both boys were unarmed.

Notwithstanding tragic outcomes like these, the Castle Doctrine, for the most part, is bedrock American law. Its roots go all the way back to before the founding of the United States, to English common law, even the Old Testament: "If a thief is caught breaking in at night and is struck a fatal blow, the defender is not guilty of bloodshed." (Exodus 22:2). The Castle Doctrine is here to stay. So powerful is the notion that a stranger entering our home is inherently a dangerous threat that we essentially allow homeowners to shoot first and ask questions later. We are willing to accept tragic accidents like these without any calls to change the law.

From the standpoint of the Japanese, or the parents of children who have been shot, the Castle Doctrine is overly expansive in protecting the rights of shooters. It forgives poor judgment, even when the bloodshed that results is the bloodshed of children. So why on earth would anyone want to expand it further?

But that's precisely what Florida, and then many other American states, did. In 2005, unsatisfied with these broad protections for shooters inside their homes, Florida enlarged the right to use deadly force, without a duty to retreat, to any situation where a person believed she was in grave danger in a place she was lawfully entitled to be present. On the street. In a park, or a car, or an office. Other states quickly followed suit. Twenty-seven states[223] now have some form of Stand Your Ground laws, allowing citizens to shoot (or stab, or fight—but mostly shoot) their way out of threatening situations, rather than remove themselves from them.

Stand Your Ground is deeply appealing to many Americans steeped in a culture of sports, war, adventure movies, and violent video games. In our way of thinking, ceding ground in football, surrendering territory on the battlefield, and running away from danger are for losers. Few of us are Mennonites, or Quakers, or pacifists who see true strength in refusing to be baited into violence. Standing one's ground has a ring of bravery and virility, of film lines that cause audiences to erupt in applause: *bring it on,* or *make my day,* or *say hello to my little friend* (as Scarface pulls out his M-16). A popular T-shirt and bumper sticker after 9/11 featured an American flag with the words, "These colors don't run," emphasizing that we are a people who stay put and fight, though no one had suggested we retreat from where we were attacked—America. Each part of Stand Your Ground resonates with these values: *stand*—plant your feet, don't run like a coward; *your*—that turf belongs to you, fight for it!; *ground*—don't lose your position, physically or in the argument. No surrender. Man up. Don't give 'em an inch.

Stand Your Ground.

Like popular culture, Stand Your Ground focuses on who is standing, not who has fallen. In tough-guy movies or video games, gun violence is an exhilarating way to obtain satisfying retribution against a two-dimensional bad guy. The next scene always features the triumphant shooter, not the impact of the shooting death. Messy real-world consequences would only muck up the story line: the life extinguished, the grieving family; the orphaned children scarred for life; the searing loss of a beloved spouse or friend; the hospital, funeral, and burial expenses; the loss of an income earner, reducing a family to homelessness. Twenty years later, Webb Haymaker still thinks of his teenaged friend often, trying to make sense of the trauma he endured witnessing Yoshi's death. "It's hard to fully comprehend what it means for someone to die when they're sixteen years old," he said[224] recently.

With the broad protections of the Castle Doctrine, why was Stand Your Ground needed? Was there a rash of people who'd peacefully extricated themselves from threatening situations on the street and later regretted it, thinking, "If only I'd stayed put and killed that guy. Unfortunately, I was well versed in the law and knew that would not comply with the rules regarding self-defense. So now I must go to my legislator and get a bill moving so that next time I'm in a perilous encounter, it can end with satisfying bloodshed"? No, that never happened.

According to a symposium[225] of prosecutors, law enforcement, government officials, public health advocates, and academics assembled from a dozen states by the National Association of District Attorneys, who exhaustively reviewed the history and status of nationwide Stand Your Ground laws, the impetus started with 9/11. One of the repercussions of the worst terrorist acts on American soil was increased fear—fear of sudden attacks by extremists, fear of crime, fear that law enforcement would not necessarily be able to respond quickly enough if another 9/11 happened. That generalized anxiety morphed into advocacy for the right of citizens to be armed and ready to protect themselves at any time from threats foreign and domestic, without worry about criminal prosecution. Since 9/11, the gun rights lobby expanded the rights of citizens to own guns, even formerly banned assault weapons, and to keep them not just in the home but holstered on the body as one goes about one's business. And hand in hand with those expansive gun rights went Stand Your Ground laws, which increase the opportunities for citizens to not just own but to *use* those guns.

Of course, a civilian with a handgun, or ten or a hundred or a million civilians with handguns, or even high-powered rifles or automatic weapons, would have been entirely ineffective against airplanes being used as missiles, unless those armed citizens were passengers on the 9/11 planes. Even the NRA does not advocate arming air travelers. But the apprehension remained, and it motivated a variety of ill-advised legislation, like the Patriot Act, which restricted civil liberties and allowed for previously illegal detentions, wiretaps, eavesdropping, and searches (several portions of the law have been struck down as unconstitutional), and Stand Your Ground laws.

Fast-forward to 2012. A month after Trayvon Martin was killed, the police were saying they could not arrest Zimmerman due to Florida's Stand Your Ground law, and the public was in an uproar. Florida Governor Rick Scott convened a nineteen-member Citizen Safety and Protection[226] task force to review the law. After its review, the bipartisan task force recommended no change in the law and concluded, "Regardless of citizenship status, (people) have a right to feel safe and secure in our state. To that end, all persons have a fundamental right to stand their ground and defend themselves from attack with proportionate force in every place they have a lawful right to be and are conducting themselves in a lawful manner."

And that, ultimately, is what Stand Your Ground is all about. That *feeling* of safety, that gut sense that we all have a *fundamental right* (so fundamental that until a few years ago, no one had even thought of it) to defend ourselves with force, even if it's not really necessary, even when walking away would prevent injury, mayhem, or death. Even if that *feeling* of safety, of the *rightness* of meeting violence with more violence, demonstrably results in more injuries and deaths, and more killers walking the streets, immunized, armed, and ready for the next altercation. To supporters it just feels right, and that's good enough.

The second justification for Stand Your Ground laws was that they were seen to go hand in hand with gun rights. In Florida, by 2005 the NRA had already persuaded the legislature to enact a sweeping set of gun rights laws,[227] granting access to firearms to most citizens over the age of twenty-one. Floridians may purchase guns without any licensing or registration. For the gun lobby, Stand Your Ground was the next logical step. Why allow so many people to carry guns if they can't fire them?

Stand Your Ground laws have typically been enacted over the strenuous objections of law enforcement, who understood that loosening self-defense rules leads to more shootings and less accountability. In other words, lawlessness. And the professionals on the ground were right. Stand Your Ground states have seen a doubling of justifiable homicides—killings where the shooter has no legal responsibility and usually is not even charged with a crime at all. In Florida, justifiable homicides doubled within two years after its Stand Your Ground law was passed. By 2011, the numbers tripled.[228] Justifiable homicides remained flat or decreased in states without the law. This reflected the nationwide trend, as justifiable homicides by civilians using firearms doubled in states with Stand Your Ground laws between 2005 and 2010,[229] while falling or remaining about the same in states lacking them.

Proponents argued that more "good people with guns" on the streets would reduce violence, as criminals would know they could be stopped by any citizen at any time. Yet the reality is that since 2005, Florida's Stand Your Ground law has allowed killers to go free where the facts of the case previously would have made that unthinkable. The *Tampa Bay Times* conducted a thorough examination of seven years of criminal cases where defendants claimed they should not be prosecuted due to their new Stand Your Ground rights. The results showed that Florida prosecutors, judges, and juries had exonerated killers[230] whose victims were in retreat and were shot in the back, killers who picked fights with their victims, and killers who left the scene of an altercation to get a gun and then returned with it to fire the fatal shots. One Florida judge,[231] Terry P. Lewis, complained that Stand Your Ground could be used to exonerate everyone in a Wild West–style shootout on the street, as they could all claim they were reacting to the others, with no duty to retreat. He said he had no choice but to grant immunity from prosecution to two gang members who had fired an AK-47 assault rifle that killed a fifteen-year-old boy.

As with so much else in our criminal justice system, African Americans fare worse, much worse, under Stand Your Ground. According to a study by the Urban Institute's Justice Policy Center, in Stand Your Ground states, whites who kill blacks are 354 percent more likely to be found justified in their killings. Similar studies[232] have also found that those who shoot black victims are far more likely to be exonerated than those who shoot members of other races. As we've seen, in considerations of whether a victim was threatening, African Americans are judged more harshly, their behavior perceived as aggressive where the identical behavior from a white person is not. Those subjective determinations are constantly at play in Stand Your Ground cases, often with only the word of the shooter to go on after the smoke has cleared. In other words, if you're going to shoot someone on the street and claim self-defense, it's a huge advantage to be white. Whites who shoot blacks are the most likely of all to be acquitted (actually, they are unlikely to even be charged).

Stand Your Ground laws immunize the shooter not just from criminal prosecution, but also from civil suits for financial compensation for the victim's next of kin. Stunningly, this is broader than the rights of the police, who are immune from neither prosecution nor lawsuits when they injure or kill citizens in the line of duty.

America's new round of Stand Your Ground laws run entirely in the wrong direction, encouraging more violence, protecting shooters from responsibility for their decisions to take lives, amplifying the lack of accountability when whites shoot blacks. The old thinking was that gun deaths on our streets were a social evil that the law should make every effort to deter. The new thinking: we'll tolerate more firearm fatalities in order to *feel better* about crime. Stand Your Ground laws are more appropriately called Shoot First Laws (as the Brady Center to Prevent Gun Violence calls them) because they bestow such powerful legal advantages on whoever shoots first in an altercation. The preservation of human life is no longer our paramount concern.

THE STAND YOUR Ground defense was officially not part of the Zimmerman murder trial, until it was. That is, shortly before the trial, the defense announced[233] that it would not invoke Zimmerman's rights under the law because his account was that he was restrained at the time he fired the shot, unable to escape. Retreat was impossible, according to Zimmerman's story, and hence the law did not apply to the facts of the case. During the trial, neither side argued that the Stand Your Ground law applied or didn't apply—it was a nonissue.

But then a curious thing happened. The language crept into the jury instructions. On page twelve of all the legalese, Judge Nelson included this sentence:

> If George Zimmerman was not engaged in an unlawful activity and was attacked in any place where he had a right to be, he had no duty to retreat and had the right to stand his ground and meet force with force, including deadly force if he reasonably believed that it was necessary to do so to prevent death or great bodily harm . . .

And Stand Your Ground was part of the jurors' decision making as well. Juror B37 said that Stand Your Ground was part of the law the jury considered in reaching its verdict. "The law became very confusing. It became very confusing," she told Anderson Cooper on CNN. "We had stuff thrown at us. We had the second-degree murder charge, the manslaughter charge, then we had self-defense, Stand Your Ground."[234] Later in the interview she said that Zimmerman was acquitted "because of the heat of the moment and the Stand Your Ground." ("Heat of the moment" was also not a defense in the case.)

How is it possible both that the defense disavowed Stand Your Ground and that the judge and jury included it? For the judge's part, she simply used the standard Florida self-defense instruction, which since 2005 includes Stand Your Ground language, whether the defendant invokes it or not. As to the jury, the answer is murkier. Stand Your Ground had been part of the public discussion in Florida, and especially the media coverage of the Trayvon Martin shooting. Floridians knew that they had the right to stand their ground and fight, even if none of the lawyers argued that as a defense in the courtroom. At any rate, there it was in that confusing booklet they took into the jury room.

In the Trayvon Martin case and in many cases, Stand Your Ground has become a proxy, shorthand for the concept that altercations can turn deadly without any legal accountability. In Stand Your Ground states, juries no longer have to parse the issue of whether there was a reasonable escape route, whether a life could have been saved by a citizen de-escalating a volatile situation. Diplomacy and nonviolence are no longer valued, or required. More broadly, Stand Your Ground is understood as a rule allowing citizens to pull out a gun and shoot in any fight, even if that's not the law.

The solution lies in returning to our shared value that the preservation of human life must be paramount, and the recognition that laws that do not facilitate that goal do not serve us. We cannot accept more killings, more street deaths, more shooters walking free, emboldened for the next time by the law that's got their back. "Feeling better" is an insufficient justification for laws that increase deaths, and how on earth do we allow ourselves to feel better about more violence anyway?

Labor organizer Cesar Chavez said, "In some cases nonviolence requires more militancy than violence." In a culture that does not find restraint sexy, we must nevertheless demand that everyone behave like adults in hostile confrontations, and we must punish those who cannot.

We must return to our law's strict insistence upon nonviolence whenever humanly possible. Shooters should know that their actions will be carefully scrutinized by authorities. The repeal of Stand Your Ground would return us to that civilized rule of law.

# CONCLUSION

## *Aligning Our Actions With Our Core Values*

*"Things don't happen. Things are made to happen."*

—PRESIDENT JOHN F. KENNEDY

WIDESPREAD IMPLICIT RACIAL bias, the enthusiasm for unrestricted gun ownership, and expansive Stand Your Ground laws combine to enable the continued shootings of African-American young people who are taking out the trash, knocking on a door, or stopping at a gas station. It's no longer just the police who are accused of racial profiling. A prolifically armed citizenry now stands ready to back up its suspicions with gunfire.

Individually, each of these three problems causes enormous harm. Unreasonable fears of "blacks as criminals" underlie the rampant discriminatory treatment of African Americans in our criminal justice—*justice*—system, the one place where fairness should be paramount. Even in our schools, where we should be educating children and correcting their immature mistakes, giving them skills for success, we push out and lock out black kids punitively, jacking up their odds of failure, cycling another generation into poverty. The fact that we have fifty million more guns than cars in the United States, with next to no requirements that gun owners be qualified to possess them, means that day after day, those firearms are used carelessly to snuff out the lives of Americans of all races and ages, as the rest of the civilized world looks on with horror. And Stand Your Ground laws not only embolden gun owners to use their weapons even when they could have ended the incident peacefully, they then immunize and exonerate killers, bestowing on them a feeling of impregnability for the next time. (After his acquittal, George Zimmerman's wife Shellie said he felt "invincible." Why wouldn't he?) No longer required to call the police, citizens become the law themselves, deciding based on a hot stew of suspicions and fears and snap judgments, finger on the trigger, that shooting is the best option. Afterward, when the deceased turns out to be unarmed and it was all a misunderstanding, no remedy follows. No justice for the victim's family. Not even compensation.

We have veered away from our core values. Thomas Jefferson wrote in the Declaration of Independence: "We hold these truths to be self-evident, that all men are created equal, that they are endowed by their Creator with certain unalienable Rights, that among these are Life, Liberty, and the pursuit of Happiness." When those lofty words were written, they could not have been further from reality. They expressed where the founders saw us going, not where we were at the time. Equality of all persons was hardly self-evident in the slave days of the eighteenth century, when only property-owning white men had any real legal rights. Jefferson's words were a promise, filled with unrealized potential, a check waiting to be cashed. A century later, after the mass carnage of the Civil War ended slavery, the Fourteenth Amendment was passed, guaranteeing each citizen the constitutional right to "equal protection of the laws." Those words too were more hope than truth, as segregation and the legally enforced discrimination of the Jim Crow era continued for another century still. The twentieth century saw the aspirational 1954 landmark ruling in *Brown v. Board of Education*, in which the U.S. Supreme Court declared public education as "a right which must be made available on equal terms," and passage of the groundbreaking 1964 Civil Rights Act barring job and housing discrimination based on race (and other factors), legal advances we could all feel good about, though glaring disparities in education, employment, and housing continue in earnest to the present day. And meanwhile, rampant racial inequality desecrates our criminal justice system, wholly unchecked by the law.

Our ancestors committed radical, brave acts by writing equality into our legal documents, in times when verbalizing support for nondiscrimination stood in opposition to much of the mainstream thinking of the day. Today, voicing opposition to racism no longer requires courage because our common values have shifted to a core belief in equal opportunity. What's required now, as before, is putting those words into action. Each generation has had to struggle to move us closer toward our often-expressed national value of equality, to bring those principles from our founding documents, our constitution, and laws into our streets, workplaces, schools, and homes. And among our human rights to life, liberty, and the pursuit of happiness, the protection of life comes first. When our laws fail to stop or even punish the squandering of human life, they run counter to that universal human right. They cry out for reform.

As Martin Luther King, Jr. said in his last speech, "All we say to America is be true to what you said on paper."[235] Our culture and laws are and should be ever evolving, as we remember to push forward, to align our institutions and rules to the values we share. The tragedy of

the senseless death of Trayvon Martin and the criminal justice system's
ineffective trial of his killer can and should wake us up to the glaring
errors we created and that we can reform because we do value life, and
we despise racism and violence.

DOWN IN DAYTONA Beach, Florida, Pastor Ron Durham talked to me
about the confusion of not knowing who among his neighbors might
racially profile members of his congregation or even him. "I could walk
out of my church today and walk to the beach side in blue jeans and
sneakers, and I wouldn't get too far before someone in the million-dollar
homes on the ocean said someone suspicious is walking in my community."[236] America is not fully liberated so long as we hold these biases
based on skin color, he said. Last year it was Trayvon Martin who was
considered criminal, followed and shot dead by a killer who now walks
free. This year it could be him, and he knows it.

One thing about George Wallace, he added slyly, was "at least you
knew where you stood." As Governor of Alabama, Wallace in 1963
stood on the spot where Jefferson Davis had been sworn in as president
of the Confederate States of America and proclaimed, "Segregation now,
segregation tomorrow, and segregation forever."[237] He spent much of
the rest of the year ignominiously standing his ground in schoolhouse
doors, attempting to block African-American college and even elementary school students from attending white schools.

Which is worse: Those, like Wallace, who espoused explicit racism
and openly made every effort to hold back the inclusion of blacks into
American life, or those, like most of us today, who claim to despise

racism and yet allow our schools, police, and justice system to relegate African Americans to the back of the bus? The straightforward segregationism of the past or the hypocrisy of "colorblind" America today, proudly claiming that we have achieved racial equality as black youth are taught in inferior schools, pushed out of education in record numbers, watched and stopped and hassled and locked up in droves for petty offenses whites escape with impunity? When the outcomes have changed so little, when African-American leaders almost—*almost*—wax nostalgic for the days of George Wallace, our eyes should open wide to the scale of the work that remains to be done.

The days when bigots drew cheers were worse, far worse, of course. We're never going back to leaders who stand and proudly proclaim the racial inferiority of African Americans. We've moved forward since then, but we haven't yet arrived at our destination, and it's still a good distance off.

Biases that impede our progress toward equality can be sloughed off, even when they're buried and we want to believe in our own defense mechanism, the denial of their very existence. Laws that are written can be unwritten. We may demonize an individual like George Zimmerman, but that's so much easier than acknowledging what we have in common with him: suspicion toward our neighbors, unreasonable fears and reactions to that suspicion, a Stand Your Ground culture where guns blaze and our children fall. Zimmerman's story is not over, but neither is ours. Like O.J. Simpson, he appears likely to bring himself down eventually with his reckless behavior. We can prevent our country from making the same mistake by deciding that the scourges of racial bias and rampant gun violence are intolerable, and that the life of each of our children, every single one, matters and is worthy of our passionate protection.

# NOTES

1  Maddy (juror in the George Zimmerman trial), interview by the author, Celebration, Florida, September 23, 2013.

2  Don West, "Zimmerman defense begins with . . . a joke," YouTube Video, posted by "HLN," June 24, 2013, www.youtube.com/watch?v=ZiI5bVurSo0.

3  Rick Kissell, "Zimmerman Trial Revs Up Ratings for Cable News Networks," *Variety*, July 12, 2013, http://variety.com/2013/tv/news/zimmerman-trial-revs-up-ratings-for-cable-news-networks-1200561565/.

4  TMZ, "Bruce Springsteen America's Still Racist . . . Trayvon Martin is Amadou Diallo," July 17, 2013, www.tmz.com/2013/07/17/bruce-springsteen-trayvon-martin-amadou-diallo/.

5  Peter Dreier, "Will the Killing of Trayvon Martin Catalyze a Movement Like Emmett Till Did?" Huffington Post, July 20, 2013, www.huffingtonpost.com/peter-dreier/will-the-murder-of-trayvo_b_3628274.html.

6  Krissah Thompson and Scott Wilson, "Obama on Trayvon Martin: 'If I had a son, he'd look like Trayvon,'" *Washington Post*, March 23, 2012, www.washingtonpost.com/politics/obama-if-i-had-a-son-hed-look-like-trayvon/2012/03/23/gIQApKPpVS_story.html.

7  Barack Obama, "Remarks by the President on Trayvon Martin," The White House Office of the Press Secretary, July 19, 2013, www.whitehouse.gov/the-press-office/2013/07/19/remarks-president-trayvon-martin.

8  Ibid.

9  Maddy (juror in the George Zimmerman trial), interview by Robin Roberts, ABC News, July 25, 2013, www.youtube.com/watch?v=eG8KZEJGtco.

10  Ibid.

11  Ibid.

12  George Zimmerman, www.youtube.com/watch?v=Z63X-yDefFE.

13    Lisa Bloom, "Zimmerman Prosecutors Duck the Race Issue," *New York Times*, July 15, 2013, www.nytimes.com/2013/07/16/opinion/zimmerman-prosecutors-duck-the-race-issue.html?pagewanted=all&_r=1&.

14    Gary Fields and John R. Emshwiller, "Federal Guilty Pleas Soar As Bargains Trump Trials," *Wall Street Journal*, September 23, 2012, http://online.wsj.com/news/articles/SB10000872396390443589304577637610097206808.

15    Lindsey Devers, PhD, "Plea and Charge Bargaining: Research Summary," Bureau of Justice Assistance, U.S. Department of Justice, January 24, 2011, https://www.bja.gov/Publications/PleaBargainingResearchSummary.pdf.

16    *New York Times*, "Criticizing Sentencing Rules, U.S. Judge Resigns," September 30, 1990, www.nytimes.com/1990/09/30/us/criticizing-sentencing-rules-us-judge-resigns.html.

17    Mike Schneider, "Martin Family Lawyer Known for Civil Rights Cases," *StarTribune*, March 30, 2012, http://m.startribune.com/nation/?id=145073445.

18    Daniel Trotta, "Trayvon Martin: Before the World Heard the Cries," Reuters, April 3, 2012, www.reuters.com/article/2012/04/03/us-usa-florida-shooting-trayvon-idUSBRE8320UK20120403.

19    Schneider, "Martin Family Lawyer."

20    Ibid.

21    Edward B. Colby and Gilma Avalos, "Nothing to Dispute Sanford Shooter's Self-Defense Claim in Miami Boy's Death: Police Chief," NBC 6 South Florida, March 21, 2012, www.nbcmiami.com/news/local/Nothing-to-Dispute-Sanford-Shooters-Self-Defense-Claim-in-Miami-Boys-Death-Police-Chief-142376875.html.

22    Mirkinson, "Melissa Harris-Perry on Trayvon Martin Killing: Remember His Name," Huffington Post, March 19, 2012, www.huffingtonpost.com/2012/03/18/melissa-harris-perry-trayvon-martin_n_1357392.html.

23    Brian Stelter, "In Slain Teenager's Case, a Long Route to National Attention," *New York Times*, March 25, 2012, www.nytimes.com/2012/03/26/business/media/for-martins-case-a-long-route-to-national-attention.html?_r=1&.

24    Michael Leslie and Stania Antoine with Tasha Shangvi, "Trayvon Martin in the International Press," University of Florida, scholarship.law.ufl.edu/cgi/viewcontent.cgi?article=1004&context=csrrr_events.

25    Leslie and Antoine with Shangvi, "Trayvon Martin in the International Press."

26    Ibid.

27  Nancy Shute, "Around the World, Gun Ownership and Firearms Deaths Go Together," NPR, September 18, 2013, www.npr.org/blogs/health/2013/09/17/223508595/around-the-world-gun-ownership-and-firearms-deaths-go-together.

28  Maddot, "Why Do So Many Americans Have Guns?" HubPages, http://maddot.hubpages.com/hub/Why-do-so-many-US-citizens-have-guns.

29  Zoe Fox, "Trayvon Martin Petition Is Fastest-Growing in Change.org History," Mashable, March 28, 2012, http://mashable.com/2012/03/28/trayvon-martin-petition-change-org/.

30  Huffington Post, "Trayvon Martin's Mom Sybrina Fulton Receives 8 Months Vacation Time Donated by Miami-Dade County Workers," May 12, 2012, www.huffingtonpost.com/2012/05/12/sybrina-fulton-trayvon-8-months-vacation-time-donation_n_1511553.html.

31  Byron Tau, "'If I had a son, he'd look like Trayvon,'" Politico, March 23, 2012, www.politico.com/politico44/2012/03/obama-i-had-a-son-hed-look-like-trayvon-118439.html.

32  Graham Winch, "Zimmerman Attorney: We Won't Take a Plea Deal," HLN, December 7, 2012, www.hlntv.com/article/2012/12/06/zimmermans-attorney-we-will-not-take-plea-deal.

33  Ronald Durham (National Action Network leader), in discussion with the author, Daytona Beach, FL, September 24, 2013.

34  New York Times, "Key Disputes in the Zimmerman Trial," July 8, 2013, www.nytimes.com/interactive/2013/07/05/us/zimmerman-trial.html?ref=us.

35  Ashley Hayes, "George Zimmerman: Trayvon Martin Threatened My Life," CNN, June 22, 2012, www.cnn.com/2012/06/21/justice/florida-teen-shooting/.

36  Ashley Hayes, "George Zimmerman: Trayvon Martin Threatened My Life," CNN, June 22, 2012, www.cnn.com/2012/06/21/justice/florida-teen-shooting/.

37  Ibid.

38  Douglas Stanglin, "Tape shows Zimmerman re-enacting Martin shooting for police," USA TODAY, June 21, 2012, http://content.usatoday.com/communities/ondeadline/post/2012/06/tape-shows-zimmerman-re-enacting-martin-shooting-for-police/1#.Up9n1cRDtiA.

39  Justifiable Use of Force, The 2013 Florida Statutes, sec. 776.012, www.leg.state.fl.us/statutes/index.cfm?App_mode=Display_Statute&Search_String=&URL=0700-0799/0776/Sections/0776.012.html.

40   Zabkowicz v. West Bend Co., 589 F. Supp. 780, 784, 35 EPD %C2%B6 34, 766 (E.D. Wis. 1984).

41   George Zimmerman, www.youtube.com/watch?v=7oTaxG51RYc.

42   "State v. Zimmerman: Evidence Released by Prosecutor," May 17, 2012, www. scribd.com/doc/93951121/state-v-zimmerman-evidence-released-by-prosecutor.

43   Alicia Stanley (Trayvon Martin's stepmother), interview by Anderson Cooper, Anderson Cooper 360, June 29, 2013, www.youtube.com/watch?v=LjkgI5ShcWs&feature=endscreen.

44   Chris Francescani, "George Zimmerman: Prelude to a Shooting," Reuters, April 25, 2012, www.reuters.com/article/2012/04/25/us-usa-florida-shooting-zimmerman-idUSBRE83O18H20120425.

45   Hal Boedeker, "Trayvon Martin: Attorney calls race 'the elephant in the room,'" Orlando Sentinel, September 29, 2012, http://articles.orlandosentinel.com/2012-09-29/entertainment/os-trayvon-martin-benjamin-crump-20120929_1_trayvon-martin-martin-george-zimmerman-benjamin-crump.

46   Sonari Glinton, "Parents of Slain Florida Teen Appear on Capital Hill," NPR, March 28, 2012, www.npr.org/2012/03/28/149512229/slain-teens-parents-appear-on-capitol-hill.

47   New York Times, "George Zimmerman's Written Statement," June 21, 2012, www. nytimes.com/interactive/2012/06/22/us/21george-zimmerman-transcript.html?_r=0.

48   Francescani, "Prelude to a Shooting."

49   Matthew DeLuca, "Did Trayvon Shooter Abuse 911?" Daily Beast, March 22, 2012, www.thedailybeast.com/articles/2012/03/23/did-trayvon-shooter-abuse-911. html.

50   http://mynews13.com/content/dam/news/static/cfnews13/documents/2013/01/zimmerman-discovery-baez-documents-010813.pdf.

51   Maddy, interview by the author.

52   http://edition.cnn.com/TRANSCRIPTS/1307/14/ndaysun.03.html.

53   Lee Dye, "Assessing American's Science Knowledge," ABC News, July 26, 2013, http://abcnews.go.com/Technology/story?id=120061.

54   Brandon Keim, "Expert Advice Shuts Your Brain Down," ABC News, March 28, 2009, http://abcnews.go.com/Technology/Science/story?id=7192000.

55 Associated Press, "Shiping Bao, Medical Examiner Who Testified in Trayvon Martin Case, Fired for Undisclosed Reasons," *NY Daily News*, September 10, 2013, www.nydailynews.com/news/national/medical-examiner-trayvon-martin-case-fired-undisclosed-reasons-article-1.1451430.

56 Joy-Ann Reid, "Zimmerman Trial Medical Examiner: Prosecutors, Police Threw the Case," Grio, September 16, 2013, http://thcgrio.com/2013/09/16/zimmerman-trial-medical-examiner-prosecutors-police-threw-the-case/.

57 Ibid.

58 George Zimmerman, http://edition.cnn.com/TRANSCRIPTS/1307/05/cnr.06.html.

59 Lydia Saad, "In U.S., 38% Have Tried Marijuana, Little Changed Since '80s," Gallup Politics, August 2, 2013, www.gallup.com/poll/163835/tried-marijuana-little-changed-80s.aspx.

60 Marc Caputo, "Poll: 7 in 10 Back Florida Medical-Marijuana Plan, Enough to Possibly Affect Governor's Race," *Miami Herald*, February 26, 2013, www.miamiherald.com/2013/02/25/v-fullstory/3253273/poll-7-in-10-back-fl-medical-marijuana.html.

61 Office of the Medical Examiner Florida, Districts 7 and 24, "Medical Examiner Report: Martin, Trayvon," February 27, 2012, lawofselfdefense.com/wp-content/uploads/2013/06/trayvon.martin.autopsy.pdf.

62 Reid, "Zimmerman Trial Medical Examiner."

63 George Zimmerman, www.youtube.com/watch?v=Jho9N15elCI.

64 George Zimmerman, www.youtube.com/watch?v=oeYhAc3UytM.

65 Dr. Vincent DiMaio (medical examiner) in cross-examination by Alan Jackson (Los Angeles Prosecutor).

66 Rachel Jeantel (friend of Trayvon Martin), interview by Piers Morgan, Piers Morgan Live, July 15, 2013, www.youtube.com/watch?v=RdSxdSPn7HM.

67 www.youtube.com/watch?v=XdzrBw-x8Xc.

68 Rachel Jeantel (friend of Trayvon Martin), interview by the author.

69 George Zimmerman, www.youtube.com/watch?v=eGvwKvdctw0.

70 George Zimmerman, www.youtube.com/watch?v=eGvwKvdctw0.

71 Urban Dictionary, "Cracker," June 29, 2003, www.urbandictionary.com/define.php?term=cracker.

72 Rachel Jeantel (friend of Trayvon Martin), interview by Nancy Grace, CNN, July 17, 2013, http://transcripts.cnn.com/TRANSCRIPTS/1307/17/ng.01.html.

73 Jeantel, interview by Grace.

74 www.youtube.com/watch?v=p2jLnUIOl4E.

75 Alana Abramson, "Radio Host Tom Joyner Offers Rachel Jeantel Full College Scholarship," ABC News, July 17, 2013, http://abcnews.go.com/blogs/headlines/2013/07/radio-host-tom-joyner-offers-rachel-jeantel-full-college-scholarship/.

76 http://edition.cnn.com/TRANSCRIPTS/1307/08/cnr.06.html.

77 www.youtube.com/watch?v=9FKF23rkUEI.

78 George Zimmerman, www.youtube.com/watch?v=Rnv8Q6FCQ8Y.

79 Seni Teinabeso and Matt Gutman, "Trayvon Martin Told Friend About Man Following Him in Final Moments," ABC News, June 26, 2013, http://abcnews.go.com/US/trayvon-martin-told-friend-man-final-moments/story?id=19490796.

80 http://transcripts.cnn.com/TRANSCRIPTS/1307/12/cnr.08.html.

81 http://transcripts.cnn.com/TRANSCRIPTS/1307/13/cnr.13.html.

82 Angela Corey, Bernie de la Rionda, John Guy, and Richard Mantei, statements during Zimmerman acquittal press conference, Sanford, FL, July 13, 2013, www.youtube.com/watch?v=cA_fxmm1Ryo.

83 Ronald Durham (National Action Network leader), in discussion with the author, Daytona Beach, FL, September 24, 2013.

84 Mark Sappenfield, "Trayvon Martin Rallies: Has Al Sharpton 'Gone Mainstream'?" *Christian Science Monitor*, July 21, 2013, www.csmonitor.com/USA/USA-Update/2013/0721/Trayvon-Martin-rallies-Has-Al-Sharpton-gone-mainstream-video.

85 Rebecca Leber, "Photos: 100 Cities Rally for Trayvon Martin," Think Progress, July 20, 2013, http://thinkprogress.org/politics/2013/07/20/2332721/trayvon-martin-rallies/.

86 Lisa Wade, PhD, "'I Am a Man': Black Men's Claims to Humanity," Society Pages, July 15, 2013, http://thesocietypages.org/socimages/2013/07/15/i-am-a-man-fighting-dehumanization-in-the-civil-rights-era/.

87  "Ann Coulter on George Zimmerman Verdict: 'Hallelujah,'" Huffington Post, July 13, 2013, www.huffingtonpost.com/2013/07/13/ann-coulter-george-zimmerman-verdict_n_3593018.html.

88  Rex W. Huppke, "Saying racism is over is the new saying you have 'a black friend,'" *Chicago Tribune*, July 23, 2013, http://articles.chicagotribune.com/2013-07-23/news/ct-met-huppke-race-20130723_1_racism george-zimmerman-trayvon-martin.

89  Evan McMurry, "O'Reilly Denounces NAACP, Celebs For 'Grievance Industry': 'It's Not About Trayvon Martin, It's About The Money,'" Mediaite, July 17, 2013, www.mediaite.com/tv/oreilly-denounces-naacp-celebs-for-grievance-industry-its-not-about-trayvon-martin-its-about-the-money/.

90  Kristen Savali, "Todd Kincannon: Former GOP Executive Director Defends Graphic Trayvon Martin Tweet," Newsone, February 6, 2013, http://newsone.com/2186779/todd-kincannon-trayvon-martin/.

91  News4Jax, "Report: Volusia County Beach Officer Suspended Over Trayvon Martin Comments," July 20, 2013, www.news4jax.com/news/report-volusia-county-beach-officer-suspended-over-trayvon-martin-comments/-/475880/21082116/-/15bxwvsz/-/index.html.

92  TMZ, "George Zimmerman Shops for Tactical Shotgun," August 22, 2013, www.tmz.com/2013/08/22/george-zimmerman-shotgun-kel-tec-trayvon-martin-shop-gun/.

93  Seni Tienabeso, "George Zimmerman's Wife Says He is 'Selfish,' Feels 'Invincible,'" ABC News, September 6, 2013, http://abcnews.go.com/US/george-zimmermans-wife-selfish-feels-invincible/story?id=20174763.

94  MSNBC, "Zimmerman Accused of Domestic Violence, Fighting With a Police Officer," March 27, 2012, http://usnews.nbcnews.com/_news/2012/03/27/10894561-zimmerman-accused-of-domestic-violence-fighting-with-a-police-officer.

95  Jonathan Capehart, "George Zimmerman's Relevant Past," *Washington Post*, May 28, 2013, www.washingtonpost.com/blogs/post-partisan/wp/2013/05/28/george-zimmermans-relevant-past/.

96  S.A. Miller, "Zimmerman Plans to Go Back to Carrying the Same Gun That Killed Trayvon Martin," *New York Post*, July 15, 2013, http://nypost.com/2013/07/15/zimmerman-plans-to-go-back-to-carrying-the-same-gun-that-killed-trayvon-martin/.

97  Richard LaPiere, "Attitudes vs. Actions" Social Forces 13, no. 2 (1934): 230-237, http://sf.oxfordjournals.org/content/13/2/230.full.pdf+html?ijkey=b6c55c0b2a1250b3a887a8cf7beeed9ecf5b81ef&keytype2=tf_ipsecsha.

98  People v. Hall (1854) 4 Cal. 399, 404.

99  Stephen Ambrose, *Nothing Like It In the World: The Men Who Built the Transcontinental Railroad 1863-1869* (New York: Simon and Schuster, 2000).

100  LaPiere, "Attitudes vs. Actions."

101  Charles M. Blow, "50 Years Later," *New York Times*, August 23, 2013, www.nytimes.com/2013/08/24/opinion/blow-50-years-later.html?hp&_r=0.

102  Pew Research, "King's Dreams Remain an Elusive Goal; Many Americans See Racial Disparities," August 22, 2013, www.pewsocialtrends.org/2013/08/22/kings-dream-remains-an-elusive-goal-many-americans-see-racial-disparities/3/.

103  Tufts Now, "Whites Believe They Are Victims of Racism More Often Than Blacks," May 23, 2011, http://now.tufts.edu/news-releases/whites-believe-they-are-victims-racism-more-o.

104  Associated Press, "Racial Attitudes Survey," October 29, 2012, http://surveys.ap.org/data%5CGfK%5CAP_Racial_Attitudes_Topline_09182012.pdf.

105  For this study, Hispanics are counted as either white or African-American, depending on how they self-identify.

106  If you are ready to bring your own hidden biases to light, try the test yourself at https://implicit.harvard.edu/implicit/. Prepare to get depressed.

107  Dexter Mullins, "Six Decades After Brown Ruling, U.S. Schools Still Segregated," Aljazeera America, September 25, 2013, http://america.aljazeera.com/articles/2013/9/25/56-years-after-littlerockusschoolssegregatedbyraceandclass.html.

108  Hazel Trice Edney, "New 'Doll Test' Produces Ugly Results," Final Call, September 14, 2006, www.finalcall.com/artman/publish/National_News_2/New_doll_test_produces_ugly_results_2919.shtml.

109  Eric Wilson, "Fashion's Blind Spot," *New York Times*, August 7, 2013, www.nytimes.com/2013/08/08/fashion/fashions-blind-spot.html.

110  Christine Rudder, "How Your Race Affects the Messages You Get," OkTrends, October 5, 2009, http://blog.okcupid.com/index.php/your-race-affects-whether-people-write-you-back/.

111  Angela Stanley, "Black, Female and Single," *New York Times*, December 10, 2011, www.nytimes.com/2011/12/11/opinion/sunday/black-and-female-the-marriage-question.html?pagewanted=all&_r=0.

112  Rudder, "How Your Race Affects the Messages."

113 Duncan BL, "Differential Social Perception and Attribution of Intergroup Violence: Testing the Lower Limits of Stereotyping of Blacks," *Journal of Personality and Social Psychology* 34, no. 4 (1976): 590-598, www.ncbi.nlm.nih.gov/pubmed/993976.

114 Sally Kohn, "The Great Debate," Reuters, March 21, 2012, http://blogs.reuters.com/great-debate/2012/03/21/trayvon-martin-obama-and-the-persistence-of-bias/.

115 Science Daily, "'Mere Presence' of a Black Face Can Lead People to Mistake Objects for Weapons More Often, Study Says," May 21, 2011, www.sciencedaily.com/releases/2001/05/010521072157.htm.

116 Lydialyle Gibson, "Shooter's Choice," *University of Chicago Magazine* 99, no. 6 (2007), http://magazine.uchicago.edu/0778/investigations/shooters_choice.shtml.

117 Michelle Alexander, *The New Jim Crow* (New York: The New Press, 2012), 264.

118 Pew Research, "50 Years After the March on Washington, Many Racial Divides Remain," August 22, 2013, www.pewsocialtrends.org/2013/08/22/50-years-after-the-march-on-washington-many-racial-divides-remain/raceinamerica_05a/.

119 Gary Langer and Peyton M. Craighill, "Fewer Call Racism a Major Problem Though Discrimination Remains," ABC News, January 18, 2009, http://abcnews.go.com/PollingUnit/Politics/story?id=6674407.

120 CBS News, "Judge Defends Denied Interracial Marriage," October 19, 2009, www.cbsnews.com/2100-500202_162-5396242.html.

121 Simon Mainwaring, "What Corporate America Can Learn from Martin Luther King Jr.," *Forbes*, October 20, 2011, www.forbes.com/sites/simonmainwaring/2011/10/20/what-corporate-america-can-learn-from-martin-luther-king-jr/2/.

122 Alexia Elejalde-Ruiz, "Interracial Marriage: Mixing in Matching," *Chicago Tribune*, July 11, 2012, http://articles.chicagotribune.com/2012-07-11/features/sc-fam-0710-dating-mixed-20120710_1_interracial-marriage-whites-blacks.

123 John R. Logan, "Separate and Unequal: The Neighborhood Gap for Blacks, Hispanics and Asians in Metropolitan America," (US2010 Project report, Brown University, 2011), www.s4.brown.edu/us2010/Data/Report/report0727.pdf.

124 Adom Cooper, "The Shocking Reason Why More Black People Are Unemployed," PolicyMic, September 11, 2013, www.policymic.com/articles/62665/the-shocking-reason-why-more-black-people-are-unemployed.

125  Drew Desilver, "Black Incomes Are Up, but Wealth Isn't," Pew Research, August 30, 2013, www.pewresearch.org/fact-tank/2013/08/30/black-incomes-are-up-but-wealth-isnt/.

126  Janell Ross, "'Insidious and Persistent' Residential Segregation Called Out in Study," Huffington Post, August 3, 2011, www.huffingtonpost.com/2011/08/02/study-race-plays-bigger-r_n_916391.html.

127  Martin Luther King, Jr. "Letter from a Birmingham Jail," April 16, 1963, www.africa.upenn.edu/Articles_Gen/Letter_Birmingham.html.

128  Kevin McCorry, "Robbing Peter to Pay Paul: 'Leveling' Philly Schools in the Time of Budget Crisis," News Works, October 9, 2013, www.newsworks.org/index.php/local/the-latest/60708-robbing-peter-to-pay-paul-leveling-philly-schools-in-the-time-of-budget-crisis.

129  Valerie Strauss, "Philadelphia Passes 'Doomsday' School Budget," *Washington Post*, June 1, 2013, www.washingtonpost.com/blogs/answer-sheet/wp/2013/06/01/philadelphia-passes-doomsday-school-budget/.

130  Valerie Strauss, "Girl Dies After Getting Sick at School Without Nurse," *Washington Post*, October 12, 2013, www.washingtonpost.com/blogs/answer-sheet/wp/2013/10/12/girl-dies-after-getting-sick-at-school-without-nurse.

131  Marian Wright Edelman, "America's Public Schools: Still Unequal and Unjust," Huffington Post, April 6, 2012, www.huffingtonpost.com/marian-wright-edelman/public-schools-minority-students_b_1408878.html.

132  Ary Spatig-Amerikaner, "Unequal Education: Federal Loophole Enables Lower Spending on Students of Color," (Washington, DC: Center for American Progress, 2012), www.americanprogress.org/wp-content/uploads/2012/08/UnequalEduation.pdf.

133  Center for American Progress, "Students of Color Still Receiving Unequal Education," August 22, 2012, www.americanprogress.org/issues/education/news/2012/08/22/32862/students-of-color-still-receiving-unequal-education/.

134  American Civil Liberties Union, "Back to School Without Books: Many CA Students Still Lack Textbooks, ACLU Charges," September 12, 2000, https://www.aclu.org/racial-justice/back-school-without-books-many-ca-students-still-lack-textbooks-aclu-charges.

135  Yoav Gonen, "Book Rack and Ruin at City Schools," *New York Post*, May 14, 2012, http://nypost.com/2012/05/14/book-rack-ruin-at-city-schools/.

136  Ugonna Okpalaoka, "Report: Only 52 Percent of Black Males Graduate from High School in 4 Years," Grio, September 20, 2012, http://thegrio.com/2012/09/20/report-only-52-percent-of-black-males-graduate-from-high-school-in-4-years/.

137  Schott Foundation for Public Education, "The Schott 50 State Report on Public Education and Black Males," (Cambridge, MA, 2012), www.schottfoundation.org/urgency-of-now.pdf.

138  Sabrina Canfield, "Another School Suspends a Student for Criticizing a Teacher on Facebook," Courthouse News Service, October 25, 2011, www.courthousenews.com/2011/10/25/40892.htm.

139  Johanna Miller and others, "Education Interrupted: The Growing Use of Suspensions in New York City's Public Schools," (New York: New York Civil Liberties Union, January 2011), www.nyclu.org/files/publications/Suspension_Report_FINAL_noSpreads.pdf.

140  Brett M. Kelman, "Study: Black Students Suspended More Often Than Others," *USA TODAY,* May 12, 2013, www.usatoday.com/story/news/nation/2013/05/12/black-student-suspensions/2151423/.

141  Daniel J. Losen and Tia Elena Martinez, "Out of School and Off Track: The Overuse of Suspensions in American Middle and High Schools," (Los Angeles, CA: UCLA Center for Civil Rights Remedies at the Civil Rights Project, 2013).

142  Dr. Michael M. Krop Senior High School, "Student Handbook," (Miami, Florida, 2013), http://kropseniorhigh.org/ourpages/auto/2013/8/12/36073645/krophandbook2013.pdf.

143  Frances Robles, "Multiple Suspensions Paint Complicated Portrait of Trayvon Martin," *Miami Herald*, March 26, 2012, www.miamiherald.com/2012/03/26/2714778_p2/thousands-expected-at-trayvon.html.

144  Lizette Alvarez, "Defense in Trayvon Martin Case Raises Questions About the Victim's Character," *New York Times*, May 23, 2013, www.nytimes.com/2013/05/24/us/zimmermans-lawyers-release-text-messages-of-trayvon-martin.html.

145  Claudio Sanchez, "A High School Dropout's Midlife Hardships," NPR, July 28, 2011, www.npr.org/2011/07/28/138741367/a-high-school-dropouts-mid-life-hardships.

146  Ibid.

147  United States Department of Education, "Impact of Inadequate School Facilities on Student Learning," April 3, 2000, http://www2.ed.gov/offices/OESE/archives/inits/construction/impact2.html.

148 Pew Research, "50 Years After the March on Washington."

149 Darren Wheelock, "A Jury of One's 'Peers': The Racial Impact of Felon Jury Exclusion in Georgia," *Justice System Journal* 32, no. 3 (2011), www.ncsc.org/ Publications/Justice-System-Journal/~/media/Files/PDF/Publications/Justice System Journal/Jury of Ones Peers.ashx.

150 Brian C. Kalt, "The Exclusion of Felons from Jury Service," *American University Law Review* 53, no. 1 (2003), http://digitalcommons.wcl.american.edu/cgi/ viewcontent.cgi?article=1090&context=aulr.

151 Keith Herbert, "Blacks Are Unusual in Prosecutor Positions," Philly.com, August 29, 2005, http://articles.philly.com/2005-08-29/news/25424078_1_national-black-prosecutors-association-african-american-prosecutors-black-representation.

152 *ABA Journal*, "Race and Gender of Judges Make Enormous Differences in Rulings, Studies Find," February 6, 2010, www.abajournal.com/news/article/race_gender_of_ judges_make_enormous_differences_in_rulings_studies_find_aba.

153 The Sentencing Project, "Reducing Racial Disparity in the Criminal Justice System: A Manual for Practitioners and Policymakers," (Washington, DC, 2008), www. sentencingproject.org/doc/publications/rd_reducingracialdisparity.pdf.

154 Hayley Roberts, "Implicit Bias and Social Justice," Open Society Foundations, December 18, 2011, www.opensocietyfoundations.org/voices/implicit-bias-and-social-justice.

155 Jamie Fellner, "Race, Drugs, and Law Enforcement in the United States," *Stanford Law and Policy Review* 20, no. 2 (2009), www.hrw.org/news/2009/06/19/race-drugs-and-law-enforcement-united-states.

156 Maia Szalavitz, "Study: Whites More Likely to Abuse Drugs Than Blacks," *Time*, November 7, 2011, http://healthland.time.com/2011/11/07/study-whites-more-likely-to-abuse-drugs-than-blacks/.

157 www.youtube.com/watch?v=xbS2ItoqKew.

158 David C. Baldus, Charles Pulaski, and George Woodworth, "Comparative Review of Death Sciences: An Empirical Study of the Georgia Experience," *Journal of Criminal Law and Criminology* 74, no. 3 (Autumn 1983), http://www2.law. columbia.edu/fagan/courses/law_socialscience/documents/Spring_2006/Class 16-Capital Punishment/Baldus_Study.pdf.

159 Keith Kamisugi, "Share Your Unconscious Bias Stories With Us," Equal Justice Society, December 11, 2009, www.equaljusticesociety.org/2009/12/11/share-your-unconscious-bias-stories-with-us/.

160 Harvard University Press Blog, "Whites Commit Crimes, but Blacks Are Criminals," January 5, 2010, http://harvardpress.typepad.com/hup_publicity/2010/01/whites-commit-crimes-but-black-males-are-criminals.html.

161 Kelly Welch, "Black Criminal Stereotypes and Racial Profiling," *Journal of Contemporary Criminal Justice* 23, no. 3 (2007), www.sagepub.com/gabbidonstudy/articles/Welch.pdf.

162 Welch, "Black Criminal Stereotypes."

163 Perry L. Moriearty, "Framing Justice: Media, Bias, and Legal Decisionmaking," *Maryland Law Review* 69, no. 4 (2012), http://digitalcommons.law.umaryland.edu/cgi/viewcontent.cgi?article=3435&context=mlr.

164 *Dred Scott v. Sandford*, 60 U.S. 393 (1857).

165 Robert A. Gibson, "The Negro Holocaust: Lynching and Race Riots in the United States, 1880-1950," (New Haven, Connecticut: Yale–New Haven Teachers Institute, 2013), www.yale.edu/ynhti/curriculum/units/1979/2/79.02.04.x.html.

166 Kahlil Gibran Muhammad, *The Condemnation of Blackness: Race, Crime, and the Making of Modern Urban America* (Harvard University Press: Cambridge, MA, 2010).

167 Richard Cohen, "Racism Vs. Reality," *Washington Post*, July 15, 2013, www.washingtonpost.com/opinions/richard-cohen-racism-vs-reality/2013/07/15/4f419eb6-ed7a-11e2-a1f9-ea873b7e0424_story.html?hpid=z2.

168 Jeffrey Goldberg, "The Color of Suspicion," *New York Times Magazine*, June 20, 1999, www.nytimes.com/1999/06/20/magazine/the-color-of-suspicion.html?pagewanted=all&src=pm.

169 Federal Bureau of Investigation, "Uniform Crime Report 2011: Arrests," October 29, 2012, www.fbi.gov/about-us/cjis/ucr/crime-in-the-u.s/2011/crime-in-the-u.s.-2011/tables/table-43.

170 Justice Policy Institute, "Crime, Correctional Populations and Drug Arrests Down in 2011: As States Reform Justice and Save Money, Crime Continues to Decrease," (Washington, DC, 2012), www.justicepolicy.org/uploads/justicepolicy/documents/fbi_ucr2011jpifactsheet.pdf.

171 Dylan Matthews, "The Black/White Marijuana Arrest Gap, in Nine Charts," *Washington Post*, June 4, 2013, www.washingtonpost.com/blogs/wonkblog/wp/2013/06/04/the-blackwhite-marijuana-arrest-gap-in-nine-charts/.

172 Alexander, *The New Jim Crow*, 103.

173  Ian Urbina, "Blacks Are Singled Out for Marijuana Arrests, Federal Data Suggests," *New York Times*, June 3, 2013, www.nytimes.com/2013/06/04/us/marijuana-arrests-four-times-as-likely-for-blacks.html.

174  Drug Policy Alliance, "10 Facts About Marijuana," www.drugpolicy.org/drug-facts/10-facts-about-marijuana.

175  *Terry v. Ohio*, 392 U.S. 1 (1967), www.law.cornell.edu/supremecourt/text/392/1.

176  As this book went to press, the case was on appeal to the federal appellate court, which stayed the remedies ordered by the lower court judge pending its full review. Judge Sheindlin was removed from the case based on the appellate court's concern that she had an "appearance of impropriety," as she had appeared to encourage the filing of the cases and facilitated their assignment to her, and she had agreed to media interviews while the cases before her were pending.

177  Aviva Shen, "White People Stopped by New York Police Are More Likely to Have Guns or Drugs Than Minorities," Think Progress, May 22, 2013, http://thinkprogress.org/justice/2013/05/22/2046451/white-people-stopped-by-new-york-police-are-more-likely-to-have-guns-or-drugs-than-minorities/.

178  Shen, "White People Stopped by New York Police."

179  Paul von Zielbauer, "Study Shows More Job Offers for Ex-Convicts Who Are White," *New York Times*, June 17, 2005, http://query.nytimes.com/gst/fullpage.html?res=9905EEDB133EF934A25755C0A9639C8B63.

180  L.A. Johnson, "Studies Find that Afrocentric Names Often Incur a Bias," *Pittsburgh Post-Gazette*, November 25, 2003, http://old.post-gazette.com/lifestyle/20031125blacknames1125fnp2.asp.

181  Jahvaris Fulton, tweet, July 13, 2013, https://twitter.com/jahvaris_martin.

182  Tom Foreman, "Analysis: The Race Factor in George Zimmerman's Trial," CNN, July 15, 2013, www.cnn.com/2013/07/14/justice/zimmerman-race-factor/.

183  Van Jones, "ARE Blacks a Criminal Race? Surprising Statistics," Huffington Post, October 5, 2005, www.huffingtonpost.com/van-jones/are-blacks-a-criminal-rac_b_8398.html.

184  Jamelle Bouie, "The Trayvon Martin Killing and the Myth of Black-on-Black Crime," Daily Beast, July 15, 2013, www.thedailybeast.com/articles/2013/07/15/the-trayvon-martin-killing-and-the-myth-of-black-on-black-crime.html.

185  Hatty Lee and Shani O. Hilton, "Fife Myths About Crime in Black America—and the Statistical Truths," Color Lines, April 13, 2012, http://colorlines.com/archives/2012/04/crime_myths.html.

186  Welch, "Black Criminal Stereotypes and Racial Profiling."

187  United States Census Bureau, "State and County Quick Facts," June 27, 2013, http://quickfacts.census.gov/qfd/states/00000.html.

188  Federal Bureau of Investigation, "Uniform Crime Report 2011: Murder," October 29, 2012, www.fbi.gov/about-us/cjis/ucr/crime-in-the-u.s/2011/crime-in-the-u.s.-2011/tables/expanded-homicide-data-table-6.

189  DiscovertheOdds.com, "What Are the Odds of Being Struck by Lightning?" October 8, 2012, http://discovertheodds.com/what-are-the-odds-of-being-struck-by-lightning/.

190  Ruth D. Peterson and Lauren J. Krivo, "National Neighborhood Crime Study (NNCS), 2000. ICPSR 27501-v1," (Ann Arbor, MI: Inter-university Consortium for Political and Social Research, 2010), www.icpsr.umich.edu/icpsrweb/RCMD/studies/27501.

191  "Where Have All the Burglars Gone?" *Economist*, July 20, 2013, www.economist.com/news/briefing/21582041-rich-world-seeing-less-and-less-crime-even-face-high-unemployment-and-economic.

192  Patrik Jonsson, "FBI: Violent Crime Down, but People Don't Feel Safer," *Christian Science Monitor*, September 15, 2009, www.csmonitor.com/USA/Justice/2009/0915/p02s04-usju.html.

193  Justice Policy Institute, "Crime, Correctional Populations and Drug Arrests."

194  Sherry L. Murphy, BS, Jiaquan Xu, MD, and Kenneth D. Kochanek, MA, "Deaths: Final Data for 2010," *National Vital Statistics Reports* 61, no. 4 (2013).

195  Ben Martin, PsyD, "Taking on Anxiety and the Irrational Fears in Your Life," Psych Central, 2006, http://psychcentral.com/lib/taking-on-anxiety-and-the-irrational-fears-in-your-life/00023.

196  Stanton BF, Behrman RE, "Death Among Children and Adolescents," in Kliegman RM and others, eds., *Nelson Textbook of Pediatrics*, 19th ed. (Philadelphia, PA: Saunders Elsevier, 2011), www.nlm.nih.gov/medlineplus/ency/article/001915.htm.

197  Lenore Skenazy, *Free-Range Kids: Giving Our Children the Freedom We Had Without Going Nuts With Worry* (San Francisco: Wiley, 2009), 16.

198  Ronald Weitzer, "Racialized Policing: Residents' Perceptions in Three Neighborhoods," *Law and Society Review* 34, no. 1 (2000), 129-155, www.jstor.org/discover/10.2307/3115118?uid=2&uid=4&sid=21102950458231.

199  Alexander R. Green and others, "Implicit bias among physicians and Its Prediction of Thrombolysis Decisions for Black and White Patients," *Journal of General Internal Medicine* 22, no. 9 (2007), http://cat.inist.fr/?aModele=afficheN&cpsi dt=19040317.

200  Jessica Cumberbatch, "Racial Bias Among Doctors Linked to Dissatisfaction With Care, Report Says," Huffington Post, May 3, 2012, www.huffingtonpost. com/2012/05/03/racial-bias-doctors_n_1472281.html.

201  Frank Partnoy, "Beyond the Blink," *New York Times*, July 6, 2012, www.nytimes. com/2012/07/08/opinion/sunday/reactions-by-nurture-not-nature.html?_r=2&.

202  Lorie A. Fridell, "Racially Biased Policing: The Law Enforcement Response to the Implicit Black-Crime Association," in Michael J. Lynch, E. Britt Patterson, and Kristina K. Childs, *Racial Divide: Racial and Ethnic Bias in the Criminal Justice System* (Monsey, NY: Criminal Justice Press, 2008) 33-59, http:// fairandimpartialpolicing.com/docs/rbp-thelaw.pdf.

203  Evidence Prof Blog, "What's the Harm?: Cynthia Lee's Making Race Salient and Jury Instructions on Racial Bias and Cross-Racial Identifications," August 21, 2013, http://lawprofessors.typepad.com/evidenceprof/2013/08/cynthia-lee-thecharles-kennedy-poe-research-professor-of-law-at-thegeorge-washington-university-law-school-presented-her-fo.html.

204  https://implicit.harvard.edu/implicit.

205  Yasmina Bekhouche and others, "The Global Gender Gap Report 2013," (Cologny/ Geneva, Switzerland: World Economic Forum, 2013), http://www3.weforum.org/ docs/WEF_GenderGap_Report_2013.pdf.

206  Annie-Rose Strasser, "George Zimmerman Had a Small Arsenal With Him When He Was Arrested on Domestic Violence Charges," Think Progress, November 26, 2013, http://thinkprogress.org/justice/2013/11/26/2998931/zimmerman-guns-arrest/.

207  Igor Volsky, "Gun Advocacy Group Sends Zimmerman $12,000 to Buy Guns," Think Progress, July 26, 2013, http://thinkprogress.org/justice/2013/07/26/2359831/ gun-advocacy-group-sends-zimmerman-12000-to-buy-guns/.

208  Aram Roston, "In Florida, It's Often Shoot First, Learn the Law Later," Daily Beast, May 17, 2012, www.thedailybeast.com/articles/2012/05/17/in-florida-it-s-often-shoot-first-learn-the-law-later.html.

209  Adam Weinstein, "How the NRA and Its Allies Helped Spread a Radical Gun Law Nationwide," *Mother Jones*, June 7, 2012, www.motherjones.com/politics/2012/06/ nra-alec-stand-your-ground.

210  Michael Luo and Mike McIntire, "Children and Guns: The Hidden Toll," *New York Times*, September 28, 2013, www.nytimes.com/2013/09/29/us/children-and-guns-the-hidden-toll.html.

211  Rick Stone, "Trayvon Martin's Uncle Says Media Should Have Challenged Pretrial Misinformation," WLRN, July 12, 2013, http://wlrn.org/post/trayvon-martins-uncle-says-media-should-have-challenged-pretrial-misinformation.

212  Sabrina Tavernise, "To Reduce Suicide Rates, New Focus Turns to Guns," *New York Times*, February 13, 2013, www.nytimes.com/2013/02/14/us/to-lower-suicide-rates-new-focus-turns-to-guns.html.

213  Henry Goldman, "Shootings Costing U.S. $174 Billion Show Burden of Gun Violence," Bloomberg Politics, December 20, 2012, www.bloomberg.com/news/2012-12-21/shootings-costing-u-s-174-billion-show-burden-of-gun-violence.html.

214  Adam Winkler, *Gunfight* (New York: W.W. Norton and Company, 2011), 289.

215  *McDonald v. City of Chicago*, 130 S. Ct. 3020 (2010).

216  Winkler, *Gunfight*, 168–9.

217  California Penal Code, sec. 12022.53, http://codes.lp.findlaw.com/cacode/PEN/3/4/2/1/2/s12022.53.

218  Steven Jansen and M. Elaine Nugent-Borakove, "Expansions to the Castle Doctrine: Implications for Policy and Practice," (Alexandria, Virginia: American Prosecutors Research Institute), www.ndaa.org/pdf/Castle Doctrine.pdf.

219  *New York Times,* "Acquittal in Doorstep Killing of Japanese Student," May 24, 1993, www.nytimes.com/1993/05/24/us/acquittal-in-doorstep-killing-of-japanese-student.html?src=pm.

220  Ibid.

221  Akiko Fujita, "Parents of Slain Japanese Student Push for Gun Control From Afar," ABC News, December 18, 2012, http://abcnews.go.com/blogs/headlines/2012/12/parents-of-slain-japanese-student-push-for-gun-control-from-afar/.

222  *Stanley M. Quaggin v. State of Florida*, 752 So.2d 19 (2000).

223  Cora Currier, "The 24 States That Have Sweeping Self-Defense Laws Just Like Florida's," ProPublica, March 22, 2012, www.propublica.org/article/the-23-states-that-have-sweeping-self-defense-laws-just-like-floridas. Utah has had a Stand Your Ground law on its books since 1994, though it's rarely been invoked. Robert Gehrke, "Utah's 'Stand Your Ground' Law Dates to 1994," *Salt Lake Tribune*, March 27, 2012, www.sltrib.com/sltrib/news/53796323-78/case-florida-force-ground.html.csp.

224 Robert Stewart, "Death of Exchange Student Painful 20 Years Later," *Advocate*, October 17, 2012.

225 Jansen and Nugent-Borakove, "Expansions to the Castle Doctrine."

226 http://www.flgov.com/wp-content/uploads/2012/11/Task-Force-Report-Draft.pdf.

227 Weinstein, "How the NRA and Its Allies Helped Spread a Radical Gun Law."

228 Ibid.

229 Ibid.

230 Kris Hundley, Susan Taylor Martin, and Connie Humburg, "Florida's 'Stand Your Ground' Law Yields Some Shocking Outcomes Depending on How Law is Applied," *Tampa Bay Times*, June 1, 2012, www.tampabay.com/news/publicsafety/crime/florida-stand-your-ground-law-yields-some-shocking-outcomes-depending-on/1233133.

231 Hundley, Martin, and Humburg, "Florida's 'Stand Your Ground' Law."

232 Rebecca Leber, "At Stand Your Ground Hearing, Ted Cruz Argues Florida Law Helps African-Americans," Think Progress, October 29, 2013, http://thinkprogress.org/justice/2013/10/29/2852451/cruz-blacks-benefit-stand-ground/.

233 Scott Hiaasen, "Zimmerman Defense: No Need for Stand Your Ground Hearing," *Miami Herald*, March 5, 2013, www.miamiherald.com/2013/03/05/3268716/zimmerman-defense-no-need-for.html.

234 Mark Caputo, "Juror: We Talked Stand Your Ground Before Not-Guilty Zimmerman Verdict," *Miami Herald*, July 18, 2013, www.miamiherald.com/2013/07/16/3502481/juror-we-talked-stand-your-ground.html.

235 Martin Luther King, Jr., "I've Been to the Mountaintop," (speech, Mason Temple, Memphis, TN, April 3, 1968).

236 Ronald Durham (National Action Network leader), in discussion with the author, Daytona Beach, FL, September 24, 2013.

237 George Wallace (inaugural address, Alabama State Capitol, Montgomery, AL, January 14, 1963).

# ACKNOWLEDGMENTS

A WRITER OF CURRENT events nonfiction must, over and over again, brazenly request favors from complete strangers. *Would you sit for an interview? Would you trust me with your story? May I ask you just a few more questions?* I asked, and remarkably, sometimes the answer was yes.

In Florida, David Chico, Dr. Shiping Bao, Maddy, Pastor Durham, Rachel Jeantel, and Rod Vereen selflessly agreed to speak with me and share their perspective on the Zimmerman trial, a case that had caused each of them pain. Their insights were valuable, and I am honored that they chose to entrust their stories to me. We are strangers no more. And to the others, whom I promised not to name, who gave me valuable background and insights: you know who you are, and I thank you.

I imposed upon friends to give me their most precious, limited asset: time. *Would you read my manuscript and give me your thoughts?* I was honored by the brilliant legal eagles Jami Floyd, Lauren Lake, and Alan Jackson who read and diligently marked up my manuscript. Dr. Lawrence Kobilinsky quickly and clearly answered my science questions. The very busy Jeffrey Toobin so kindly wrote the foreword.

Then there are the publishing professionals, who inspire me with their brains and hard work. Laura Dail, my literary agent, continues to shepherd me through the world of publishing and push me to aim higher, think deeper. All the while she has my back. Dan Smetanka always strives for excellence, is a model of calm amidst the storm, and is the wise editor and publisher every writer wants. Barrett Briske swiftly and ably provided copy editing and kind encouragement. Megan Fishmann helped announce the book to the world.

While I covered the Zimmerman trial for NBC and MSNBC, I could not have worked with more dedicated, ethical, insightful folks. Phil Griffin and Elena Nachmanoff entrusted this challenging assignment to me. So many producers, anchors, and reporters dug deep to cover the trial accurately and thoughtfully, and I was especially lucky to work with Stefanie Cargill, Craig Melvin, and Ugonna Okpalaoka. Joy-Ann Reid, the smartest human on the planet, spurred me on and extended herself to lend a hand behind the scenes, taking the leap to believe in this project. Rich Greenberg took the time to vet the manuscript.

What a pleasure it was from start to finish to have the outstanding research assistance of Sam Wong, who doubles in his off hours as my son. Keep dancing! And reading and thinking! And dancing some more!

Big love to my friends and family, including my daughter Sarah and my mama Gloria, who cheerfully tolerate my habit of disappearing to the dark side of the moon while I write books, emerging months later, blinking into the light of day and picking back up where we left off.

And as always, my fiancé Braden Pollock, an author's dream partner, roots for my books and understands my need to write them, or pretends to, taking care of our lives while I hole up and tap away on my keyboard. No one was more surprised than I that when this trial was over, I could not move on, sweetheart. I hope this book explains why.